The Uneven Offshore World

Informed by world-systems analysis, this book examines the shifting patterns of accommodation and resistance to the offshore world, with a particular focus on Mauritius as a critical but underappreciated offshore node mediating foreign investment into India and Africa. Drawing on a large pool of financial data and elite interviews, the authors present the first detailed comparative study of the Mauritius–India and Mauritius–Africa offshore relationships. These relationships serve as indicative test cases of the contemporary global tax reform agenda and its promise to rein in offshore finance. Whereas India's economic power and multilateral track record have enabled it to actively shape this agenda and implement it in a robust manner, most African countries have found themselves either unable to meet its stringent criteria or unwilling to do so out of fear that it might discourage investment. Its impact on offshore financial centers has likewise been limited. A few of the least sophisticated ones appear to have fallen by the wayside, but the rest have either remained largely unaffected, or, like Mauritius, succeeded in consolidating their operations and surviving the current round of regulatory headwinds. The findings suggest that the contemporary global tax reform agenda has thus far not only failed to make good on its promise but also actually reinforced numerous existing power hierarchies. *The Uneven Offshore World* is written in an accessible style and aimed at readers without specialized knowledge of tax issues.

Justin Robertson is an associate professor in the Department of Asian and International Studies at the City University of Hong Kong. His most recent research explores the extent to which hedge funds, private equity funds, and offshore structures are materializing in emerging markets.

Michael Tyrala is a postdoctoral fellow at the Institute for Emerging Market Studies of the Hong Kong University of Science and Technology. His research focuses on the historical and contemporary trajectories of the global offshore economy and its evolving impact on the global capitalist system.

Routledge Advances in International Relations and Global Politics

The Frontiers of Public Diplomacy
Hegemony, Morality and Power in the International Sphere
Colin R. Alexander

Security and Safety in the Era of Global Risks
Edited by Radomir Compel and Rosalie Arcala Hall

Laws of Politics
Their Operations in Democracies and Dictatorships
Alfred G. Cuzán

Climate Change and Biodiversity Governance in the Amazon
At the Edge of Ecological Collapse?
Joana Castro Pereira and Eduardo Viola

Mega-regionalism and Great Power Geo-economic Competition
Xianbai Ji

De Facto State Identity and International Legitimation
Sebastian Klich

Perspectives on the State Borders in Globalized Africa
Edited by Yuichi Sasaoka, Aimé Raoul Sumo Tayo and Sayoko Uesu

Making Sense of Cyber Capabilities for Small States
Case Studies from the Asia-Pacific
Francis C. Domingo

The Uneven Offshore World
Mauritius, India, and Africa in the Global Economy
Justin Robertson and Michael Tyrala

For information about the series: www.routledge.com/Routledge-Advances-in-International-Relations-and-Global-Politics/book-series/IRGP

The Uneven Offshore World

Mauritius, India, and Africa in the Global Economy

Justin Robertson and Michael Tyrala

Routledge
Taylor & Francis Group
LONDON AND NEW YORK

First published 2022
by Routledge
4 Park Square, Milton Park, Abingdon, Oxon OX14 4RN

and by Routledge
605 Third Avenue, New York, NY 10158

Routledge is an imprint of the Taylor & Francis Group, an informa business

British Library Cataloguing-in-Publication Data
A catalogue record for this book is available from the British Library

Library of Congress Cataloging-in-Publication Data
Names: Robertson, Justin, 1972– author. |
Tyrala, Michael, 1985– author.
Title: The uneven offshore world : Mauritius, India, and Africa in the global economy / Justin Robertson and Michael Tyrala.
Description: Abingdon, Oxon ; New York, NY : Routledge, [2022] | Series: Routledge advances in international relations and global politics | Includes bibliographical references and index.
Identifiers: LCCN 2021048609 (print) | LCCN 2021048610 (ebook) | ISBN 9780367751128 (hardback) | ISBN 9780367751111 (paperback) | ISBN 9781003161011 (ebook)
Subjects: LCSH: Investments, Foreign—Mauritius. | Tax incentives—Mauritius. | Corporations, Foreign—Taxation—Mauritius. | Mauritius—Foreign economic relations—India. | India—Foreign economic relations—Mauritius. | Mauritius—Foreign economic relations—Africa. | Africa—Foreign economic relations—Mauritius.
Classification: LCC HG5890.3.A3 R63 2022 (print) | LCC HG5890.3.A3 (ebook) | DDC 332.67/3096982—dc23/eng/20211019
LC record available at https://lccn.loc.gov/2021048609
LC ebook record available at https://lccn.loc.gov/2021048610

ISBN: 9780367751128 (hbk)
ISBN: 9780367751111 (pbk)
ISBN: 9781003161011 (ebk)

DOI: 10.4324/9781003161011

Typeset in Galliard
by Apex CoVantage, LLC

Contents

Figures

Tables

Boxes

Abbreviations

AfDB – African Development Bank
AML – Anti-Money Laundering
ATAF – African Tax Administration Forum
AU – African Union
BCEAO – Banque Centrale des États de l'Afrique de l'Ouest
BEAC – Banque des États de l'Afrique Centrale
BEPS – Base Erosion and Profit Shifting (OECD)
BIT – Bilateral Investment Treaty
BMG – BEPS Monitoring Group
BTT – Bilateral Tax Treaty
BVI – British Virgin Islands
CbCR – Country-by-Country Reporting
CBGA – Centre for Budget and Governance Accountability
CCCTB – Common Consolidated Corporate Tax Base (EU)
CDIS – Coordinated Direct Investment Survey (IMF)
CFA – Colonies Françaises d'Afrique / Communauté Financière Africaine
CFC – Controlled Foreign Company
CFP – Center for Freedom and Prosperity (US)
CFT – Combating the Financing of Terrorism
CGT – Capital Gains Tax
CIJ – Centre for Investigative Journalism (UK)
CIT – Corporate Income Tax
CRS – Common Reporting Standard (OECD)
CSO – Civil Society Organization
CSP – Corporate Services Provider
DFI – Development Finance Institution
DFTC – Deemed Foreign Tax Credit (Mauritius)
DIT – Department for International Trade (UK)
DPIIT – Department for Promotion of Industry and Internal Trade (India)
DTA – Double Taxation Agreement
DTAA – Double Taxation Avoidance Agreement
DTT – Double Tax Treaty
EOIR – Exchange of Information on Request (OECD)

EC – European Commission (EU)
EP – European Parliament (EU)
EU – European Union
EUSD – European Union Savings Directive
FATCA – Foreign Account Tax Compliance Act (US)
FATF – Financial Action Task Force
FDI – Foreign Direct Investment
FOC – Flag of Convenience
FPI – Foreign Portfolio Investment
FSC – Financial Services Commission (Mauritius)
FSF – Financial Stability Forum
FSPA – Financial Services Promotion Agency (Mauritius)
FTC – Financial Transparency Coalition
G7 – Group of Seven
G20 – Group of Twenty
G77 – Group of Seventy-Seven
GAAR – General Anti-Avoidance Rule
GBC – Global Business Company (Mauritius)
GBI – Global Business Institute (Mauritius)
GDP – Gross Domestic Product
GILTI – Global Intangible Low-Taxed Income (US)
HNWI – High-Net-Worth Individual
HTCI – Harmful Tax Competition Initiative (OECD)
ICIJ – International Consortium of Investigative Journalists
ICTD – International Centre for Tax and Development
IFA – International Fiscal Association
IFF – Illicit Financial Flow
IFI – International Financial Institution
ILO – International Labour Organization
IMF – International Monetary Fund
IP – Intellectual Property
IPE – International Political Economy
IRS – Internal Revenue Service (US)
ISDS – Investor-State Dispute Settlement
ITF – International Transport Workers' Federation
ITIO – International Tax and Investment Organization
ITT – Income Tax Treaty
KYC – Know Your Client
LOB – Limitation-on-Benefits
MAP – Mutual Agreement Procedure
MC – Management Company (Mauritius)
MCAA – Multilateral Competent Authority Agreement
MIPA – Mauritius Institute of Professional Accountants
MLI – Multilateral Instrument (OECD)
MNC – Multinational Corporation

MNE – Multinational Enterprise
MRA – Mauritius Revenue Authority
MTC – Model Tax Convention
NIEO – New International Economic Order
OECD – Organization for Economic Cooperation and Development
OEEC – Organization for European Economic Cooperation
OFC – Offshore Financial Center
PEP – Politically Exposed Person
POEM – Place of Effective Management
PPT – Principal Purposes Test
PR – Public Relations
PwC – PricewaterhouseCoopers
RBI – Reserve Bank of India
SAR – Special Administrative Region (China)
SEBI – Securities and Exchange Board of India
SEZ – Special Economic Zone
SME – Small- and Medium-sized Enterprise
SOE – State-Owned Enterprise
TIEA – Tax Information Exchange Agreement (OECD)
TJN – Tax Justice Network
TPG – Transfer Pricing Guideline
TUAC – Trade Union Advisory Committee to the OECD
UAE – United Arab Emirates
UK – United Kingdom
UN – United Nations
UNCTAD – United Nations Conference on Trade and Development
UNECA – United Nations Economic Commission for Africa
US – United States
VCC – Variable Capital Company
WHT – Withholding Tax
WTO – World Trade Organization

1 Introduction

> "*What Mauritius is providing is not a gateway but a getaway car for unscrupulous corporations dodging their tax obligations.*"
>
> – Alvin Mosioma
>
> (Executive Director of Tax Justice Network Africa)

Mauritius has served as the central financial entry point to India for over 20 years, largely because of its tax advantages. By structuring inward and outward investments through Mauritius, individuals and businesses have been able to eliminate capital gains liabilities and lower other forms of taxation, such as withholding taxes on dividends, interest, and royalties. Due to the significant offshore role that Mauritius serves in the Indian economy and the global economy in general, companies registered in Mauritius hold over US$774 billion in assets according to the island state's own Financial Services Commission ([FSC], 2020a; 2020b). The offshore relationship between Mauritius and India, although emblematic of the financially unregulated offshore world, has been unfamiliar to many students of the global political economy.

Following the global financial crisis of 2007–2008, there has been a renewal of efforts to regulate the offshore economy, with prominent action taken at the level of both policy and discourse by the newly empowered Group of Twenty (G20)[1] and the Organization for Economic Cooperation and Development (OECD). As with the response to any financial crisis, it is worth asking whether such attempts of structural financial reforms will persist once the crisis conditions abate. One of the surprising and under-reported outcomes of the global financial crisis has been the manner in which India seized this moment to undertake significant reforms in the area of taxation. The country's dealings with Mauritius, which had long been criticized by social forces within India but never substantially altered, were drastically rewritten under a 2016 bilateral agreement that removed many of Mauritius's special tax benefits. The reaction by investors and the financial press was swift, typified by a headline that declared "Mauritius Is Now a Tax Paradise Lost for Investors in India" (Shrivastava & Beniwal, 2016). In the wake of India's tougher stance on Mauritian offshore structures, Mauritius has aggressively sought to market itself as the financial gateway to Africa, replete with slick advertising campaigns in global media outlets such as CNN and on social media

DOI: 10.4324/9781003161011-1

platforms. As was the case with India in previous decades, significant tax advantages can still be obtained by using offshore vehicles registered in Mauritius to conduct business in many African countries.

Larger debates and research questions

These developments form a part of a larger debate in the International Political Economy (IPE) research area focused on the trajectory of the post-crisis world. Specifically, it is contested whether the global financial crisis has led to continuity or change in global economic processes (Grant & Wilson, 2012; Helleiner, 2014; Mackintosh, 2014; Keaney, 2017). The question examined in this book is whether the number of offshore routes and the volumes of capital flowing through them are substantially decreasing.

The aim of tax justice, a cause which has in recent years risen to the top of the global policy agenda, is to ensure that individuals and firms are held accountable for their economic behavior. A major facet of this is to challenge offshore tax evasion and avoidance, and the offshore secrecy they so frequently rely on, within and across borders, to support a fairer international tax system. More stringently regulating the offshore system is a key objective in the global pursuit of tax justice. OECD officials maintain that the reforms undertaken following the global financial crisis, namely the Common Reporting Standard (CRS), the Base Erosion and Profit Shifting (BEPS) project, and the ongoing BEPS 2.0, have begun to constrain the offshore system (OECD, 2021a). Similarly, we have attended a range of international conferences in Europe, and in the China Offshore series and the Asia Offshore series in Mainland China and Hong Kong, at which tax practitioners from the "Big Four" accounting firms (Deloitte, EY, KPMG, and PricewaterhouseCoopers [PwC]) have consistently affirmed that the new standards negotiated at the OECD are reframing the terms of global business. However, other observers are unconvinced that any truly substantive change has taken place (Johannesen & Zucman, 2014; ActionAid, 2015; BEPS Monitoring Group [BMG], 2015; Avi-Yonah & Xu, 2016; Trade Union Advisory Committee to the OECD [TUAC], 2016a). Picciotto (2019, p. 29) calls the BEPS project an important starting point but states that it contains no more than "temporary palliatives." The BEPS project, coordinated by the G20 and the OECD, stipulates that signatories will aim to legislate domestically and internationally broadly agreed-upon minimum standards in over a dozen areas to counter the profit shifting of multinational enterprises (MNEs).

Christensen and Hearson (2019a) propose that a new political economy of global tax governance has arisen in the wake of the global financial crisis. The previously unchallenged autonomy of the tax policy expert community has been reduced. It is no longer isolated from the pressures of international negotiations and the concerns of a much broader segment of societal actors. Moreover, the greater willingness of governments to act unilaterally has created conditions for a sovereignty-constraining cooperation, and that has led to the adoption of new global tax rules. In short, these authors believe that a decisive move has been taken against offshore financial centers (OFCs), which had been tolerated for many years. This contention is examined throughout the remainder of the book. As such, the economic relationships between Mauritius and India and between Mauritius and Africa are studied, as the nature of these relationships is indicative of the extent of changes in tax rules and practices in the post-crisis global political economy.

In this context, the following questions are addressed:

- What do India's actions tell us about the gathering resistance to the outsized role played by the offshore system in the global economy? Is there a new role for emerging markets to provide global tax policy leadership?
- Does the Mauritius–Africa relationship exhibit continuity, suggesting that there is still significant space for offshore transactions, or does it have similarities with the Mauritius–India relationship?
- Can small states, such as Mauritius, stabilize their financial sectors by moving beyond the provision of basic offshore incorporations and the exploitation of a few loopholes?
- What are the broader implications of these developments in the study of global political economy, especially as it relates to Africa?

Argument and significance

The evidence presented in the seven chapters of this book shows that the global offshore economy has been inhibited but certainly not eliminated. It seems unlikely that tax reform will be truly comprehensive and will result in the offshore path becoming inaccessible to all countries equally. Instead, it is more likely that the patterns of offshore engagement will vary according to a country's level of power and development. This is reflected by the fact that the Mauritius–India pairing has undergone deeper restructuring than the Mauritius–Africa pairing. These comparative differences underscore the need for a holistic analysis that takes into account both historical and systemic considerations, while also incorporating global, regional, and national influences. The space that is available for global offshore activity is undoubtedly shrinking because of the international consensus that offshore structures must be better regulated. Yet, it is premature for the OECD's top tax official, Pascal Saint-Amans (as quoted in the Economist, 2018), to declare that the OECD's new agreement on tax treaties means that "treaty shopping is dead." The financial playing field remains uneven. Core OECD members have signed on to more stringent global standards and norms, which could create more offshore financial opportunities for clients doing business in emerging and developing markets. Accordingly, Mauritius is still able to intermediate investment in Africa, albeit in a more constrained fashion.

Beyond OFCs, many recipient countries in emerging markets are likely to accommodate offshore capital in the belief that such a choice is necessary to attract foreign capital, particularly given local capital deficits. An important facet in analyzing the approaches of economic elites to offshore politics is to determine their dominant ideologies on foreign investment. Historically, many key elites from emerging markets accepted the "aspirational propositions" of neoliberalism (Bracking, 2012, p. 628), which emphasized the necessity of offshore structures in the development process. Such governing elites believed that it was imperative to attract highly competitive foreign investment to their economies. Obtaining offshore capital entails a trade-off between the anticipated gains from higher foreign investment and losses of tax revenue, primarily from missed capital gains taxes and the inability to effectively impose withholding taxes (Mehta, 2014). As Moore (2014a, p. 2) notes, "virtually all governments compete heavily for investors and investment, and are willing to forego quite a lot of their potential tax revenue in the process." Sometimes this entails tax incentives but often it also means allowing offshore finance. India is an exemplar of a country that has accommodated the demands of offshore capital in recent decades. In defending India's determination to continue its offshore relationship with Mauritius, a Minister in the Indian government, Yashwant Sinha, was explicit that the inflow of Mauritius-registered foreign investment outweighed any tax revenue losses (Union of India v. Azadi Bachao Andolan, 2003).

What are the mechanisms through which national elites facilitate foreign investment via offshore channels? Two frameworks are pivotal: double taxation agreements (DTAs) and bilateral investment treaties (BITs). DTAs mandate how a corporation's taxable income is treated, while BITs outline the principle of non-discrimination and protect against expropriation. BITs offer investors certainty, setting out clear rules and dispute settlement procedures for use in the case of expropriation for instance. These treaties are therefore technical but vital texts for foreign investors because they provide a legal framework and enhance the confidence of foreign investors seeking to allocate capital. Moreover, because these agreements largely follow OECD principles, which tend to represent neoliberal orthodoxy, they have thus far overrepresented the interests of investors and have been subject to very little societal scrutiny.

DTAs and BITs are pro-investment tools that give investors confidence and underpin the flows of capital in a global economy. In signing DTAs, countries are necessarily negotiating away some part of their economic sovereignty. ActionAid (2016, p. 5) concludes that countries have signed away their rights to tax capital gains in nearly half of the DTAs that exist. DTAs between Mauritius and African countries deliver lower tax rates than would be the case if foreign entities invested into African countries directly. The outlier – but possibly the model of the future – is India, which has been able to fully reacquire from Mauritius its right to tax capital gains. The analysis in this book seeks to delineate the understudied phenomena of DTAs and BITs.

Much of Africa has been following in the footsteps of India in seeking to attract investment flows by means of advantageous tax terms. Nonetheless, expectations of these flows approaching the levels reached in the Mauritius–India case should be tempered. Using FSC (2020a; 2020b) data, we calculated that Mauritius-mediated foreign investment into Africa is significantly lower than that into India. In 2019, the latest available year, Mauritius-mediated direct investment into India was worth over three times all Mauritius-mediated direct investment into African countries, and when portfolio investment was added to the tally, it was worth over five times that. Moreover, African economies, on balance, represent a more challenging business environment for foreign firms, especially because many new entrants lack the experience of doing business in Africa, whereas returnees and non-resident Indians have guided investment projects into India via Mauritius. The staggering volume of capital that has flowed to India via Mauritius represents a unique chapter in the period marked by ascendant globalization. The extent to which India's actions constitute a decisive shift in the global political economy of development needs to be carefully examined.

Will Africa's approach to Mauritius reverse faster than was the case in India? Many African countries have a shorter history with attracting offshore-mediated capital, and their national political economies feature limited resistance to and less experience with the multilateral system as well as less competent governments and administrations. Still, as Chapter 6 demonstrates, there is change afoot domestically and regionally within the African continent. Moreover, global reform efforts, largely pushed by the European Union (EU) and several major emerging markets, including India, are intensifying. Because of these factors, it is doubtful that the Mauritius–Africa story can run as long as the multi-decadal Mauritius–India story. Still, African economies generally hold less negotiating power with Mauritius than India ever did as a large emerging market. Larger emerging markets hold leverage over global capital in ways that smaller ones do not (Walter, 1998). This pattern is also perceptible within Africa, as evidenced, for example, by larger African countries negotiating somewhat more favorable DTAs with Mauritius.

The growth in the number of African regimes being accommodative of Mauritius as an offshore financial gateway has not been linear, nor has it been without political conflict. Opponents such as Picciotto (2019, p. 16) have been direct in their criticisms of Mauritius's role in the global political economy:

> Any benefits to Mauritius are also highly disproportionate to the damage they cause to other countries. Essentially, this amounts to providing facilities that enable an MNE to avoid tax in countries such as Kenya where they have substantial activities, in exchange for the creation of a few relatively well-paid professional service jobs in Mauritius. This can fairly be described as a beggar-thy-neighbour policy.

Difficult negotiations, renegotiations, and even terminations of existing bilateral agreements have taken place and some African countries have opted against signing new DTAs and BITs with Mauritius. Nevertheless, the trend has been one of opening up to economic transactions with Mauritius. This outcome is surprising in light of several other trends: the global financial crisis has led to pressures for regulatory change; tax collection has become a political issue in both developed and emerging markets; potential fiscal resources have been foregone by governments that accommodate offshore finance; and a diminished corporate tax base is especially worrisome for developing countries, which are more dependent on these revenues as compared to developed countries. Corporate income tax generates twice as much tax revenue in developing countries as in developed countries (United Nations Conference on Trade and Development [UNCTAD], 2015, p. 181). Moreover, taxes paid by foreign affiliates in Africa are significantly more important to total government revenue than even in other developing economies (UNCTAD, 2015, pp. 184–187).

This leads to the broader question of domestic resource mobilization in Africa and other developing regions, the vital importance of which has also been confirmed by its inclusion in the UN's 2015–2030 Sustainable Development Goals. Forstater (2018) argues that the problem of far lower tax revenues as percentage of Gross Domestic Product (GDP) found in Africa and most developing countries as compared to developed countries is nowhere near as much caused by corporate tax avoidance and the OFCs that enable and facilitate these practices as it is by the inability of developing countries to tax their domestic tax bases. While this is technically true, such a superficially narrow, purely domestically focused approach ignores a range of crucial historical and systemic power dependencies that influence developmental outcomes, especially in Africa.

To begin with, the offshore world enables and facilitates not only corporate tax avoidance but also tax evasion, money laundering, corruption, regulatory arbitrage, capital flight, and numerous other illegal, illicit, and/or immoral practices that undermine developmental efforts. Therefore, the problem is considerably more multifaceted. Compounding it are the still all too present legacies of colonialism, with the offshore world itself argued to serve as a direct extension of colonial control and exploitation, contributing not only to the arrested development in many African and other developing countries but also to global inequality. It is important to note that the ultimate beneficiaries of these practices are some of the wealthiest individuals and MNEs in the world. These foreign individuals and entities, still more often than not Western ones, have naturally benefited the most from the offshore world, as it was essentially built and maintained for them by the developed countries from which they originate, the very same ones that now claim to be serious about clamping down on these exploitative practices. Aside from that, effectively taxing domestic tax bases is a considerably more difficult task for most developing countries than it is to compel foreign MNEs to act more responsibly with regard to their tax obligations. After all, even many emerging economies have not been able to effectively tax their domestic tax bases. It is a complicated matter of state building that requires ample state capacities and even then it can take a long time, especially in a region that is still feeling the impacts of colonialism and the ethnic conflicts the colonizers either themselves created or at least exacerbated, whether through arbitrary placement of borders, displacement of populations, or other catastrophic interventions. Finally, there is also the question of fairness. Foreign MNEs do not operate in developing countries out of charitable concerns, but first and foremost because it is profitable for them. They are there to extract resources and expand their customer bases and are certainly better placed than regular African citizens to afford to pay their share of taxes.

In terms of the larger significance of developments in India and Africa for Mauritius, this case directs attention to the challenges of governance in small OFCs. Even though Mauritius is seen as a promising regional financial center, it is struggling to replace the demand for offshore business in India and to seize new business opportunities in a global financial economy shaped by unyielding market niches and professional networks. While room may still exist in the global and regional political economies for OFCs, Mauritius is not as well positioned as advertisements make it out to be and Africa is unlikely to be as big a market for it as India was. Moreover, Mauritius has suffered reputational damage because of the Mauritius Leaks and the Luanda Leaks, for which it was unprepared. In the Mauritius Leaks, the records of an offshore law firm revealed the prevalence of treaty shopping and the extent to which Mauritius has been involved in this particular form of offshore tax avoidance. The Luanda Leaks are a collection of over 700,000 documents on the business dealings of Isabel dos Santos, one of Africa's wealthiest individuals, and her extensive use of Mauritius and other parts of the offshore system. As the director of the International Consortium of Investigative Journalists (ICIJ), Gerard Ryle (as quoted in Cano, 2019) observed of Mauritius:

> I think they were just a bit surprised that they could be viewed in that way and I think that probably goes to a lot of other countries as well where they think that for them it is commerce and they're not harming anybody.

Case selection

The aim of this book is to develop a fuller picture of global financial services that lie outside the traditional foundations of the global economy. Amid newfound global pressures, this book contributes to the study of the offshore economy by probing key cases of emerging markets and the underappreciated role of Mauritius as a player in the global economy. The study of the offshore economy is gaining prominence in IPE (Palan et al., 2010; Harrington, 2016; Garcia-Bernardo et al., 2017; Seabrooke & Wigan, 2017; Sharman, 2017; Vlcek, 2017; Hakelberg & Schaub, 2018; Christensen & Hearson, 2019a), but Africa has remained a weak spot. For example, we carried out a content analysis of all issues of the outstanding journal *Review of African Political Economy* and found no mention of Mauritius as an OFC. The best analyses have been published by civil society organizations (CSOs), think tanks, and international institutions, as is evident throughout the book, with additional scholarship of interest found in law and tax journals (Burgers & Mosquera Valderrama, 2017; Mosquera Valderrama, 2015). However, much of the latter work is less accessible and understood only by a technical audience. Area studies and IPE need to be more engaged with the fast developing dynamics of tax issues at the global, regional, and national levels. This book attempts to fill some of this gap through a conceptual and empirical analysis of emerging markets and the global offshore economy. Few analysts are aware of the fundamental role that DTAs have played in the global economy, or that over a half of the world's current DTAs involve developing countries (Mehta, 2014), unlike earlier periods when nearly all DTAs involved only developed countries. Information on trends found in India and Africa is needed to balance out the sometimes excessively Western-oriented nature of offshore studies. The book emphasizes capital inflows over capital outflows, as justified by data illustrating a rise in the use of offshore jurisdictions for investments into emerging markets in recent years and an opposite pattern in the case of developed economies (UNCTAD, 2015, pp. 198–199).

Lower-middle-income countries in Africa represent an important test because they are presently in a position similar to that of India in the early 1990s. There has been a process of economic opening and African societies have a more positive outlook toward globalization and liberalization than most other regions (Pew Research Center, 2014). In the difficult choice between foreign investment and tax revenue, African countries have largely chosen capital flows, reflecting their desire for injections of foreign investment. This is in line with India's experience over the last two decades. However, it is a genuine trade-off. One major investigation into DTAs concluded that African countries have given up more power to tax multinationals than developing countries in other parts of the world (ActionAid, 2016).[2] Because of offshore structures, capital gains receipts in most African countries are negligible (Bracking, 2012, p. 621). Tension is mounting in Africa between the accommodation of offshore capital and the global, regional, and national efforts against the offshore economy. One instructive CSO report highlights Mauritius as "a particularly corrosive tax haven, especially in the region" (Etter-Phoya et al., 2019, p. 4).

Despite being a small country of 1.2 million residents, Mauritius intermediates large volumes of global capital. The choice of Mauritius as a focal point of the book's analysis reflects an acknowledgment that an analysis undertaken purely at the global scale would have remained too abstract and that it is in less known bilateral offshore relationships that global economic patterns are sometimes most apparent. Mauritius differs substantially from other OFCs such as the Netherlands, Luxembourg, and Ireland, which overwhelmingly intermediate flows of capital between Western countries. As Hers et al. (2018) point out, 79% of Mauritius's foreign investment travels to developing economies.[3] Mauritius's outsized role in India's political economy is evident in the following statistic: from 2000 to 2016, Mauritius was responsible for the largest amount of foreign direct investment (FDI) into India, which equated to 34% of the total FDI (Department for Promotion of Industry and Internal Trade [DPIIT], 2021). Mauritius's structures were first known generically as offshore companies before the Mauritius government rebranded such vehicles as Global Business Companies (GBCs) because of the negative connotations of the term "offshore." According to the robust database produced by Tørsløv et al. (2020), Mauritius collects 97% of its corporate tax receipts by artificially attracting US$7.2 billion in corporate profits shifted from higher-tax countries, without substantial underlying business activity taking place in Mauritius.

Vlcek (2011, p. 147) highlights how potential OFCs make choices in a world of offshore competition:

> As long as offshore financial services exist at some place in the world economy the negative features attributed to them would remain present while any localised economic benefits produced by the OFC would accumulate in that place. The creation of an OFC in Ghana represents an effort to capture the rents of offshore finance in Ghana, rather than leaving them to be collected in other locations. In other words, rather than continuing to enrich the banks in Europe and North America, the OFC in Ghana offers the opportunity to keep the wealth in Africa and potentially it will also attract money avoiding taxes in Europe and North America.

Mauritius is following the same logic as it seeks to assert itself in the global offshore system and continue to capture a share of the available rents. While Ghana continues to struggle, Mauritius has successfully carved out a niche for itself. Its future prospects, however, are far from assured.

Careful examination of the behavior of multinationals within emerging markets is needed. Large MNEs are the archetypal abusers of offshore structures (Desai et al., 2006, p. 20). Historically, tax systems have been written to the advantage of large companies rather than smaller companies. By exploiting loopholes in the international tax system and taking advantage of tax subsidies, MNEs outcompete smaller, locally based competitors (Shaxson & O'Hagan, 2013; OECD, 2015). There is a widespread misconception that there is a clear line between tax evasion and tax avoidance. According to this misconception, tax evasion is by definition illegal, but tax avoidance, although ethically questionable, is perfectly legal. However, as Shaxson (2019) explains, while tax evasion is indeed indisputably illegal, tax avoidance is a considerably more complicated matter. Tax avoidance lies in a vast grey area in which it is frequently tax authorities and courts that are called on to decide on the legality of any given tax avoidance scheme and while the rulings sometimes do go in favor of MNEs, very often they do not. Reflecting this more nuanced reality, in recent years, several major UN bodies, high-level panels, and task forces have been opting to bypass the question of legality as much less important than the fact that both tax evasion and tax avoidance "foster inequalities, deprive countries of resources that could be used for financing public goods, and undermine trust in governance and the social contract" (FACTI Panel, 2021, p. 7). As a result, much of the focus has shifted toward illicit financial flows (IFFs), which include outright financial and tax crimes like money laundering and tax evasion, but also tax avoidance. In this book, we make a distinction between tax evasion and tax avoidance whenever such a distinction is sufficiently clear and appropriate, but our interest likewise lies more with the impacts of these phenomena than with their legality.

Structure of the book

The book's analysis proceeds in six parts. In Chapters 2 and 3, we present our analytical framework, which is based on the historical macrosociological approach of world-systems analysis and the conflict between a set of global, regional, and national forces that are accommodative to offshore finance, and those that are resistant to it, eventually resulting in the promulgation of new global standards and norms negotiated in the wake of the global financial crisis. This context is producing an uneven offshore world, in the sense that there are differentiated outcomes between developed, emerging, and developing economies. Differentiated outcomes are also found among OFCs, with the least viable ones falling by the wayside as the offshore system consolidates toward fewer but better established jurisdictions offering a broader range of more sophisticated services. While it is often global and regional factors that are emphasized in these debates, national factors are critical as well, as it is the interplay of all three that is shaping outcomes in several key respects:

- The more forceful and comprehensive implementation of new rules by developed and emerging economies (this applies especially to India);
- The limited implementation of new rules by developing economies eager to attract offshore investment (this applies especially to many African countries);
- The ability of higher tier OFCs to protect themselves; and
- The inability of lower tier OFCs to protect themselves.

With this larger context established, Chapters 4 and 5 examine the patterns of change and continuity in India's and Africa's relationships with the offshore system. Aside from the usual combination of academic sources, national and international statistics, reports from private research firms and international financial institutions (IFIs), and accounts from national and international media outlets used throughout the book, these chapters are also based on over 125 elite interviews. Fieldwork was conducted in Mauritius in 2014 and 2016, during which over 40 interviews were conducted with financial sector elites, public sector administrators, and government officials. Building on these initial findings, follow-on research was carried out in India in 2017 and 2018, consisting of over 25 meetings in New Delhi and Mumbai with informants from the financial services industry, the public sector, and the civil society sector. Follow-on research was also carried out again in Mauritius in 2019, consisting of over 30 additional interviews. Throughout this whole period, over 30 additional in-person, telephone, or online interviews were conducted with informants spanning all three sectors from around a dozen European, Asian, and African countries.

Chapter 6 contrasts the outcomes in India and Africa, drawing out the significance of recent events. These include India's taking on of global tax leadership, the slow emergence of questioning from many African countries about the role of Mauritius as an OFC, and the ambitious aspirations of Mauritius to advance into the top ranks of global finance – a goal that is implausible. Chapter 7 recapitulates the primary theoretical and empirical findings, outlines possible future scenarios, and raises several lines of future enquiries concerning China's offshore engagement, specifically its potential to replace India as a major user of Mauritian offshore companies.

Notes

1 The members of the G20 are Argentina, Australia, Brazil, Canada, China, France, Germany, India, Indonesia, Italy, Japan, Korea, Mexico, Russia, Saudi Arabia, South Africa, Turkey, the United Kingdom, the United States, and the European Union. Spain is also invited as a permanent guest.
2 See Sauvant and Sachs (2009) for a larger global discussion on the economic contribution of DTAs and BITs.
3 Similarly, Singapore transfers 69% of its outward FDI stock to developing economies (Hers et al., 2018).

2 Analytical framework part one

World-systems analysis, global finance, and regional specialization in the global offshore economy

The following two chapters set out the book's analytical framework, which combines key concepts and theories derived from world-systems analysis with dominant patterns and processes that shape the context in which Mauritius's engagement with India and Africa need to be understood. This chapter represents the first part of this theoretical and empirical contextualization. We begin by delving into world-systems analysis, which informs our thinking about the historical and systemic sources of unevenness within the global economy and the roles of differently positioned states, ideologies, and social movements within it. After that, we look at two prominent patterns related to the history of the offshore world: the rise of truly global finance since the early 1970s, and the roots of the regional specialization of offshore hubs in the global offshore economy.

World-systems analysis

Almost five decades ago, Immanuel Wallerstein (1974a, 1974b) laid the foundations of one of the two main strands of historical macrosociology, world-systems analysis. This formidable research paradigm, which was essentially a synthesis of continental European historicism, Marxism, and "Third World" radicalism, especially dependency theory, went on to revolutionize the study of modern social change through the use of an ambitious conceptual framework and a sweeping metanarrative. One of the foundational axioms of world-systems analysis is the replacement of the standard unit of analysis in the social sciences, most often the nation state, with the system as a whole, which in our era specifically means the capitalist system. The argument is not against simplifying the immense complexity of the real world for illustrative purposes but against getting lost in the simplifications and running with them, which has all too often plagued the social sciences. For example, it is perfectly fine to study any events or phenomena by focusing primarily on their endogenous or exogenous factors; or on their global, regional, national, or other aspects; or perhaps on their economic, political, social, cultural, or other dimensions; or to approach them from the specific point of view of intergovernmental organizations, nation states, corporations, social movements, individuals, or any other actors; however, we should never forget that each of these factors, aspects, dimensions, actors, or any

DOI: 10.4324/9781003161011-2

other descriptors is part of the same social reality, each one constantly influencing the others and in turn being influenced by each of them. Social reality is not easily simplified without incurring losses and thus sacrificing analytical accuracy. As such, world-systems analysis insists that regardless of what the specific focus is, in order to mitigate these losses, all events and phenomena should be studied within their historical and systemic contexts, which is exactly what we are striving for in this book.

Like all successful research paradigms, world-systems analysis has not remained static over the decades. It has undergone several transformations and continues to evolve to this day. Consequently, there is no single unified world-systems consensus but rather many different world-systems perspectives with distinct and sometimes contradictory central theories and metanarratives (Amin, 1976; Frank, 1978; Chase-Dunn, 1998; Arrighi, 2010). In this book, we specifically engage with the original world-systems analysis as it was developed and refined by Wallerstein (1974a, 1974b, 1979, 1984, 2004). Moreover, it should be stressed that the following outline is not intended to capture the full complexity of Wallerstein's conceptual framework and metanarrative but merely to serve as a simplified frame of reference through which we approach the subsequent sections and chapters. With this caveat out of the way, we can proceed to the outlining of the three interwoven sets of central concepts and theories that we believe are helpful in conceptualizing the multidimensional unevenness of the offshore world and the growing resistance against it.

The first and most recognizable set of concepts pertains to the axial division of labor, which divides production in the capitalist system into core production processes and peripheral production processes, with the pair being relationally bound together by an invisible axis. Core production processes are capital-intensive, requiring high-skilled labor and cutting edge technology. They are the least accessible and thus the most profitable ones, and since profitability is directly related to monopolization, they are run by global monopolies and oligopolies and are therefore subject to minimal competition. Peripheral production processes are labor-intensive, requiring only low-skilled labor and rudimentary technology. They are the most accessible and thus the least profitable ones, and are therefore subject to the highest degree of competition. When trade occurs, core processes are in a far stronger position than peripheral ones, which results in unequal exchange, a worldwide mechanism by which surplus value constantly flows from the periphery to the core. It is primarily, though not exclusively, through this exploitative mechanism that the axial division of labor has led to the creation of a stark systemic hierarchy which divides the capitalist system into core, semiperipheral, and peripheral zones and states. This division of the capitalist system largely depends on particular mixes of core and peripheral processes taking place within their territories, which essentially determine their overall levels of power and development. There exists a certain degree of bounded dynamism within this division in that it is common for some states to ascend and others to descend the rungs of the ladder, but the systemic hierarchy itself is set and constantly maintained with every successive cycle of capital accumulation. Hence, there always exists an exploitative core, an exploited periphery, and in between them a semiperiphery that both exploits and is exploited.

The second set of concepts pertains to the interstate system, which explains much of the bounded dynamism that takes place within the aforementioned systemic hierarchy. States are crucial arenas of class struggle and play an indispensable role in cycles of accumulation by distorting the world market to favor their respective dominant class forces. The key determinant in their ability to do so is state power, the starting point of which, aside from natural and demographical endowments, is the modern bureaucratic apparatus, which leads to increasingly effective tax collection. Tax revenue then forms the basis for the development of the productive, commercial, financial, cultural, diplomatic, military, and other capacities of the state. Stronger states use these capacities to distort world markets, militarily through direct imperialism and colonialism, diplomatically through alliances and agreements, and economically through various forms of foreign and domestic coercion, regulation, taxation, and rule-setting, enforcing and reinforcing mechanisms of unequal exchange. When done successfully, the distortion generates a more favorable mix of core and peripheral processes, and thus a more favorable position in the systemic hierarchy. Periodically, the ongoing rivalry between the most powerful core states ends in one of them achieving hegemony, a rare preeminent status characterized by simultaneous supremacy in so many domains of power that for a period of time it enables the hegemon to impose its own rules within the capitalist system. This was the case with Great Britain from the mid-nineteenth century until 1945, and with the United States (US) from 1945 to around 1968, which marked the beginning of its ongoing hegemonic decline, although despite the gradual loss of influence in comparison with the past, its position remains unmatched. Accordingly, it is state interference rather than the free market that is synonymous with capitalism. The free market is merely one of the many myths legitimizing the capitalist system, a function of ideology.

The third set of concepts pertains to the dominant geoculture, which refers to the assortment of widely accepted truths, ideas, values, and norms that make up the cultural and ideological framework on which the capitalist system operates and which constrain social action within it. For most of the history of the capitalist system, the dominant geoculture has been that of centrist liberalism, the middle-of-the-road ideology positioned between right-wing conservatism and left-wing radicalism. The fundamental differences between the three ideologies lie in how far and how fast they propose that progress in terms of class, racial, gender, and other traditional social hierarchies should go. Of course, given the baseline of these hierarchies, what centrist liberalism delivered in practice was merely a milder form of the old bourgeois, white, male, and other forms of dominance. However, it also promised continued progress, and so, through the combination of its moderating influence, repression, and cooption, it kept the antisystemic forces of both the right and the left in check, maintaining relative stability. This lasted until around 1968, when the global wave of social unrest and general strikes in response to falling profitability and rising unemployment shattered the dominance of centrist liberalism over the other two ideologies, freeing them to begin reasserting themselves. In an immediate effort to retain control and stabilize the capitalist system, the centrist liberal establishment strategically aligned with the antisystemic movements of the radical left on the sociocultural front, leading to unprecedented progress in issues of race, gender, and sexuality, and with the antisystemic movements of the conservative right on the economic and political fronts, leading to the neoliberal class campaign that reversed much of the progress achieved by the middle and lower classes in the preceding decades. By the early 2000s, the radical left began pushing back on the economic and political fronts and the conservative right on the sociocultural front, leaving the increasingly divided and desperate centrist liberal establishment clinging to appeals for a return to the status quo ante "normalcy" that had caused the chaos in the first place.

This, of course, represents only an extremely abridged version of the world-systems analysis metanarrative but it is sufficient in highlighting the key concepts and theories guiding our analysis here. In short, the capitalist system is by its nature a highly uneven structure of social organization that is based not only on a complex top-down exploitation that takes place within individual countries along class, racial, gender, and other lines but also, and even more importantly, on a complex top-down exploitation that takes place between individual countries along the core, the semiperiphery, and the periphery lines. Essentially, in every country, elites – whether political, business, or other – have to a greater or lesser degree been exploiting their own masses, but core elites have also been exploiting semiperipheral and peripheral masses, and semiperipheral elites have also been exploiting peripheral masses. Semiperipheral and peripheral elites sometimes collude with core elites for a portion of the profits, and sometimes they compete with them, although generally they are in a weaker position to do so. Since a portion of the extracted wealth is taxed and used for national development, core masses tend to benefit more than semiperipheral and peripheral masses, and semiperipheral masses tend to benefit more than peripheral masses. The masses as such are of course not just passive observers; they struggle constantly, often by organizing and starting social movements. As the capitalist system matures, requiring greater amounts of increasingly educated labor, the masses as a whole are becoming more aware of their exploitation and the mechanisms through which it is conducted. This has led not only to a proliferation of social movements in completely new issue areas but arguably also to increasingly effective social movements. As we shall see, these key concepts and theories have a lot to contribute to our understanding of the past, present, and future dynamics of the offshore world, to which we turn to next.

The rise of global finance

The first prominent pattern relating to the history of the offshore world we need to take a closer look at is the spread and growth of global finance since the early

1970s. It was in this period that neoliberalism began to replace Keynesianism as the dominant ideological paradigm and by the end of the 1980s resulted in a fundamental restructuring of the global economy. Neoliberalism is a notoriously slippery term that still arouses a great deal of controversy. For its most fervent adherents, it represents nothing more than the belief that human well-being can best be advanced by unleashing the individual entrepreneurial spirit within an institutional framework characterized by strong private property rights, free markets, and free trade, with as little state intervention as possible. For its most ardent critics, it represents nothing less than a concerted campaign for the maintenance, reconstitution, and restoration of capitalist class power over all areas of social life, with its political rhetoric of freedom and liberty merely serving as a veil behind which the capitalists hide their true intentions. In spite of this sizable disconnect, what both sides generally can agree on is that neoliberalism is associated with a specific set of policy prescriptions for development that include, among others: fiscal austerity; low taxation achieved by broadening tax bases and cutting marginal tax rates; liberalization of trade, interest rates, and inward FDI; privatization; and deregulation. Together, these policy prescriptions have produced a particularly fertile ground for the global process of financialization (Williamson, 2004; Harvey, 2005; Mirowski & Plehwe, 2009; Davies, 2014).

In our usage, global finance denotes financial structures that are: relatively common across different jurisdictions; accessible around the world because they are supplied by a network of professionals that is global in reach; and utilized by a rising number of actors globally rather than exclusively Western-based actors. These conditions have largely been met in the field of offshore finance. Consider the tremendous spread and growth that have occurred across the multiple main structural elements that constitute the offshore world (Palan, 2003; Ogle, 2017):

- Offshore financial centers (OFCs);
- Flags of convenience (FOCs);
- Special economic zones (SEZs); and
- Professional intermediaries.

OFCs, commonly referred to as tax havens or secrecy jurisdictions, are jurisdictions that attract foreign clientele with a mix of low or zero tax rates, light and flexible incorporation, ample secrecy provisions, and a host of other advantages that enable so-called high-net-worth individuals (HNWIs) and MNEs to engage in various forms of tax and regulatory arbitrage and even outright financial crime. The number of OFCs has risen dramatically from about two dozen in the early 1970s to anywhere between 60 and 100 such jurisdictions actively operating today, depending on the exact definition used. Even more troubling than this dramatic rise in their number has been the substantial increase in their impact on the global economy in that same period. Once marginal players, OFCs are now home to millions of offshore structures, including international business companies, captive insurance companies, trusts, mutual funds, and even most of the various shadow banking instruments such as hedge funds, special purpose entities, structured investment vehicles, collateralized debt obligations, and others that have gained notoriety for their role in the global financial crisis. About 50% of all international lending is routed through OFCs and they are also estimated to account for as much as 40% of all FDI, even though most of this is completely artificial, passing through empty corporate shells that exist only on paper, for no other purpose than the reduction or elimination of tax and regulatory obligations (Hampton, 1996; Palan et al., 2010; Garcia-Bernardo et al., 2017; Damgaard et al., 2019; Tax Justice Network [TJN], 2020a, 2021).

FOCs, sometimes also referred to as flags of registry, represent one of the ways in which the offshore world extends into commercial maritime transportation. Jurisdictions providing FOCs allow ships to be registered under their flag, and thus to be subject to their laws, regardless of the actual national origin of the owners. More often than not, these jurisdictions are OFCs themselves. However, even when this is not the case, just like OFCs, FOCs attract their foreign clientele with a mix of low or zero tax rates on shipping income, minimal regulations regarding ships and crews, and greater anonymity throughout, thereby significantly reducing the registry and operating costs of the owners as well as their accountability to potential stakeholders. To complicate matters further, it is common for flag registries to be managed from a different jurisdiction than the one providing the FOCs to insulate the owners even more. Similarly, as has been observed with OFCs, there has been a substantial rise in FOCs, both in terms of the number of jurisdictions providing them and in terms of the share of ships operating under them. In the early 1980s, there were only about 10 jurisdictions, with their FOCs collectively accounting for approximately 25% of world shipping tonnage. Today, there are more than 30 such jurisdictions, and their FOCs collectively account for as much as 70% of world shipping tonnage (Metaxas, 1981; Rodrigue, 2020; International Transport Workers' Federation [ITF], 2021).

SEZs, a generic term increasingly used to cover all types of free zones, free trade zones,[1] export processing zones, free economic zones, and freeports, refers to clearly demarcated geographical areas within which governments attempt to foster domestic industrial development by attracting FDI with a mix of preferential fiscal and regulatory regimes, infrastructure support, and other incentives that are unavailable in the rest of the national economy. Because the primary aim of SEZs has in general more credibly and more demonstrably been to use their inward FDI for genuine economic activity, such as to build, diversify, and upgrade industries, or to support complex cross-border supply chains, they have rightly not been considered to be as harmful or as controversial as OFCs, which have sometimes claimed a similar primary aim but in practice have clearly been content with collecting their fees for letting all sorts of financial flows pass through artificially, regardless of the serious tax and regulatory consequences for other economies. Notwithstanding this difference, SEZs have earned their place among the main structural elements of the offshore world because the incentives they provide and the ways in which they have all too often been providing them have consistently been shown to be tied to IFFs as well as to human rights, labor, environmental, and other abuses (Padilla et al., 2020). Even worse, most of these costs appear to have been suffered in vain. A recent study that analyzes the performance of 346 SEZs in 22 emerging economies between 2007 and 2012 finds that 81% of the SEZs performed equally or worse relative to national GDP growth, and among the remaining 19% that performed better, the average differential over national growth never exceeded 5% (Frick et al., 2019). Nevertheless, as in the case of OFCs and FOCs, the number of jurisdictions setting up SEZs and the number of SEZs themselves have risen substantially from 47 jurisdictions setting up 176 SEZs in the mid-1980s to 147 jurisdictions setting up nearly 5,400 SEZs today (International Labour Organization [ILO], 2014; UNCTAD, 2019).

Finally, there are the professional intermediaries from the accounting, legal, finance, banking, and other related sectors, which arguably edge out OFCs as the most important structural element of the offshore world because they not only grease the wheels of the entire offshore juggernaut and connect all of its constituent parts to its individual and MNE clientele but together with receptive political and business elites from around the world have also been actively shaping and steering it. Put another way, these professional intermediaries are not just the software that runs the offshore hardware and makes it accessible to the end users but also the programmers of the software, and the designers of the hardware, constantly working to make both as user-friendly, efficient, and safe for the end users as possible. Regarding the spread and growth of these professional intermediaries, it is sufficient to point out that the ones dominating the global offshore economy are by and large the same household names dominating their respective sectors in the global economy as a whole. Examples include the "Big Four" accounting firms; New York's white shoe law firms; London's Magic Circle law firms; the Offshore Magic Circle law firms, connected to the United Kingdom (UK); and the notoriously too-big-to-fail financial services and banking giants like JP Morgan Chase, Citigroup, Goldman Sachs, Lloyds, Royal Bank of Scotland, Deutsche Bank, Commerzbank, UBS, BNP Paribas, ABN Amro, Santander, HSBC, and many others that nowadays operate either directly or through their local partnerships in nearly every jurisdiction in the world. While offshore secrecy and regular commercial confidentiality make it difficult to pinpoint exactly how much of their overall activity relates to the global offshore economy, the numerous offshore-related scandals, data leaks, and data hacks strongly suggest that this offshore portion has been rising hand in hand with the other main structural elements of the offshore world (OECD, 2008; Sikka & Willmott, 2013; Taylor & Derudder, 2016; Schumann, 2017; De Groen, 2017; Murphy & Stausholm, 2017; Jones et al., 2018; ICIJ, 2021a, 2021b).

Naturally, supply of this magnitude could not have sustained for such a long time, let alone continued to expand as much as it has, had there not been corresponding demand. We begin with the contemporary offshore exposure of the world's leading MNEs. In the US, 366 (73%) of the Fortune 500 companies voluntarily disclosed that between them, they maintained 9,755 subsidiaries in OFCs, based on a list of 50 OFCs that excluded US states from consideration (Phillips et al., 2017). In the UK, only two of the FTSE 100 companies did not maintain any subsidiaries in OFCs. The 98 that did maintained a combined 8,311 of them, which amounted to 38% of all the foreign subsidiaries controlled by the FTSE 100 companies (ActionAid, 2013a). In Australia, 61 of the ASX 100 companies maintained 692 subsidiaries in OFCs (Zirnsak, 2013). Similar patterns exist for France and its CAC 40 companies (Observatoire des Multinationales, 2020), for Spain and its IBEX 35 companies (Oxfam Intermón, 2020), as well as for many other countries and their largest companies. The exposure is thus evidently significant. However, the crucial takeaway is that in all of these examples, maintaining subsidiaries in OFCs correlated with average effective tax rates that were 7% to 14% lower than the respective statutory tax rates and also lower than the respective average effective tax rates of companies that did not maintain any subsidiaries in OFCs (TJN Australia & United Voice, 2014; Osborne, 2016; Gardner et al., 2017). This was also indirectly confirmed by the OECD (2015), which estimates the effective tax rates paid by large MNEs in general to be 4% to 8.5% lower than those paid by enterprises with similar domestic-only operations.

The offshore exposure of individuals is more difficult to gauge, as they generally have far fewer reporting obligations and far less public visibility. Nonetheless, as already touched on in the introduction, it is individuals that are ultimately the beneficiaries of MNE profits, and we are learning more about the composition of both this MNE portion and the remainder with every new scandal, leak, and hack, of which at least one has dominated the global headlines every year since 2013. It was then that the ICIJ, a global network that today encompasses 267 investigative reporters from over 100 countries, territories, and media organizations, released its original Offshore Leaks bombshell. This was followed by the China Leaks and the Luxembourg Leaks in 2014, the Swiss Leaks in 2015, the Panama Papers in 2016, the Paradise Papers in 2017, the West Africa Leaks in 2018, the Mauritius Leaks in 2019, and the Luanda Leaks and the FinCEN Files in 2020 (ICIJ, 2021a, 2021b). In 2021, we are already off to a solid start with the publication of Le Monde's OpenLux investigation, which involves 64,458 beneficiaries representing 157 nationalities, including at least 279 of the more than 2,000 billionaires listed by Forbes magazine, and 55,000 offshore shell companies managing assets worth at least US$7 trillion (Baruch et al., 2021).

The ICIJ data currently cover a period of over 40 years and contain information on close to one million offshore entities linked to individuals and MNEs in more than 200 jurisdictions. Thanks to this ever-growing treasure trove of data and the development of newer and more innovative estimation methods, we now know that the individual beneficiaries of offshore services have always been more geographically diverse than what was portrayed by the old stereotypical narratives according to which these services were mostly the domain of transnational organized crime syndicates, so-called "Third World" and "Second World" authoritarian kleptocrats, oligarchs, and corrupt officials, and perhaps the occasional shady businessperson or wayward celebrity from the otherwise "clean" Western countries of the "First World." While the old stereotypes certainly continue to be amply represented among the offshore clientele even today, for their "First World" counterparts, be they run-of-the-mill wealthy businesspeople, celebrities, and athletes, or political and business elites at the highest echelons of power and influence, the offshore escape has from the outset been at least as common of an avenue for managing their financial affairs.

We also know that the offshore wealth held by this geographically diverse clientele has swelled to enormous proportions. According to what are arguably the two most comprehensive studies that have attempted such a measurement, from the early 1970s to around 2014, the amount of concealed private wealth that this clientele has siphoned off offshore was conservatively estimated to range somewhere between US$7.6 trillion and US$36 trillion, or 8% to 38% of total global financial wealth, which amounted to about US$95.5 trillion in 2014 (Henry, 2012, 2016; Zucman, 2015). Regardless of whether it is Zucman's lower estimate or Henry's higher one that more accurately approximates reality, it is worth underscoring that both studies focused strictly on tax evasion, and on financial wealth with at least some form of an electronic footprint. This means that, as the authors openly acknowledge, at least three non-negligible sources of offshore wealth were excluded from their assessments. The first and likely the least significant is cash in high-denomination bank notes, of which Zucman estimates as much as US$400 billion could be held in vaults in OFCs. The second is tax avoidance, which generally results in significantly higher tax revenue losses than tax evasion, and at least some portion of it is likely held offshore in properly declared bank accounts after the tax schemes have run their course. The third and likely the most significant is non-financial wealth, which includes real estate, art, airplanes, yachts, racehorses, diamonds, gold bricks, and other commodities and holders of value of which a large proportion is registered offshore. With all this taken into account, it is clear that the offshore stash must be substantially larger than Zucman's lower estimate, although is also plausible for it to exceed even Henry's higher estimate. Whatever the true sum may be, we know that the offshore stash continues to grow. The most recent and arguably the most authoritative of the studies designed to capture this dynamic estimates that as much as US$427 billion in direct tax revenues is being added to the stash every year (Cobham et al., 2020). Of this, US$182 billion (43%) is attributed to offshore tax evasion by wealthy individuals and US$245 billion (57%) to offshore tax avoidance by MNEs. To be clear, the US$427 billion figure is not an estimate of the total financial wealth that is being stashed offshore every year, but only of the taxes that are lost as a result. This means that the total financial wealth that is being stashed offshore every year is actually about four to five times larger than the US$427 billion.

Another thing we know is that the wealth held offshore is extremely concentrated. In the most sophisticated study on the topic to date, Alstadsæter et al. (2019) analyzed micro-data from the Swiss Leaks, the Panama Papers, and tax amnesties conducted in the aftermath of the global financial crisis and matched them to the population-wide administrative income and wealth records of Norway, Sweden, and Denmark. Their findings indicate that the top 0.01% of the wealthiest households own approximately 50% of offshore wealth and the top 0.1% own nearly 80%. As before, these estimates are strictly based on concealed offshore assets that amounted to tax evasion, while excluding all properly declared offshore assets, at least a portion of which likely amounted to tax avoidance and would have likely skewed the resulting distribution of wealth toward the top even more had it been taken into account. Thus, as diverse as the offshore clientele is geographically, it is anything but that in terms of class. Offshore wealth is exclusively owned by the world's wealthy and even more so its super wealthy, and based on what we know about race and gender at the very top of the global wealth distribution, most of it disproportionally by white men, further exacerbating global inequality across all three of the traditional social dividing lines (Chancel, 2021).

In short, the offshore world is no longer something to be found in a few select enclaves on the margins of the global economy, but rather something that already stretches from its very center to every corner of it, and is well on track to continue making gains almost everywhere. To understand how this monumental transformation was possible in the first place, and where Mauritius fits into all of it, we must first understand some of the technical inner workings of the offshore world, and to do that, we must take a brief detour into history and understand three basic principles upon which the international tax system has been based on ever since its creation in the 1920s at the League of Nations (Picciotto, 1992; Devereux & Vella, 2014):

- The primacy of residence over source principle;
- The separate entity principle; and
- The arm's length principle.

The primacy of residence over source principle was the result of an uneasy and still highly contentious historical compromise on the allocation of taxing rights between all of the jurisdictions with a legitimate claim to some portion of the total taxes paid by MNEs operating within their borders. According to this principle, the jurisdiction of source, which is the jurisdiction hosting an investment, is generally limited to taxing only the active income of the local branch or subsidiary of an MNE, in other words, its local business profits. The jurisdiction of residence, which is the jurisdiction where the parent company or investor resides, is generally entitled to tax the MNE's worldwide passive income, in other words, the dividends, interest, royalties, capital gains, and other forms of investment income from all sources, although subject to the circumscribed right of source jurisdictions to impose a minor withholding tax on them. As a consequence of these terms, the international tax system has become heavily skewed in favor of what have mostly been developed capital-exporting countries where the beneficiaries of the economic activity reside, at the expense of what have more often than not been developing capital-importing countries where the economic activity actually takes place, and this despite the clearly valuable role of the latter for MNEs as markets for the selling of their products and services, extraction of raw materials, and exploitation of cheaper labor or more permissive business environments. However, reaching a compromise is not the same as being able to implement it, which has forced the experts charged with resolving the numerous quandaries involved in the process of forging functional international tax rules to devise another principle.

The separate entity principle was a consequential piece of legal fiction designed to get around one of the main problems in the original debates on the allocation of taxing rights, which was the difficulty of treating MNEs as the unitary legal entities they are without a high degree of multilateral cooperation. According to this principle, tax authorities had to treat each MNE subsidiary as if it was its own independent entity, even though subsidiaries are of course centrally controlled in every single way that matters. With this approach, tax authorities would have their jobs made relatively straightforward, as they would only be dealing with the accounts of local entities that were fictionally separated from their respective MNEs. However, it was not lost on the experts that by itself, this blunt solution would likely raise another serious problem, because once tax authorities began treating related entities as separate, there would be nothing to stop MNEs from artificially structuring any trade and investment taking place between their entities by manipulating the transfer prices of the transactions to shift their worldwide profits to low-tax jurisdictions, and their worldwide losses to the higher-tax jurisdictions where they genuinely operate, effectively reducing or even eliminating their tax obligations, all without any knowledge by the affected tax authorities, or indeed any recourse available to them. To mitigate the worst effects of this eventuality, the experts were forced to devise another principle.

The arm's length principle was another consequential piece of legal fiction, one specifically designed to ensure that the separate entity principle would not result in as much international tax avoidance as it potentially could, and thus be at least somewhat practicable. According to this principle, any transaction between related entities within a single MNE had to be priced as if it was undertaken between unrelated entities operating at arm's length, in other words, by using market prices. If a tax authority discovered and proved that arm's length pricing between related entities was not adhered to, it now had the right to rectify the situation by penalizing the offending MNE and adjusting its taxes accordingly. However, far from empowering tax authorities, the new power afforded by the arm's length principle thrust them into a state of legal schizophrenia. On the one hand, they had to treat local entities as completely separate, but on the other, they had to scrutinize the transfer prices of their transactions undertaken with related entities, about which they had little to no information under normal circumstances. Even if the tax authorities did arduously obtain the relevant information, their task was still much easier in theory than in practice, because finding comparable market transactions on the basis of which to determine what constitutes a legitimate arm's length price has always been difficult and time-consuming, and this has only grown more so with the global economy constantly maturing into ever-greater complexity. Instead of being an effective way to address transfer pricing manipulation, the arm's length principle gave rise to an increasingly complex jumble of transfer pricing rules and calculation methods, as well as to an army of transfer pricing professionals specializing in delivering the results desired by MNEs while minimizing the risk of successful challenges by tax authorities.

The primary motivation behind the creation of the international tax system and its design on the basis of these three basic principles has been to facilitate cross-border trade and investment by removing the various tax-related obstacles that businesses encountered as they increasingly began to internationalize their operations and set up subsidiaries in foreign markets. By far the most important of these obstacles was double taxation, generally defined as the imposition of comparable taxes by two or more jurisdictions on the same taxpayer in respect of the same income or profit in the same period. However, broader questions of tax certainty loomed large as well, leaving businesses in the dark about how much tax they could expect to pay in each of the jurisdictions where they operated. Understandably, this raised the risk of any foreign venture considerably, undermining exchange in goods and services, and movements of capital, labor, and technology. To give credit where it is due, the international tax system has largely succeeded in preventing double taxation and in providing at least some amount of tax certainty to MNEs and other investors. Nonetheless, the single-minded focus with which these particular objectives had been pursued at the expense of nearly all other considerations, and the shortcuts taken to achieve them, have all but guaranteed that the international tax system would lead to serious structural consequences down the line.

Leaving aside for the moment that the international tax system practically opened the gates to international tax avoidance, with the only remedy put in place amounting to little more than an honor system, its reliance on the source/residence dichotomy and the active/passive income dichotomy have also made it, in the words of even pro-business moderates such as Devereux and Vella (2014, p. 461), "arbitrary" and "ill-suited to dealing with multinationals operating in a truly global business environment," as well as "manipulable," "distortive," and "often incoherent and unprincipled." Worse than that, the authors continue, by structuring international tax relations in this way, the system practically encouraged all participants to engage in a destabilizing competitive race to the bottom in tax rates and other tax-related incentives. This was not only a matter of potential host jurisdictions desperate to attract mobile capital and not having much else with which to attract it, but even home jurisdictions such as the US, which on several occasions actively aided its MNEs in their use of aggressive tax avoidance schemes, and continued doing so as long as their gain was greater than the reduction in its domestic tax base, in other words as long as more of the cost of this subsidy was borne by competing jurisdictions (Altshuler & Grubert, 2005). Regardless of the extent to which the international tax system's exceptional conduciveness to international tax avoidance and tax competition was unintended or incidental, the key takeaway for our purposes is that they emerged as two of its defining characteristics and laid the foundations for the eventual rise of the offshore world.

Of course, this did not happen overnight. The seeds had been planted, but it would take decades before the conditions were just right for them to sprout. For one, the international tax system was still new, and since the long negotiation phase over its substance and form was mostly dominated by the UK, the US, and several major colonial powers of continental Europe, while most of the remaining three to four dozen far less influential countries that at one point or another comprised the membership of the League of Nations only played marginal roles, the resulting agreements were fragile and the uptake of the three basic principles only gradual and slow. The main vehicles of dissemination by which the principles eventually spread globally to become an important part of international law were double taxation agreements (DTAs), commonly also known as double taxation avoidance agreements (DTAAs), double tax treaties (DTTs), bilateral tax treaties (BTTs), and income tax treaties (ITTs). The League of Nations process led to the development of several early soft law model tax conventions (MTCs) on which actual DTAs were meant to be based. The separate entity and arm's length principles were broadly accepted in all of them, but the primacy of residence over source principle remained an enduring point of contention. This continued to be the case even after the dissolution of the League of Nations, when it was the OECD and to a much lesser extent the United Nations (UN), which were put in charge of international tax matters, eventually coming up with their own respective MTCs and even their own respective transfer pricing guidelines (TPGs). Regardless, both the 1977 OECD MTC and the 1980 UN MTC, including all of their subsequent revised versions, ended up supporting the contentious principle, with the only difference being that the OECD MTCs have done so more stringently than the UN MTCs, which have been more moderate (see Box 2.1).

Box 2.1: A Brief History of Double Taxation Agreements (DTAs) and the Main Controversies Surrounding Them

DTAs are based on a set of common principles designed to prevent double taxation and provide tax certainty to MNEs and other investors in order to facilitate cross-border trade and investment (Picciotto, 1992; Lennard, 2008; Avi-Yonah, 2009). The existing network of more than 3,000 DTAs that are in force today dates back to the 1920s and the soft law MTCs that were being developed at the League of Nations.

The first League of Nations MTC was approved in 1928, and laid many of the basic principles of international taxation, including the primacy of residence over source principle, the separate entity principle, and the arm's length principle. It was followed by the 1935 Draft Convention, which was never approved by a formal intergovernmental meeting, nor used on its own as the basis for DTAs, but has nevertheless left a strong imprint. It further developed the three basic principles and many of its provisions were later incorporated into successive MTCs, including, if we allow for some rewording, contemporary ones. The original 1928 MTC was then directly superseded by the 1943 MTC of Mexico and the 1946 MTC of London.

While both of these new MTCs broadly reaffirmed support for the separate entity and arm's length principles, they differed fundamentally on the allocation of taxing rights between jurisdictions of source and jurisdictions of residence. The 1943 Mexico MTC completely flipped the script, and in no uncertain terms stipulated the primacy of source over residence. Not only did it provide that all income, dividends, interest, and royalties were to be taxable where the underlying business or activity was carried out, with the jurisdiction of residence required to grant a credit for all these source taxes should that be necessary to prevent double taxation, but in the case of the export of raw materials, even the entire income resulting from the sales at world market prices was to be considered as realized in the jurisdiction of source. However, this unexpected twist was only made possible because representatives from many of the capital-exporting colonial powers that normally dominated such negotiations were unable to travel to Mexico during the war, so for once, the reins were left in the hands of representatives from capital-importing countries, many of which, mostly from Latin America, had not been represented at all at the 1928 and 1935 meetings. As soon as the war ended and all of the representatives were once again able to reconvene, the matter was reconsidered at a new round of negotiations in London, resulting in the 1946 London MTC, which fully reasserted the primacy of residence over source, but did not go as far as to supersede the 1943 Mexico MTC. Instead, the Mexico and London MTCs were published together with a commentary, a testament to how significant, and as it would turn out, how lasting, the disagreement on some of the most basic principles of international taxation has been.

Following the 1946 dissolution of the League of Nations, the work on international tax matters was transferred to its institutional successor, the UN, which set up a Fiscal Commission to carry on with what was still a sizable agenda with many unresolved questions and gaps. However, the combination of existing differences, a broader membership, and Cold War tensions proved to be a crippling one, and the Fiscal Commission stopped meeting altogether after 1954. In 1955, the US-led bloc of predominantly Western European powers delegated the work on international tax matters to the Organization for European Economic Cooperation (OEEC), which with the 1961 accession of the US and Canada evolved into the more transatlantic OECD. In 1963, the OECD adopted its own Draft Convention, which after a major round of revisions led to the publication of the 1977 OECD MTC. As a consequence of the rapid acceleration of globalization, liberalization, and technological change in this period, the OECD published a revised version of the OECD MTC in 1992, and this time in a loose-leaf format, in recognition of the need for an increased frequency of updates, which have since been made in 1994, 1995, 1997, 2000, 2003, 2005, 2008, 2010, 2014, and most recently in 2017

(OECD, 2017). Given the composition of the OECD membership over the decades, it should come as no surprise that the starting point for the OECD Draft Convention and the OECD MTCs has been the London MTC, and that every new update has only solidified adherence to the three basic principles further.

In an attempt to at least partially counter these developments, the UN reentered the field of international taxation in 1968, when at the request of developing countries, and very much to the displeasure of some OECD members, it set up the Ad Hoc Group of Experts on Tax Treaties between Developed and Developing Countries. The experts were nominated by their governments, but acted in their personal capacity, and were supported only by a small secretariat. Despite numerous challenges, its work eventually led to the publication of the 1980 UN MTC, with revised versions published in 2001, 2011, and most recently in 2017 (UN, 2017). While the UN MTC is often portrayed as the successor to the Mexico MTC, it has never exhibited anywhere near as much of the commitment to the primacy of source over residence as the Mexico MTC did. In fact, much of the work that went into the UN MTC was instead based more closely on the OECD Draft Convention, and even the text of the UN MTC clarifies that it only represents "a compromise between the source principle and the residence principle" (UN, 2017, p. vi). As a result, the OECD MTC and the UN MTC are actually remarkably similar, with the topics covered, the order of articles, and even about 75% of the actual words being almost identical. In the remaining 25%, the UN MTC does allocate more taxing rights to the jurisdiction of source, but only moderately so. The main differences pertain to when and under what conditions MNEs can be considered as having a permanent establishment in the source jurisdiction, for which the UN MTC provides a slightly lower threshold than the OECD MTC; withholding tax rates on dividends, interest, and royalties, which the UN MTC leaves open to negotiation, while the OECD MTC specifies maximum rates; and the treatment of business profits, capital gains, international shipping, and other items, for which the UN MTC provides a few similarly minor tweaks in favor of source taxation.

Since it was set up, the Ad Hoc Group of Experts was allowed to broaden its focus beyond treaty-related issues, and in 2005, it was upgraded to become the Committee of Experts on International Cooperation in Tax Matters. Still, throughout its existence, whether in its original Ad Hoc Group form or its current Committee form, it has continued to suffer from chronic understaffing and almost non-existent funding, and it has never reached the status of an official UN intergovernmental body, as is once again made explicit even in the text of the UN MTC, which clarifies that its provisions "should not be construed as formal recommendations of the United Nations" (UN, 2017, p. vii). Considering the sizable asymmetries in staffing, financing, and status, the very existence of a regularly updated UN MTC – even one that does not really challenge any of the basic principles of the OECD MTC – can be seen as a real achievement. At the same time, partly due to these asymmetries and partly due to the stark differences in the bargaining power between many developed and developing countries, the UN MTC has been far less influential than the OECD MTC, even as the number of new DTAs steadily increases.

Prior to the wider spread of DTAs, three other important developments laid the foundations for the rise of the offshore world, and further solidified those already laid down by the international tax system. The first, in 1957, was the emergence of the City of London-centered Euromarket, the earliest completely unregulated offshore financial market. The second, from the 1960s onwards, was the process of decolonization, which freed dozens of newly independent sovereign jurisdictions to look for niches in the global market, and the offshore route appeared the most viable for many of them. The third development, occurring throughout this same period, was the tremendous strides made in transportation, communication, and information technologies, with the first successful commercial passenger jet airliners entering service in 1958, the first fax machines in 1964, and the first microprocessors in 1971, greatly facilitating the free movement of goods, services, people, and capital, and making the early offshore enclaves vastly more accessible and efficient than they could have ever hoped to be before (Palan et al., 2010).

With this, our brief detour into history dovetails back into the main path of the spread and growth of global finance, and the onset of the ideological dominance of neoliberalism, the policy prescriptions of which began to build atop all the offshore foundations that had been laid down until then, supercharging virtually every factor that has contributed to the rise of the offshore world. For those offshore foundations stemming directly from the international tax system, the key process set off by the new neoliberal orthodoxy was the feverish scramble for FDI that had taken over the global economy. As a result of this scramble, and to a lesser extent also the geopolitical shift caused by the end of the Cold War, the 1990s ushered in a whole new era of bilateral investment treaties (BITs) and DTAs, with the numbers of both skyrocketing.

As for the BITs, while only 404 (12%) of them had been signed in the four decades between 1950 and 1989, that number jumped by an incredible 2,663 (76%) new signings between 1990 and 2007. Only after that did new signings slow down again to just 410 (12%) between 2008 and April 2015, a period also marked by the renegotiation and termination of hundreds of BITs (UNCTAD, 2015, pp. 121–125). The main reason behind this turnaround was the combination of the system-wide shock of the global financial crisis, the shift in priorities toward sustainable development that had occurred in its aftermath, and several highly controversial investor-state dispute settlement (ISDS) cases. In the latter, MNEs attempted to use BITs to exert influence over the domestic policymaking of host states, to the clear detriment of internationally recognized health, safety, environmental, and labor standards. What is arguably the most notorious of these cases was launched in 2011 by the US tobacco giant, Philip Morris, shortly after it moved ownership of its Australian operations from its subsidiary in Switzerland to a Hong Kong limited liability company under the administration of its subsidiary in the Netherlands. This was done to exploit the ISDS clause of the Hong Kong–Australia BIT, and sue to claim compensation for losses allegedly caused by the introduction of Australia's new plain cigarette packaging laws. Even though the MNE ultimately lost the case in 2015 on an abuse of rights technicality, because it was found to have changed its corporate structure to gain the protection of the BIT only well after the Australian government announced its intention to pass the disputed laws, Australia still had to cover half of its own legal costs, which by then ran into millions. Also of interest is the fact that in an attempt to avoid losing on the basis of this technicality, Philip Morris argued that one of its main motivations for the restructuring was "to minimize its tax liability" by securing "a tax advantage relating to the payment of intercompany debt" (Philip Morris Asia Limited v. Commonwealth of Australia, 2015, p. 145; Ranald, 2019).

As for the DTAs, their upward trajectory has been similarly impressive, except much steadier, and in contrast to the BITs, neither the global financial crisis nor any other development that had taken place in its aftermath thus far appear to have suppressed the appetite for more new DTAs anywhere near as significantly. This is not to say that the DTA ecosystem has not witnessed its own tidal wave of renegotiations and terminations in the last decade, because it very much has. However, none of the increasingly numerous high-profile scandals sustaining this wave have quite yet reached the globe-spanning impact of the Philip Morris moment, in other words, an impact that would put in question the very concept of these types of treaties, or at least their political viability, although as we shall see as we move forward, some have come very close to it at the national and potentially the regional level. Still, according to the Tax Treaties Explorer data set (International Centre for Tax and Development [ICTD], 2021a), which contains detailed information on 2,005 of the more than 3,000 DTAs that are in force today, while only 339 (17%) of the DTAs from this sample were signed in the four decades between 1950 and 1989, that number nearly tripled to 898 (45%) new signings between 1990 and 2007 and has kept the pace after that, with 768 (38%) new ones signed between 2008 and 2019. Alternatively, without adhering to the periodization set by the data on BITs and going simply by decades, the number of new DTAs has been growing steadily since that first batch of 339 (17%), specifically by 487 (24%) in the 1990s, by another 539 (27%) in the 2000s, and by another 640 (32%) in the 2010s. In terms of the overall balance of taxing rights they strike between the jurisdictions of residence and the jurisdictions of source, of the 1,889 DTAs from this sample for which such data is available, 1,327 (70%) are closer to the more stringently residence-oriented

OECD MTCs, and only 562 (30%) to the more moderate but likewise residence-oriented UN MTCs.

Owing to this explosion of BITs and DTAs, as well as the other processes set off by the neoliberal orthodoxy, international tax avoidance and tax competition both intensified to an unprecedented degree. The resulting race to the bottom in tax rates and other tax-related incentives ravaged public budgets in developed and developing countries alike. Between 1980 and 2020, the unweighted average worldwide statutory corporate income tax rate plummeted from 40.11% to 23.85%, representing a 41% reduction over the period (Asen, 2020). However, because of rampant tax avoidance, and the wide range of available preferential tax regimes, tax breaks, tax rulings, and other tax incentives, the effective tax rates have actually been substantially lower throughout, and sometimes even zero or negative for extended periods of time (Gardner & Wamhoff, 2021). In addition, much of this tax avoidance has been enabled by the separate entity and arm's length principles, just as was feared but never adequately addressed during the League of Nations process. In 2002, the long-time Head of the Tax Treaties, Transfer Pricing & Financial Transactions Division at the OECD, John Neighbour (2002, p. 29), called it a "fact" that "more than 60% of world trade takes place within multinational enterprises," and while much of this intra-firm trade has been perfectly legitimate, much of it has also been due to tax-motivated abuse of transfer pricing. As pointed out by Finér and Ylönen (2017, p. 70), even though "separate entities within an MNE are fictional," MNEs "have excessive powers to operate as separate entities when it suits them for tax purposes, while planning their operational supply chains as an integrated entity."

This is globalization in practice, as offshore structures are deployed to create any number of artificial entities across the world to game the international tax system by taking advantage of the very principles upon which it has been based. Aside from a few exceptions, some of which have already been mentioned (Picciotto, 1992; Hampton, 1996; Palan, 2003), the field of IPE has generally been slow in catching up with this reality. Nevertheless, some notable advances have been made in recent years. One example is the growing literature on global wealth chains, which repurposed the familiar and established concept of global value chains and began to demonstrate, in a more theoretically grounded and systematic manner, just how extensively MNEs have been minimizing their global tax obligations with the assistance of professional intermediaries and their schemes (Seabrooke & Wigan, 2017). Over the decades, this global network of increasingly offshore-oriented accountants, tax advisors, lawyers, bankers, wealth managers, consultants, and other related experts that specialize in the design of these schemes and the provision of the structures, nominee directors, bank accounts, and records necessary to make them work has become exceptionally proficient in identifying and exploiting the numerous loopholes, gaps, frictions, and mismatches that are to be found whenever domestic tax laws of different countries interact. Thus, once DTAs began to proliferate, it did not take the professional intermediaries long before they recognized the potential profitability of dragging the decades-old practice of tax-motivated treaty shopping from the margins of obscurity and growing it to an industrial scale (Grady, 1983).

Treaty shopping refers to schemes through which individuals and MNEs that are not residents of either of the countries party to a DTA attempt to gain access to its benefits, for instance by establishing a letterbox company in one of the contracting countries, similarly to the way that Philip Morris had in the earlier example concerning BITs. In specifying further, SEATINI and ActionAid (2014, p. 10), two prominent CSOs, define the practice as typically involving the following three features:

- The beneficial owner of the treaty shopping entity does not reside in the country where the entity is created;
- The conduit has minimal economic activity in the jurisdiction in which it is located; and
- The income is subject to minimal (if any) tax in the country of residence.

As a testament to how much treaty shopping has grown over the decades, the OECD (2013) has recently come to identify the practice as one of the most important contemporary sources of tax avoidance that is in need of addressing. This is particularly relevant with regard to Mauritius, which has managed to emerge as a relatively well-rounded regional OFC with its very own FOC registry, SEZs, and even several more sophisticated offshore services, precisely because it has built its entire offshore model around being a tax treaty hub, one which has succeeded in attracting countless HNWIs, as well as the subsidiaries of many of the aforementioned Fortune 500, FTSE 100, ASX 100, CAC 40, IBEX 35, and other companies, and this despite most of them not having any major operations in the jurisdiction. Of course, as is very much in line with the general messaging of most OFCs, Mauritius categorically denies its involvement in any kind of wrongdoing. It has maintained this position even its veneer of propriety has been pierced time and time again, not least by its own professional intermediaries marketing the jurisdiction to clients in very clear terms whenever they believe to be behind closed doors.

In one telling case from 2013, ActionAid obtained and passed on to the media documentation from a conference for international businesses attended by dozens of major global banks and law firms, in which Deloitte Mauritius touted the many advantages of the jurisdiction as an OFC (Deloitte, 2013; Doward, 2013). In the presentation, the contents of which were meant to remain confidential to all but the attending audience, the Deloitte team explained that investing by means of a Mauritian structure entailed, among numerous other benefits, a flat individual as well as corporate income tax (CIT) rate of 15%, which in most circumstances could be lowered further by 80% to a maximum effective tax rate of 3%, and in some cases even lower than that thanks to various exemptions and a generous deemed foreign tax credit (DFTC); no capital gains tax (CGT); no inheritance, wealth, or gift taxes; no controlled foreign company (CFC) legislation[2]; no thin capitalization legislation[3]; no transfer pricing rules[4]; no withholding tax (WHT) on dividend, interest, and royalty payments; and a vast DTA network with full or partial tax sparing provisions.[5] The team then demonstrated these advantages in a comparison between two hypothetical scenarios, one in which a Chinese holding company invests in Mozambique directly, and another in which it deploys a Mauritian structure to invest in Mozambique. If it invests directly, its profits from the venture would be subject to the full 32% CIT in Mozambique, and as there is no DTA between China and Mozambique, it would also incur the full 20% WHT on any dividend, interest, and royalty payments it may wish to send back to China, as well as the full 32% CGT on any realized capital gains should it ever decide to sell some or all of its shares in the venture. If it invests through Mauritius, it still has to pay the full 32% CIT in Mozambique, although without having to pay any additional CIT in Mauritius thanks to the DFTC, so the move is tax neutral from that standpoint, but because Mauritius has a very favorable DTA with Mozambique, the WHT on any dividend, interest, and royalty payments would be significantly lower, and the 32% CGT would be avoided altogether (see Figure 2.1).

In another such case, this time from 2015, but exposed only in 2019 from a leaked planning document in the Mauritius Leaks, KPMG Mauritius advised Ubongo Group, Africa's largest producer of educational television programs for children, whose shows nowadays reach over 24 million households in more than 40 African countries (KPMG, 2015; Fitzgibbon, 2019). In facilitating the Tanzania-based company's plans for expansion, KPMG proposed the following tax-efficient restructuring. It would start with the establishment of a holding company in Mauritius, and the transfer of all shareholding from Tanzania to Mauritius, making the parent company, Ubongo Tanzania, a wholly owned

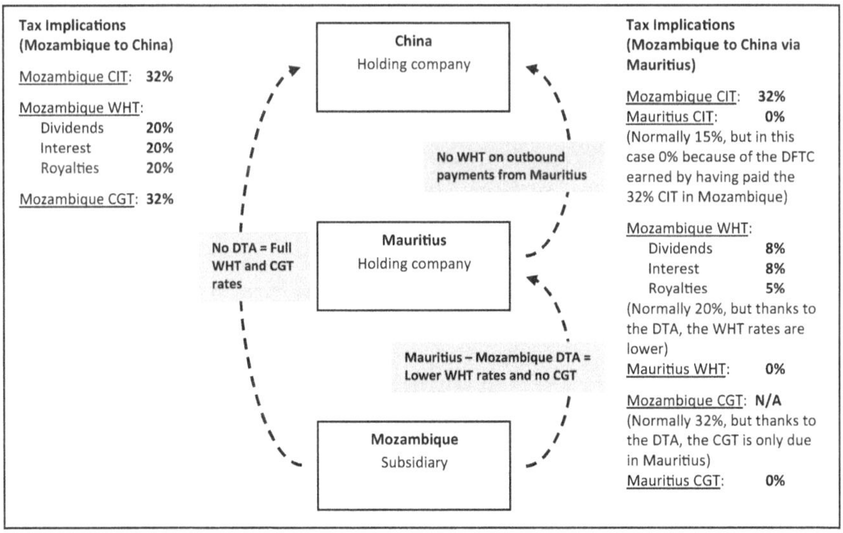

Figure 2.1 Deloitte – Investing in Africa Through Mauritius

Source: (Deloitte, 2013).

subsidiary of Ubongo Mauritius, the newly established holding company. The Mauritius side of the restructuring would be handled by Codan, the Mauritius affiliate of the Offshore Magic Circle law firm Conyers Dill & Pearman, which was the source of the more than 200,000 emails, contracts, bank statements, and other documents that formed the basis of the Mauritius Leaks. Codan would register Ubongo Mauritius as a Category 1 Global Business Company (GBC 1), arguably the most famous of the offshore structures offered by Mauritius, and provide the two resident directors and the registered office address that are required from a compliance perspective. After that, Ubongo Tanzania would sell all of its existing intellectual property (IP) to Ubongo Mauritius, which would then become responsible for the entire group's financing and licensing, despite only being staffed by the two resident directors, who at the same time would likely serve as directors to dozens if not hundreds of other companies. Once all of this was in place, Ubongo Mauritius would be ready to begin "extracting profits," as KPMG (2015, p. 1) phrased it. The extraction was to be carried out in the form of regular interest and royalty payments from all subsidiaries to Ubongo Mauritius. The interest, which as an added benefit is tax deductible, would be generated by having Ubongo Mauritius provide all subsidiaries with short-term loans, ostensibly to fund the creation of new content. The royalties would be generated by having Ubongo Mauritius provide all subsidiaries with licenses for the use of the group's IP. In this way, a substantial portion of the group's taxable profits would artificially be shifted from countries where they would normally be subject to an average CIT of 28% into Mauritius, where they would normally be subject to a lower CIT of 15%, but because they would also qualify either for an 80% exemption or for an 80% DFTC, the CIT in Mauritius would actually be brought down to only 3%. The shifted profits in the form of interest and royalties would still be subject to WHTs in the countries of the subsidiaries, but the scheme would still be worthwhile even if the shifted profits were subject to full WHT rates in every country, although this would of course not happen. As demonstrated by Deloitte in the preceding example, Mauritius's vast DTA network would ensure that the WHTs due in many of these countries would be significantly lower, and that any potential CGT would be avoided altogether, resulting in a significant reduction of Ubongo Group's overall tax obligations (see Figure 2.2).

To its credit, Ubongo Group reportedly decided not to follow through with the proposed restructuring, but these two cases are nevertheless strongly indicative of how the offshore world in general and Mauritius in particular function. This leaves us with several strands of inquiry, which we explore in greater detail in the following sections as well as throughout the rest of this book. At this point, it suffices to underscore that treaty shopping and profit shifting are not just tolerated in Mauritius, but are in fact legislatively encouraged, and that the primary focus of the professional intermediaries operating there has been to continue expanding its role as a financial gateway to Africa, in accordance with the far wider tendency toward regional specialization in the offshore world.

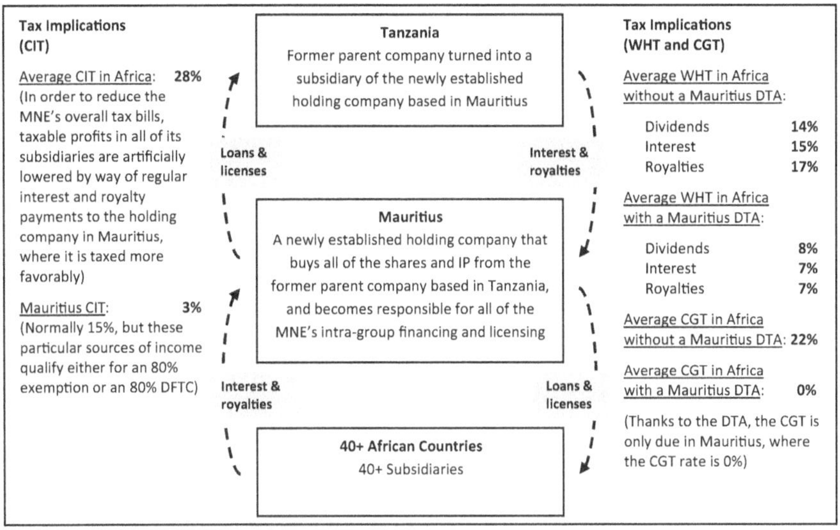

Figure 2.2 KPMG – Proposal for a Tax-Efficient Restructuring in Mauritius

Source: (KPMG, 2015; averages calculated by authors based on MRA, 2020; EY, 2020; PwC, 2021).

Regional hubs in a global world

The second prominent pattern relating to the history of the offshore world that we need to consider is the distinct regional orientation of most of the world's OFCs. Nearly 20 years ago, Hampton and Christensen (2002, pp. 1667–1668) predicted that "the cumulative pressures for reform will significantly re-configure the offshore finance industry," which "may return onshore to the large, functional financial centers such as London or New York." As they elaborated, since OFCs add little to no genuine value to transactions beyond tax and regulatory arbitrage, once the most obvious loopholes are closed, there will no longer be any economic reason to route transactions through them, and the allure of OFCs will fade, although "it is unlikely that the effects will be uniform across all OFCs." Their logic was sound, but their timing, according to which this return onshore would already be the likely outcome of their "current re-configuration of the global financial architecture," proved to be overly optimistic. While this still remains the most viable theory of the offshore world's trajectory in the long run, until only very recently, the ensuing period saw OFCs across the board, and especially regional ones like Mauritius, hold their place and even increase their market share.

This should not be interpreted as any kind of shift in the balance of power in the global offshore economy. London and New York are still integrally connected to it, and securely maintain their positions as two of its most influential command and control centers (Taylor & Derudder, 2016). Nonetheless, regional hubs that play a gateway role have been on the rise. Mauritius, servicing India, and now increasingly turning its sights on Africa, is one such example. Other examples are plentiful, such as the Cayman Islands vis-à-vis the US; the Channel Islands of Guernsey and Jersey vis-à-vis the UK; Dubai vis-à-vis the Middle East; the Seychelles vis-à-vis Russia and the Middle East; Hong Kong vis-à-vis China; Singapore vis-à-vis India and Southeast Asia; and the Netherlands, Luxembourg, Malta, and Cyprus vis-à-vis Europe, among others. Some of the most comprehensive data on the regional orientation of OFCs are presented by Haberly and Wójcik (2015a, 2015b), who analyze and map the global offshore FDI network. Their results suggest that while this network is on the whole highly globalized, it is also internally differentiated and organized into four identifiable regional subnetworks, and that the most important determinants that underpin their composition are historical, geographical, and political.

Historically, the most important factors determining the contemporary patterns of offshore FDI flows were found to be European colonialism, with British colonialism looming particularly large, followed by the post-World War II hegemonic alliance between the US and Western Europe, then by the fall of the Soviet Union, and most recently by the rise of China. According to Haberly and Wójcik (2015b, p. 271), "the metropolitan core of the former European imperial system," to which we can also attach Switzerland and Luxembourg in strong supporting roles, "is clearly the center of the global offshore network," but it is the British colonial legacy in particular that is "of singular importance" here, with the UK's vast archipelago of formerly and currently controlled entrepôt city-states surrounding the world's continents, and controlling many commercial networks, especially Arab, Indian, and Chinese ones, but also those of South and East Africa. Remarkably, the authors also find that the dominance of this British financial empire is so overwhelming that instead of displacing the spheres of postcolonial financial influence of other former metropoles, it has been incorporating them into its own, as has already been the case with the Netherlands, and some evidence suggests that such blurring may also be occurring with regard to France. This echoes the findings of several other authors, who have for years referred to this City of London-centered, Euromarket-fueled part of the offshore world as "Britain's second empire" (Palan et al., 2010; Palan, 2015; Shaxson, 2011, 2018). This view is further solidified when one considers how the UK's contemporary sphere of postcolonial financial influence is exerted through an unrivaled web of offshore nodes that includes, among others, its three current Crown Dependencies of Guernsey, Jersey, and the Isle of Man; many of its current Overseas Territories, such as the Cayman Islands, the British Virgin Islands (BVI), Gibraltar, Bermuda, Anguilla, the Turks and Caicos Islands, and Montserrat; many of its current Commonwealth jurisdictions whose court of final appeal is still the UK's Judicial Committee of the Privy Council, such as the Bahamas, Mauritius, and Saint Kitts and Nevis; as well as many of its other former colonies and protectorates, such as Hong Kong, Singapore, Dubai, Malta, Cyprus, Bahrain, and, of course, its very first colony, Ireland. Together, the UK's offshore nodes make for a list that, aside from a few notable absences, is barely distinguishable from most of the comprehensive lists of OFCs that have ever been compiled.

Like all empires, this one too has been based on extraction, dominated by capital from the same colonies ultimately flowing to the same metropoles by way of the predominantly UK-run financial infrastructure, except this time they were called the former colonies and the former metropoles; some of the smaller former colonies were promoted to OFCs and allowed to benefit by keeping a cut from the proceeds; and it was the US that through its sprawling web of financial and corporate interests eventually emerged as one of the main users and profiteers of this system (Helleiner, 1994). While the methods and some of the beneficiaries have changed, the underlying principle has not, indeed so much so that the offshore world could in many ways be seen as a more privatized revamp of the old colonial extraction engine. The way in which the old colonial structure morphed into its neocolonial offshore form is superbly elucidated by the historian Vanessa Ogle (2017, p. 1438), who explains that while the colonial tax systems were incredibly exploitative when applied to native populations, the "tax codes as they applied to Europeans and other non-natives in colonies were extremely varied, laced with exemptions, and often simply hard to enforce," and the "tax rates were much lower in colonies and other dependent territories than in metropolitan centers." As a consequence, when Europeans began to retreat from their colonies, sometimes under pressure from national liberation movements that threatened to nationalize or otherwise expropriate colonial property, the settlers, civil servants, business owners, and investors became increasingly eager to transfer their assets out of the colonies but not quite into the metropoles, where they would face higher taxes. This new demand for an offshore escape was quickly discovered and seized upon by the ever-industrious professional intermediaries, mostly British and American, but also some continental European, who began to lobby their own governments as well as others, and succeeded in shoring up support for the offshore push. As Ogle (2017, p. 1439) reports:

> Between 1945 and 1970, some of the most important new or improved tax havens and offshore markets were set up, and older ones expanded, with government involvement from London and Washington, D.C. Even where governments were not directly involved, they at least tolerated these developments. Especially in the case of tax havens in the British Empire, dependent territories normally required approval from London in order to pass tax haven legislation.

The motivations of the professional intermediaries, which aside from the typical assemblage of accountants, tax advisors, lawyers, bankers, and such also included former diplomats, politicians, and intelligence officials turned businessmen at the end of their careers, were clear enough. They were looking for ways to promote private enterprise in the more dependent and therefore safer reaches of the developing world, while simultaneously expanding opportunities for tax avoidance, often their own. The legislation, which in most cases they literally wrote themselves, not only turned dozens of these jurisdictions into OFCs, but often gave so much influence to the authors or clients they represented that it turned them "into virtual suzerains of the territories" (Ogle, 2017, p. 1443). Some of the more important examples include the Cayman Islands, the BVI, and the Bahamas from within the UK sphere, but also the US former quasi-colony of Liberia, whose FOC registry, which despite the country's civil wars has in most years remained second only to Panama's, was created by a former US secretary of state in conjunction with corporate interests such as Standard Oil, and is still headquartered and managed from the US today (Carlisle, 1980; Palan et al., 2010; Bernstein, 2017; Ogle, 2017; Shaxson, 2018). The efforts of the professional intermediaries extended to DTAs as well. One early example includes the exploitation of the DTAs between the Netherlands, the US, and the UK, which also covered the Netherlands Antilles and the BVI, effectively turning the two budding OFCs into popular treaty shopping bases for UK and US companies (Bernstein, 2017; Ogle, 2017). Following that, pressures on authorities to initiate treaty negotiations with more developing countries only grew stronger. Contrary to the traditional narrative, the main concern was not to prevent double taxation, but to limit source jurisdiction taxation. According to Hearson (2018a, p. 649):

> Negotiators from the Inland Revenue argued that there was rarely any double taxation problem to resolve, only a concern that developing countries might tax British investors in ways that were not 'acceptable', and that those firms risked 'losing out' to their competitors in the absence of a treaty.

The motivations of the UK, US, and other Western governments to actively or even just passively go along with all of this are more complicated, because the individual decisions were ultimately the result of internal power struggles and often contradictory priorities of different governments, ministries, departments, regulatory bodies, and other state authorities. The most obvious reason was that the professional intermediaries and their clients were politically well-connected and financially well-endowed, and thus more often than not got their way. However, beyond this simple reality of essentially subsidizing the City of London and Wall Street, there were also far grander international political considerations that made the offshore push more palatable. A particularly important and multifaceted matter was the economic development of the former colonies and protectorates, and the various other former or current territorial arrangements under their control. Some of this concern was genuinely altruistic, but it was immediately exploited by the professional intermediaries. They succeeded in convincing many of the officials charged with the handling of overseas affairs that since these jurisdictions had little to no natural resources or other advantages with which to attract international business, the OFC route was the only one that held prospects for any more or less self-sufficient growth. Many of the officials nevertheless remained skeptical and warned of the potential dangers of the OFC route, but because their counterproposals generally required more sustained efforts and financial support from the metropoles, and would in any case take longer to get off the ground, the skeptics were quickly brought into line under the sheer weight of broader political concerns. This was especially the case given that appearances mattered even more than they normally would during the Cold War era. It would not do having the world see these jurisdictions languishing in poverty and descending into violent chaos, or even worse than that, as the Western governments saw it, having the world see them falling under the influence of the ever-looming specter of communism. The same concerns of course applied to the larger former colonies as well, especially those that continued to have considerable strategic value due to their ample natural resources and other advantages. Some of these had already embraced communism, and others were about to. In doing so, they threatened the commercial interests of the metropoles as well as their still considerable post-independence influence. By propping up the offshore infrastructure, the metropoles gained not only another lever with which to exert influence over their former colonies, but also another method by which to continue their exploitation, without any of the costs of the freshly dismantled empires.

By this point, we are obviously already in a deep overlap between Haberly and Wójcik's (2015b) first historical determinant of offshore FDI flows, European colonialism, and the second one, the post-World War II hegemonic alliance between the US and Western Europe, as the overwhelmingly British and continental European offshore infrastructure increasingly turned to the servicing of the new hegemon and its growing informal empire, which by then already included Latin America, Japan, and much of Southeast Asia, and upon decolonization promptly expanded to fill much of the influence vacuum left in the wake of the European retreat as well. Consequently, the overwhelmingly European-colonial patterns of offshore FDI flows expanded to become more transatlantic-colonial ones instead. The two symbiotic relationships – one between the Anglo-American and continental European professional intermediaries and governments, and the other between the US and Western Europe – contributed to the rise of the offshore world. In turn, the offshore world contributed to the process of structural dependence by financial subordination, as described by world-systems analysis and several other strands of critical literature.

This financial subordination has taken many different forms. In the African context, one of the most conspicuous examples has been the persistence of the Colonies Françaises d'Afrique/Communauté Financière Africaine (CFA) franc,[6] a colonial era currency that still serves as the national currency of 14 countries in sub-Saharan Africa. The CFA franc is issued in two currency blocks by two separate African central banks, the Banque Centrale des États de l'Afrique de l'Ouest (BCEAO), and the Banque des États de l'Afrique Centrale (BEAC), but France has retained its right to veto their decisions. The central actor in the CFA system is the French Treasury. It guarantees the CFA franc's fixed rate of exchange and unlimited convertibility with the euro (and prior to that with the French franc), as well as free capital transferability within the zone. It also requires the BCEAO and the BEAC to deposit 50% of their foreign reserve holdings into an operations account at the Treasury, which essentially means that all cross-currency transactions involving the CFA franc have to be mediated by the Treasury. Because of this, the CFA system has been widely criticized as amounting to a French colonial tax, and as representing French monetary imperialism. In the words of Pigeaud and Sylla (2021, pp. 3–4):

> It is the most powerful weapon of the 'Françafrique', this peculiar neocolonial system of domination that the French state established on the eve of the independence of the former colonies, with the precise aim of preserving the advantages of the colonial pact.

Others, like Kvangraven et al. (2021), have focused on financial market and banking sector development as examples of the financial subordination of Africa. These authors demonstrate that the only African countries that have managed to steadily increase their financial depth have been OFCs like Mauritius. Furthermore, just like during the colonial period, most African countries have continued to be dominated by foreign banking oligopolies, which have continued to prioritize the financing of West-bound exports and the repatriation of the profits of Western MNEs at the expense of local economic development, such as through productive lending to small- and medium-sized enterprises (SMEs).

Regardless of its particular form, financial subordination has consistently resulted in capital flight, often motivated by tax and regulatory concerns. It is here that the offshore world has been particularly instrumental, with disastrous results for many former colonies. Based on the latest update of the long-running series of estimates produced by Ndikumana and Boyce (2003, 2011, 2018), between 1970 and 2015, the combined real capital flight from a representative group of 30 African countries amounted to about US$1.4 trillion, and once imputed interest earnings were taken into account, the amount rose to about US$1.8 trillion. This vastly exceeds not only the stock of external debts owed by these countries (US$496.9 billion) as of 2015, but also the inflows of official development aid (US$991.8 billion) they received during the 46-year period examined in the report, making the group a net creditor to the rest of the world. While the financial hemorrhaging experienced by Africa has been exceptionally egregious in its intensity and impact, much of Latin America, Asia, Eastern Europe, and other developing regions have not been spared either (Dooley, 1986; Errico & Musalem, 1999; Kar & Spanjers, 2015).

The pull of the Anglo-American and continental European offshore infrastructure has been so strong that when the transatlantic-colonial patterns of offshore FDI flows expanded yet again by way of Haberly and Wójcik's (2015b) third and fourth historical determinants, the fall of the Soviet Union and the rise of China, the new capital began flooding into it almost immediately. The former Eastern Bloc, and Russia especially, have mostly plugged in via the British-influenced BVI-Cyprus axis and Malta, with the UK itself ranking highly as a host but not as a source of Eastern European offshore FDI, and then via the continental European OFCs like Gibraltar, Liechtenstein, Luxembourg, Switzerland, and the Netherlands. China, and to an extent several other regional economies dominated by ethnic Chinese business networks, such as the Philippines, Thailand, Indonesia, and Malaysia, have mostly plugged in via the British-influenced financial gateways of Hong Kong and Singapore. However, as these two gateways have over time evolved into high-priced business locations, China and the regional economies have increasingly also plugged in via the Cayman Islands, the BVI, and Bermuda, often in conjunction with the gateways (Sharman, 2012; Vlcek, 2014; Robertson, 2021), while the UK itself again ranked highly as a host but not as a source of Chinese offshore FDI.

These four key historical processes and events have also had a fundamental influence on the development of Mauritius as an OFC. Although its complicated past as a former colony of the Dutch, the French, and then the British means that its ties extend further than just to the British Empire alone, and it is also true that neither British nor any other foreign authorities were directly involved in turning it into an OFC, its place within the UK's contemporary sphere of post-colonial financial influence is nevertheless undeniable, whether we consider the institutional and legal structure of its offshore sector, or its focus on India, Africa, and by way of Hong Kong to an increasing extent also China, with Haberly and Wójcik (2015b, p. 270) emphasizing the importance of Mauritius as a "key linkage" between all of them. Of course, just as these four historical factors have overlapped with each other in determining the contemporary patterns of offshore FDI flows, so too have they overlapped with the following geographical and more recent political factors, which are significant in their own right as determinants, and may even grow to overshadow some of the earlier historical legacies given certain circumstances and sufficient time.

Geographically, the most important factor was found to be physical proximity, contrary to the common assumption that electronic communication has rendered offshore financial relationships essentially footloose and placeless. This may work in theory and in certain individual cases, but in practice, the highly sensitive nature of offshore finance is still largely based on trust, necessitating frequent face to face interactions, and thus frequent travel of offshore professionals and clients alike, which was found to be the main driver of this sensitivity to distance (Haberly & Wójcik, 2015a). As a consequence of the wake-up call provided by the ongoing COVID-19 pandemic, and what we now know to be the relatively high likelihood of future pandemics, it is not far-fetched to postulate that despite the rapid pace of technological progress, physical proximity is likely to remain important as a factor, and may even grow in importance. Surprisingly, neither time zone proximity nor cultural proximity was found to be anywhere near as significant, but both are naturally closely intertwined with physical proximity, and are often cited as highly relevant to clients in other literature as well as in many of our interviews (Roberts, 1994; Bloningen & Piger, 2014). After all, one of the enticements of regional OFCs is that they offer Anglo-American or continental European business services while comprehending the cultural particularities of doing business in the locations of their specialization and being deeply enmeshed in the requisite sociopolitical networks. As Crawford (2001, p. 49) put it in a persuasive description of the Chinese context, "Hong Kong, for instance, must be Chinese, but not too Chinese," meaning it must mirror global standards, while acting as a bridge to China's unique market. The same logic applies to the intermediary role of Mauritius vis-à-vis India and Africa. Aside from its professional expertise, it is also its physical proximity and strong, historically-determined cultural affinities with both India and much of Africa that attract fund managers and other clients to use Mauritius as a regional hub as well as a financial gateway into these markets.

Politically, the last few years have given rise to several developments with the potential to fundamentally reshape the global offshore FDI network. The most important of these developments have arguably been the continuing proliferation of DTAs, the OECD's ongoing campaign against offshore tax evasion and avoidance, the shocking and rather disorderly exit of the UK from the EU, and what appears to be an imminent if not already unfolding new Cold War, this time with China. Given the recency of especially the latter two developments, Haberly and Wójcik (2015a) could naturally only have addressed the former two in their research, and with the second one of these two, their focus was necessarily confined only to the very earliest stages of what has been a prolonged and disjointed reform process dating back to the late 1990s. Nevertheless, they found both to be important factors that nowadays shape the global offshore FDI network. With regard to the continuing proliferation of DTAs, their results confirmed the high frequency with which offshore FDI flows are "routed along zero withholding tax pathways," providing further evidence of "widespread third-country treaty shopping," and by extension of the key role of treaty shopping hubs like Mauritius (Haberly & Wójcik, 2015a, p. 78). With regard to the earliest stages of the OECD's ongoing campaign against offshore tax evasion and avoidance, their results confirmed the findings of several other scholars (Eden & Kudrle, 2005; Rawlings, 2005; Sharman, 2006, 2009). Two findings stood out in particular. First, by only targeting offshore FDI flows connected to non-OECD OFCs while ignoring those connected to the OECD's own OFCs, the OECD did not reduce overall offshore FDI flows but merely forced their restructuring in a way that principally benefited OECD OFCs at the expense of non-OECD OFCs. And second, the non-OECD OFCs that were affected the least happened to be directly linked to OECD member states, most of them to the UK and the Netherlands, strongly suggesting that these OECD "patrons" have helped their dependencies "weather anti-offshore initiatives" (Haberly & Wójcik, 2015a, p. 90). As it would turn out, these and other forms of double standards and preferential treatments were not to be the exception but rather the staple of all future anti-offshore initiatives. But before we get to that, it is important to understand the circumstances that finally prompted such initiatives in the first place.

Notes

1 Not to be confused with free trade areas, which are agreements between two or more countries.

2 CFC legislation aims to minimize opportunities for profit shifting and long-term or even indefinite deferral of taxes. It does so by enabling jurisdictions to tax the

income of resident taxpayers held in foreign subsidiaries if it can be determined, on the basis of certain tests and analyses, that the taxpayers exercise sufficient direct or indirect control over the subsidiaries and that the subsidiaries are either wholly artificial or at least not sufficiently engaged in substantial economic activities.

3 Thin capitalization refers to a situation in which MNEs exploit the fact that interest is tax deductible by financing their operations through a much higher proportion of debt instead of equity, and then strategically shifting that debt within their own respective groups to artificially reduce their overall tax obligations. Thin capitalization legislation aims to minimize the extent to which this is possible, typically by limiting the amount of interest that can be deducted for tax purposes.

4 Transfer pricing rules set out the various terms and conditions that taxpayers have to abide by when making their transfer pricing determinations and preparing their transfer pricing documentation, such as which transfer pricing methods may be used under which circumstances, whether there is a preference for domestic comparables over foreign comparables, whether and under which circumstances tax authorities may make adjustments or impose penalties, and many others. The absence of transfer pricing rules generally means that there is no legal requirement for taxpayers to prepare transfer pricing documentation at all, or at the very least that they are given significant leeway in how to prepare them. In either case, the scope for tax avoidance is expanded considerably.

5 Tax sparing provisions are special tax treaty provisions by which the contracting jurisdiction of residence agrees to grant its resident MNEs relief from residence taxation with respect to source taxes that have been spared, or in other words that have not actually been paid, because of a tax incentive offered by the contracting jurisdiction of source. While tax sparing provisions have generally been accepted as a way of preventing DTAs from undermining the tax incentive regimes of source jurisdictions, the OECD (1998a, p. 28) has long argued against their use because they often actually work against the interests of source jurisdictions. They do this by encouraging foreign investors to repatriate their profits instead of re-investing them to consolidate or to expand on their original investment, and also by offering "wide opportunities for tax planning and tax avoidance".

6 It was originally known as the franc des Colonies Françaises d'Afrique (franc of the French Colonies in Africa) and later renamed to the franc de la Communauté Financière Africaine (franc of the African Financial Community).

3 Analytical framework part two:

Growing resistance, new global standards, and the uneven nature of the offshore world

This chapter represents the second part of the theoretical and empirical contextualization through which we situate and approach Mauritius's engagement with India and Africa. We begin by exploring the new forms of contestation that the two prominent patterns covered in the previous chapter have been subjected to since the early 1990s and then even more so since the global financial crisis. We demonstrate that the resulting revisions of the standards and norms governing international taxation only produce a significant effect when they align with national political economies. We argue that this contestation over the offshore world has further exacerbated the unevenness of what has already been an uneven landscape, and that this new structural configuration, rather than threatening the viability of the offshore world, will for the time being only lead to its upward consolidation.

Accommodation and resistance at multiple levels

The offshore world has always been a contested space, featuring a spectrum of opposing forces at the global, regional, and national levels. Actors at any of these levels can be accommodative, passive, or resistant toward offshore finance, with the passive posture typically resulting in outcomes similar to those from the accommodative approach, which by itself already indicates that the spectrum as such has been stacked in favor of accommodation to offshore finance. Thus far, we have already encountered the most aggressive of the accommodative actors in the form of the professional intermediaries and governments that helped set up the offshore world, largely in order to benefit their individual and MNE clients, and by extension themselves, whether financially, politically, or ideologically. Naturally, they have almost exclusively represented the core of the global economy, such as the largely developed capital-exporting countries, the former colonial powers, the US, and of course the OFCs themselves, whether core, semiperipheral, or peripheral ones, in other words, all those that have, comparatively speaking, been among the main beneficiaries of the offshore world. However, since in reality, benefits are typically never distributed equally within countries, referring to countries as beneficiaries, as accurate as it is at a higher level of abstraction, also glosses over the fact that the real beneficiaries are actually certain coalitions

DOI: 10.4324/9781003161011-3

of actors within these countries, and in this specific context, it is the accommodative ones. Of course, this also means that such accommodative coalitions of actors also exist in countries that have, comparatively speaking, been among the main victims of the offshore world, mostly representing the periphery and the semiperiphery of the global economy, such as the largely developing capital-importing countries and the former colonies.

Not surprisingly, professional intermediaries across the developing world have generally supported closer cooperation with OFCs. For example, a Kenyan tax consultant, Kairo Thuo (as quoted in Mutegi, 2014), spoke encouragingly about the highly controversial DTA between Kenya and Mauritius, insisting that "the net effect" would be "that Kenya now becomes a favourable environment for companies registered in Mauritius who are seeking to invest locally since they will not only avoid double taxation but enjoy friendlier taxes." Similarly, as part of the process of globalization, many governments across the developing world have chosen to embrace offshore finance or at least to adopt a non-confrontational approach toward it. For example, Durst (2019, p. 5) interprets offshore tax avoidance not as a purely corporate-driven transgression but also as an outcome of "the desire of governments to facilitate that avoidance to encourage inbound investment," with many having purposefully codified investment-friendly policy frameworks that liberally offer tax incentives in pursuit of this goal. As before, the motivations of these particular accommodative actors tend to range from the purely self-serving to ones reflecting genuine beliefs about the potential of offshore finance to foster national development, whether such beliefs have been supported by reality or not. Regardless of their individual motivations at any given time, most of the history of the offshore world has been dictated by this nexus of accommodative forces that have coalesced at the global, regional, and national levels to not only cut a path toward the offshore escape but also cultivate it and defend it against any resistance that might arise to threaten it.

Given the composition of this nexus of accommodative forces, it is not difficult to discern why the offshore world was able to thrive for such a long time without having to face any significant challenges. As aptly summarized by Shaxson (2013):

> Tackling this system pits the world's citizens against one of the most well-entrenched interest groups. And there is no interest group more rich and powerful than the rich and powerful, who are the biggest beneficiaries and protectors of this system.

Aside from the immense financial and political backing behind the offshore world, its rise and resilience were also greatly abetted by the following three structural supports: the tolerance of its secrecy provisions, which kept much of what was going on relatively under wraps; the dominance of neoliberalism, which created a particularly permissive environment for it in both ideological and practical terms; and the general rise of global finance, which allowed it to blend in more easily, and made any of its visible excesses seem like aberrant externalities that were well worth tolerating given the huge societal benefits that the financialization of the global economy was supposed to deliver. To be sure, the will of even this richest and most powerful of interest groups does not just manifest into reality automatically, immediately, or directly. In most cases, their will is still subject to at least some political struggles against resistance at the national level, since it is states that ultimately serve as the executors of this will whether by way of legislation and enforcement or by refusing to act, depending on what the given situation requires. When it comes to international matters, whether at the regional or the global level, the situation naturally becomes even more complicated by involving more states with their own sets of accommodative and resistant forces, which means that the political struggles have to be fought and won on more fronts. Of course, because the political struggles over the creation of the offshore world had been fought and won decades ago, the nexus of accommodative forces has only had to ensure its continued existence since then and the side that seeks continuity always has a distinct advantage over the side that seeks change because the former only needs to convince enough states to continue doing nothing instead of beginning to do something. This represents another way in which the spectrum of opposing forces has been stacked in favor of accommodation to offshore finance.

In spite of these odds, the offshore world has never gone completely unchallenged, although attempts to rein in its excesses have until only recently never amounted to much. Typically, such attempts originated at the national level, and thus tended to be unilateral, piecemeal, and defensive, largely aimed at the individuals and MNEs at the center of specific scandals rather than at the offshore world itself, let alone the systemic underpinnings behind its rise and resilience. Even with stakes this low, any resistance to offshore finance would immediately run up against the full lobbying might of those profiting from it and either lose outright or technically win but only after the initiatives had been stripped of their bite (Rixen, 2008). At the global level, the first promising show of resistance that had the potential to also affect the offshore world materialized in the 1970s from within the UN, when the Group of Seventy-Seven (G77), a coalition of developing countries, launched the New International Economic Order (NIEO), a sweeping set of proposals advocating for the establishment of a more equitable system of international economic relations (UN, 1974a, 1974b). While the G77 did not target the offshore infrastructure directly with the NIEO, many of its proposals called for better regulation and control over the conduct of MNEs, which included improvements to their financial transparency frameworks and completely new public reporting requirements that would have made any offshore tax avoidance they engaged in significantly more difficult to hide from tax authorities. The NIEO found strong support among developing countries, but it was seen as a threat by the US and its closest OECD allies, as well as by the leading business lobby groups that represented what were still almost exclusively their MNEs. The proposals were rejected one by one, and by the early 1980s, most of the NIEO agenda was dead and buried (Cobham, Janský, & Meinzer, 2019).

The tables finally began to turn in the 1990s, when the tremendous spread and growth of the offshore world became a source of concern even in the US and the newly established EU, which grew increasingly worried about the impact of the offshore infrastructure on their ability to effectively raise revenues. At the 1996 summit in Lyon, the Group of Seven (G7) heads of state commenced the first serious global effort aimed directly against the offshore infrastructure. The task was given to the OECD, which in 1998 launched the Harmful Tax Competition Initiative (HTCI) with the express purpose of "discouraging the spread of tax havens and harmful preferential tax regimes," as they were found to have a "large adverse impact on the revenue bases of other countries" (OECD, 1998b, pp. 8, 22). Breaking new ground, the OECD proposed that member states and non-member states alike adopt a common framework within which they could operate individually and collectively to limit the problems presented by tax havens and harmful preferential tax regimes and provided a list of 19 recommendations concerning domestic legislation, tax treaties, and international cooperation to facilitate this process. With regard to tax treaties, among other things, the OECD recommended countries to improve and intensify exchanges of information with tax havens, to include provisions that restrict the entitlement to treaty benefits for entities and income tied to any harmful tax practices, and to ensure that domestic anti-abuse rules and judicial doctrines are compatible with tax treaties. But most importantly, it recommended that they consider terminating their DTAs with tax havens or at least refrain from negotiating new ones. In what was probably the sharpest departure from past practice, the OECD even began compiling a blacklist of uncooperative tax havens to serve as the basis for further coordinated defensive measures against them, although crucially, as already mentioned earlier, none of this applied to the uncooperative tax havens that happened to be OECD member states (OECD, 2000).

In addition to the mostly tax-focused initiative undertaken by the OECD, which represented the main thrust of the whole anti-offshore campaign, OFCs were also probed by the Financial Action Task Force (FATF) because they were considered to pose a much higher risk regarding money laundering and terrorist financing, by the Financial Stability Forum (FSF) because they were considered to pose a potential systemic threat to global financial stability, and by the International Monetary Fund (IMF) because of their negative impact on the more vulnerable financial systems of emerging market economies, and on good governance in general. Each of these four organizations identified Mauritius as a tax haven or as an OFC, depending on their preferred terminology, and placed it on their lists of jurisdictions requiring closer scrutiny, with the FSF going as far as to place it among its Group III OFCs, which were perceived as posing the greatest threat to global financial stability (OECD, 2000; FATF, 2000; FSF, 2000; IMF, 2000). Showing better judgment and foresight than many other OFCs, Mauritius made a high-level political commitment to cooperate with the OECD and the FATF, which at least spared it from being added to their blacklists, although not from the FATF's greylist, reserved for cooperative jurisdictions under increased monitoring.

The speed and intensity with which the multi-pronged campaign unfolded initially took the nexus of accommodative forces by surprise and temporarily put them on the defensive, but by late 2000, they regrouped and kicked up a global lobbying storm. The governments of the targeted OFCs banded together, with some pooling their resources to found the International Tax and Investment Organization (ITIO) to represent their common interests, and began appealing to individual OECD member states bilaterally as well as by way of their old colonial links, such as the Commonwealth Secretariat, in order to get the OECD to back down, using every forum at their disposal to decry the glaring injustice of being subjected to blacklists and other defensive measures while the likes of Switzerland and Luxembourg, which were just as uncooperative, faced no equivalent repercussions. As Haberly and Wójcik (2015a) have demonstrated, this part of the lobbying effort was somewhat effective in its own right, at least for the OFCs with direct links to OECD member states, but what really turned the tide against the HTCI as a whole was the founding of the Center for Freedom and Prosperity (CFP), a US lobbying outfit led by a group of veteran libertarian Washington, DC insiders and backed by some of the most influential corporate-funded think tanks in the world. The group leaned heavily on the tenets of the still dominant neoliberal orthodoxy and succeeded in convincing a large number of Republican establishment heavyweights that by referring to any kind of tax competition as harmful, the OECD was essentially pushing an anti-market and thus an anti-American agenda with the HTCI.

In April 2001, soon after the Clinton administration gave way to the new Bush administration, the US, initially a key driver of the HTCI, publicly denounced the initiative, and watered it down beyond recognition. What started as a flawed but highly ambitious and for its time relatively aggressive campaign against the worst excesses of the offshore world was effectively reduced to politely asking OFCs if they were willing to sign tax information exchange agreements (TIEAs) based on the OECD's Exchange of Information on Request (EOIR) standard, a notoriously costly and time-consuming method of information exchange which requires that the requesting authority already possesses evidence of a crime or other kinds of wrongdoing before sending a request (Sheppard, 2009; Palan et al., 2010). Similar conclusions have also been reached by Seabrooke and Wigan (2016):

> Our field research reveals that such requests can take up to six months. This may be the best-case scenario – information exchange between friendly countries with well-developed bureaucracies. Imagine how long it takes to get information from unfriendly jurisdictions with little organizational resources. Perpetrators can move money at will and at great speed. This means that police and tax investigators usually prefer to deal with purely domestic cases, which are easier, rather than dealing with thornier international investigations, even though the latter might reveal where the big money is.

The EOIR standard is better than nothing, as it can still be useful for assessing the financial extent of a given crime or wrongdoing, but it is utterly ineffective as a deterrent against offshore tax evasion and avoidance. Nevertheless, in most cases over the ensuing years, the OFCs politely declined to sign the TIEAs, unless bilaterally coerced into doing so by one of the major global or regional powers, usually the US. Yet again, the forces resistant to offshore finance had failed (Sharman, 2006). This failure was not like any other before it though because while it did mean a return of the accommodative status quo for those supplying and demanding offshore financial services, far from demoralizing or deterring the forces of resistance, it actually served to embolden them. The failure of the HTCI proved to be a watershed moment for two groups of actors in particular, the tax justice community and the EU.

In the 1990s, it was not just the Western governments that found the tremendous spread and growth of the offshore world disconcerting but also their civil society sectors. Whether they were household names like Oxfam or newer ones like Global Witness, CSOs focusing on development grew increasingly aware of just how detrimental OFCs had been for the developmental prospects of much of the periphery and the semiperiphery, with offshore tax evasion and avoidance, corruption-related money laundering, and destabilizing capital flight all emerging as major developmental issues. When the HTCI came crashing down and it became clear that Western governments were not only unable or unwilling to tackle these issues, but were themselves a part of the whole problem, CSOs increasingly began to adopt a more tax justice-oriented focus. Tax justice, broadly conceived, was hardly a novel concept by then, but it was only in 2003 that a small group of activists and academics founded the Tax Justice Network (TJN), the first CSO exclusively dedicated to taking on the offshore world, and with that took the first major step in the rise of the tax justice community (TJN, 2015). Members of the TJN argued that effectively taking on the offshore world would require nothing less than systemic change, identifying the international tax system with its three basic principles as the main problem to be addressed. Not long after, they released the details of their tax justice agenda, which consisted of four key policy solutions:

- Automatic exchange of tax information;
- Beneficial ownership registers;
- Country-by-country reporting; and
- Worldwide unitary taxation with formulary apportionment.

In its ambition, this tax justice agenda far surpassed even the HTCI before it was gutted, and as such was widely derided as naïve and impossible to succeed with. Instead of giving into these pressures, the tax justice community at large has remained steadfast not only in its awareness-raising, campaigning, and advocacy for these four key policy solutions but in the process of its own steady growth and diversification has over time built on them and expanded the tax justice agenda further (see Box 3.1).

Box 3.1: The Tax Justice Agenda

The steady growth and increasing diversity that have over the years come to define the global tax justice community have also meant that what constitutes the tax justice agenda has constantly been evolving (TJN, 2020b; FACTI Panel, 2021). However, four key policy solutions have remained at the forefront of the tax justice agenda from the very beginning.

Solution 1: Automatic Exchange of Tax Information – A new transparency measure and data sharing practice, which would prevent individuals and MNEs from abusing foreign bank accounts to hide the true value of their wealth from tax, regulatory, and other relevant authorities, often to escape their legal obligations. It would essentially be the next logical step from the OECD's EOIR standard, surpassing it in every way by automatically and on a regular basis providing all relevant authorities everywhere around the world with accurate information about the wealth of their residents held abroad.

Solution 2: Beneficial Ownership Registers – Another new transparency measure, which would prevent individuals from hiding their ultimate beneficial ownership or control of companies or other legal vehicles behind layers upon layers of opaque offshore structures, nominee directorships, and other convoluted methods of purchasing anonymity, often for the evasion or avoidance of taxes, the circumvention of competition laws, the concealment of conflicts of interest when applying for public procurement contracts, or for various other nefarious purposes. With the introduction of beneficial ownership registers, professional intermediaries would have a legal obligation to know all of the ultimate beneficial owners of any structures they are involved in setting up or in any way administering, and register them accordingly, essentially outlawing this kind of anonymity. In addition, since beneficial ownership information is a matter of significant public interest, and is not sensitive in the way that the financial account information covered under automatic exchange of tax information is, it should be subject to full public accountability. As such, beneficial ownership registers should be made accessible online to the public for free.

Solution 3: Country-by-Country Reporting – Yet another new transparency measure, which would prevent MNEs from concealing the ways in which they artificially structure their operations and manipulate transfer prices, often to lower their effective tax rates or secure other improper benefits. With the introduction of this reporting standard, MNEs would have to provide every country in which they operate with detailed annual financial statements on all their companies anywhere in the world, including their profits, losses, taxes paid, and other important indicators of financial performance and break them down by country, so that the tax authorities can easily spot, scrutinize, and address any irregularities, unlike without it, when MNEs would normally only provide information on their local operation, alongside aggregate figures for their global operation, leaving tax authorities essentially blind to profit shifting and other forms of offshore tax avoidance. Once again, since this information is a matter of significant public interest, and is generally not sensitive, perhaps aside from a few carefully defined and individually evaluated exceptions in which publication might lead to the disclosure of legitimate trade secrets, it should be subject to full public accountability and made accessible online to the public for free. Together, automatic exchange of tax information, beneficial ownership registers, and country-by-country reporting have been thought of as so fundamental to the tax justice agenda that they had been dubbed as the ABCs of tax justice.

Solution 4: Worldwide Unitary Taxation with Formulary Apportionment – A paradigm shift in international taxation, which not only would do away with the separate entity and arm's length principles but could also go a long way in rectifying the inequities resulting from the primacy of residence over source. It has been discussed as one of the possible alternatives already during the League of Nations process and has long been in operation at the sub-central level among the various federal units within several countries, including the US, Argentina, Canada, and Switzerland. Under worldwide unitary taxation with formulary apportionment, MNEs would be treated as the unitary entities that they really are and their consolidated profits would be apportioned and taxed according to a formula that better reflects their real economic presence in each country, such as one based on a combination of their sales, assets, and employees, as opposed to just where they formally happen to declare their profits, as is currently the case. By treating MNEs as unitary entities and taxing them based on factors that are less mobile and more representative of genuine business activities than profits alone, many of the currently available opportunities for profit shifting and other forms of offshore tax avoidance would be significantly diminished.

Other Solutions – Aside from these four key policy solutions, the global tax justice community has also been actively advocating for a wide range of other specific measures and general policy directions that are too numerous to cover here in detail. Some notable examples include advocacy for a greater empowerment of tax authorities, which are often understaffed and underfunded even in the highly developed countries of the core, despite an abundance of research and practical experience consistently demonstrating that every dollar spent on tax enforcement is returned several-fold through higher tax revenues; or for the need to curb tax competition in its various guises, such as through the adoption of a global minimum corporate income tax rate; or for a variety of other ways in which a harder line should be taken against not just the individual and corporate tax dodgers, but also the tax havens and professional intermediaries that enable them, such as through stricter disclosure requirements and penalties for non-compliance. Many more such measures and policy directions can also be found among, or derived from, the 20 "secrecy indicators" used to produce the Financial Secrecy Index (TJN, 2020a) and the 20 "haven indicators" used to produce the Corporate Tax Haven Index (TJN, 2021). Two other calls by the global tax justice community that have been getting considerable attention and even some traction in the last few years concern the establishment of an intergovernmental tax body under the auspices of the UN and the adoption of a UN tax convention. The former would allow international tax matters to be discussed and agreed on through a more representative process than at the OECD and the latter would enshrine the principles of tax justice in international law.

As for the EU, the lobbying effort against the HTCI proved nowhere near as effective as it did in the US and could even be argued to have backfired. Many of the EU's key institutions, especially the European Commission (EC) and the European Parliament (EP), as well as most of its non-OFC member states saw the offshore world as a threat to be dealt with even before, and witnessing the viciousness of the reaction to what they considered to be a perfectly reasonable endeavor only served to cement their views further, motivating them to continue strengthening the EU's regulatory infrastructure against the offshore threat, albeit only at the regional level within the confines of the EU. Roughly from this point onward, the EU has consistently and increasingly proven itself to be a trailblazer in the area of anti-offshore legislation and regulation, even though its ambition has often been thwarted or undermined by its own nexus of accommodative forces, in this case mostly consisting of its OFC member states. One of the earliest major examples of this is the European Commission's proposal for a Common Consolidated Corporate Tax Base (CCCTB), which would introduce unitary taxation with formulary apportionment across the EU. Work on the CCCTB began in October 2001, a few months after the US singlehandedly derailed the HTCI. Despite having the support of some of the biggest member states like Germany, France, and Italy, in May 2011, the proposal was rejected by eight member states, including the usual suspects like the UK, Ireland, Malta, and the Netherlands (Gilleard, 2011). Another example is the European Union Savings Directive (EUSD), which constituted the first major automatic exchange of tax information standard, although it only applied to the investment income of non-resident savers from other EU countries and a few of their dependent territories. It was enacted in 2003, and even though it was riddled with loopholes and thus ultimately proved nowhere near as effective as its drafters initially hoped (Sharman, 2008; Rixen & Schwarz, 2012), it represented not only significant progress, but also the hardening stance of the EU toward the offshore world.

The position of the growing forces of resistance was further bolstered by the increasingly frequent eruptions of major scandals with a distinct offshore footprint, such as Enron in 2001, WorldCom in 2002, or Madoff and UBS in 2008, with the last one even partially bringing the US into the anti-offshore fold, prompting US authorities to initiate an unprecedented crackdown against Swiss banking secrecy, resulting in convictions, fines, and bank closures, but most importantly, a rethinking of the US approach to foreign bank accounts of US taxpayers (Emmenegger, 2017). Then came the global financial crisis, and for the first time since the rise of the offshore world, the global scales tipped from favoring accommodation to favoring resistance in a way that no lobbying effort, regardless of how professional or well-funded, could tip back anytime soon. After all, it was the offshore world that served as a base to most of the toxic shadow banking instruments, helped conceal much of the misconduct and speculation, whether criminal or not, and as such played an undeniably significant role in the crash (Palan et al., 2010; Shaxson, 2011; Rixen, 2013). As one of the key consequences of the global financial crisis, the G20 rose to become one of the most important forums of global governance. This shift was a highly relevant one with regard to the offshore world, because the G20 counts not only several EU member states as its full members but also the EU itself. Aside from that, and perhaps even more importantly, the composition of the G20 also significantly increased the influence of the emerging semiperiphery, most of which has not only long sought to reform the international tax system, but has historically been more hostile to the offshore world than much of the core, bolstering the position of the still growing forces of resistance even more. As a result of all these developments, the three structural supports that had for decades ensured the offshore world's resilience began to deteriorate. Its secrecy provisions were targeted for complete dismantling. Neoliberalism, while still prevalent, lost much of its credibility and continues to persist in the way that it does only due to the absence of a widely adhered to alternative. And global finance, while eventually having rebounded and once again finding itself on the rise by most conventional economic metrics, continues to be viewed with suspicion, if not outright resentment by the masses virtually anywhere around the world. The forces of accommodation, while still wielding immense financial and political power, and thus remaining highly influential, nevertheless found themselves decidedly on the defensive.

With the new balance of power in place, the stage was set for another global anti-offshore campaign, except this time, within a few years, the campaign would evolve into a full-blown reform of the international tax system. Just as the G7 did in 1996, in 2008, the G20 delegated the main thrust of the campaign and the subsequent reform effort to the OECD. Naturally, with the G20 and the OECD being the central actors of the ensuing campaign, most of the media and academic attention shifted to the global and the regional levels, while neglecting the national level. However, no analysis of these recent developments will be complete if it is focused only on the agreements brokered by the G20 and the OECD. After all, it is still ultimately up to individual countries to decide, based on the results of their internal political struggles, whether to implement the

OECD standards at all, how faithfully they will implement them, or whether they will unilaterally move beyond them. This is a powerful moment precisely because a significant number of global, regional, and national forces have aligned against the offshore world. As is argued throughout this book, it is not only global and regional attitudes but also national attitudes that will determine whether the offshore world will retreat in the face of this unprecedented scrutiny.

New global standards and the continuing role of national factors

In spite of the favorable conditions in which it emerged, the new anti-offshore campaign did not get off to an impressive start in the immediate aftermath of the global financial crisis. The OECD, still reeling from the HTCI fiasco, proceeded cautiously. Following the April 2009 G20 summit in London, during which the G20 leaders famously declared that "the era of banking secrecy is over" (G20, 2009), it fired its opening salvo against the offshore world. Despite the action only consisting of pushing another round of TIEAs based on the EOIR standard on OFCs, this time, the OECD was at least demanding instead of asking. In order to avoid the new OECD blacklist and any potential economic sanctions that might follow, OFCs were required to sign at least 12 TIEAs. In just five days, all OFCs committed to meeting this goal, and by the November 2011 G20 summit in Cannes, more than 700 new TIEAs had been signed. However, the effects were nevertheless underwhelming. According to Johannesen and Zucman (2014, p. 65), many of the TIEAs were signed between the OFCs themselves and the available data suggests that "rather than repatriating funds," tax evaders merely "shifted deposits to havens not covered by a treaty with their home country," causing "a relocation of deposits at the benefit of the least compliant havens."

In the meantime, what was arguably the first meaningful piece of anti-offshore legislation following the global financial crisis transpired at the national level in 2010, when the Obama administration enacted the precedent-shattering Foreign Account Tax Compliance Act (FATCA). FATCA requires financial institutions anywhere in the world to register with the US Internal Revenue Service (IRS) and annually report to it all applicable information on all their US clients. Although the registration is technically voluntary, non-participating financial institutions face an automatic 30% WHT on certain US source payments including dividends, interest, rents, premiums, and many other forms of income. More than that, FATCA also requires the participating financial institutions to withhold on payments to non-participating financial institutions, which means that its regulatory and punitive reach extends to hundreds of thousands of professional intermediaries regardless of whether they choose to register or not, and for most, it is no choice at all, because the 30% WHT would essentially make them uncompetitive on the lucrative US market, which few internationally operating financial institutions could afford (Palan & Wigan, 2014). It would be a stretch to credit FATCA with being the first global automatic exchange of tax information standard. After all, the only jurisdiction receiving information from all over the world is the US itself, with all other jurisdictions only receiving information on the accounts of their taxpayers based in the US, and even there, in a glaring display of hegemonic arrogance that continues to agitate even its closest international partners, the US does not practice full reciprocity in its exchanges, which means that it "typically receives far more information from foreign governments than it provides" (EP, 2019, p. 51). However, this clear one-sidedness notwithstanding, FATCA can rightly be credited with being the first automatic exchange of tax information standard with a global reach, raising the bar for what is possible.

The enactment of FATCA resonated throughout the G20 membership, but especially in India, whose government was growing increasingly frustrated with the lack of ambition of the OECD's initial response and impatient at the lack of meaningful progress that it entailed. At the November 2011 G20 summit in Cannes, the Indian Prime Minister, Manmohan Singh (as quoted in The Economic Times, 2011), made a forceful case for the adoption of a global automatic exchange of tax information standard, and even argued that it should be retroactive so as to deal with past cases of tax evasion, specifically declaring that:

> G20 countries should take the lead in agreeing to automatic exchange of tax-related information with each other, irrespective of artificial distinctions such as past or present, for tax evasion or tax fraud, in the spirit of our London Summit that 'the era of bank secrecy is over'.

The call represented an important validation of the work of the tax justice community and was received with general enthusiasm in the EU, most of its member states, the other emerging powers of the G20, the G77, and even the US, which, following the enactment of FATCA, was eager to level the regulatory playing field with the rest of the world so that it would not stand out to international investors as more unwelcoming than its competitors (Hakelberg, 2020). With that, the OECD was cleared to step up its efforts, and as requested, began work on the first global automatic exchange of tax information standard, which came to be known as the Common Reporting Standard (CRS). The CRS was officially approved in July 2014, with the earliest exchanges among signatories taking place in 2017. Despite not being retroactive beyond 2017, and suffering from a number of deficiencies, the general consensus has been that the CRS is a huge improvement over the EOIR standard and represents important progress in the fight against offshore tax evasion (see Box 3.2).

Box 3.2: G20/OECD – Common Reporting Standard (CRS) for Automatic Exchange of Financial Account Information in Tax Matters

The CRS is the G20/OECD's most important attempt to tackle offshore tax evasion to date and is widely considered to be a transparency milestone (OECD, 2014). For the foreseeable future, the CRS is still only a complement to the older and more cumbersome EOIR standard but should gradually replace it as more jurisdictions sign on. The CRS requires signatory jurisdictions to collect financial account information from their respective financial institutions and annually exchange that information with other signatory jurisdictions with which they had established a bilateral exchange relationship. This provides tax authorities with a significantly greater level of information on the wealth held abroad by their residents than they ever had before. The adoption of the CRS by the EU has led to the immediate repeal of the much weaker EUSD, and even though it is unlikely to achieve the same in the US with regard to FATCA, it equals or surpasses its slightly older predecessor in several crucial ways.

The CRS generally has a broader scope in terms of the financial institutions required to report, the type of account holders subject to reporting, and the financial information that is to be reported. The financial institutions covered by the standard include custodial institutions, depository institutions, investment entities, and specified insurance companies. Reportable accounts include accounts held by individuals and entities, which includes trusts, foundations, and certain types of charities. The standard even has a requirement to look through passive entities to report not only on the beneficial owners of accounts but also on their relevant controlling persons. The financial information to be reported includes account balance or value, interest, dividends, income from certain insurance products, as well as sales proceeds from financial assets and other income generated with respect to assets held in the account or payments made with respect to the account. The CRS also has fewer reporting exemptions. Whereas FATCA exempts all pre-existing and new individual accounts below the reporting threshold of US$50,000, the CRS has no de minimis thresholds for individual accounts. Unlike FATCA, the CRS is also fully reciprocal, unless a signatory jurisdiction explicitly chooses not to receive information from any of its exchange counterparts.

The one notable weakness of the CRS is that it lacks the blunt force of FATCA's devastating 30% WHT with which to address cases of non-compliance. However, it does partially make up for it by requiring signatory jurisdictions to establish their own penalty schemes, and monitors their implementation and enforcement through regular peer reviews by members of the OECD's Global Forum on Transparency and Exchange of Information for Tax Purposes. Aside from these peer reviews, the OECD has also committed to preserving the integrity of the CRS by establishing information channels to continuously gather, improve, and share intelligence on any actual or perceived loopholes of the standard, systematically analyzing their potential impact, and addressing them by developing appropriate anti-abuse provisions, as well as evaluating whether the standard is in need of more fundamental modifications.

In parallel with this activity on the offshore tax evasion front, two other fronts were being opened as part of the overall reform effort. One was against offshore tax avoidance, and the other, relatedly, against the three basic principles of the international tax system. The key actor behind the opening of both fronts was the tax justice community. With regard to offshore tax avoidance, it was the years of work by the tax justice CSOs that was among the main contributing factors leading investigative journalists to increasingly focus on corporate tax abuse. Reports on scandals featuring MNEs not paying their fair share began pouring in, forcing governments to respond. Among the most widely publicized of the initial responses was the UK's November 2012 House of Commons Committee of Public Accounts hearing with representatives of Google, Amazon, and Starbucks (BBC, 2012), which was reputationally damaging to the MNEs and contributed to the launching of dozens of further hearings, probes, and even formal investigations all over the world, including the European Commission's highly controversial state aid investigations, as epitomized by its ongoing US$15.7 billion plus interest case against Ireland because of its arrangement with Apple (EC, 2021; White, 2021). What became one of the most powerful symbols and rallying cries against offshore tax avoidance during this period was the "Double Irish with a Dutch Sandwich" scheme, and not only because it was associated with Google and several other Big Tech household names that happen to be some of the most profitable entities on the planet but also because in one tight package it contained the most important tricks of the trade enabled by the three basic principles of the international tax system, such as transfer pricing manipulation and treaty shopping (Drucker, 2010; IMF, 2013). Not only did it expose in relatively clear terms to the general public that Ireland, the Netherlands, the UK, and numerous other supposedly "clean" jurisdictions were just as much of a problem when it comes to these schemes as the Bermudas of the world but also that the international tax system itself is the problem, a problem to which the tax justice community already had a concrete solution in the form of worldwide unitary taxation with formulary apportionment. While this particular solution did not necessarily find uniform support even among some of the countries that have suffered the most under the status quo, the idea that the international tax system itself must be changed in order to effectively fight offshore tax avoidance most certainly did.

Several other concurrent factors contributed to the perfect storm that was brewing against offshore tax avoidance and the international tax system, many of them taking place at the national level. In the US, it was the upcoming 2012 presidential elections, the Occupy Wall Street movement, and corporate inversions, which US MNEs increasingly began resorting to in an attempt to escape their tax obligations. Across the EU, it was the lingering sovereign debt crisis and the unpopular politics of austerity that accompanied it. Among the non-OECD members of the G20, it was the growing frustration with how Western MNEs were able to undermine their tax bases and with the OECD for not going far enough with its work to effectively address it, combined with the realization that a more serious reform of the international tax system could potentially also serve as an opportunity to finally renegotiate the contentious primacy of residence over source principle. While most developing countries shared the same frustrations as the non-OECD members of the G20 with regard to Western MNEs and the OECD and would themselves like to see a more equitable reallocation of taxing rights, their overriding grievance was of a more fundamental kind, specifically that the global standards, which were supposed to apply to the entire world, naturally including them, were being negotiated and set largely without their input.

From around 2011, the G77, as well as many of its members or smaller member groupings in their own national or regional capacity, began giving more voice to this long-held grievance at a variety of different forums on a regular basis, calling for the establishment of an intergovernmental tax body under the auspices of the UN, where international tax matters would be discussed and agreed to with every state represented and having an equal voice, unlike at the OECD, which has first and foremost been representing the views of its comparatively small and mostly developed membership. These calls raised uncomfortable questions about the dominance of the OECD in the area of international taxation, and not only because the G77, despite retaining its historical name, grew to represent 134 countries, but also because several of its most vocal members also happened to be non-OECD members of the G20 (Financial Transparency Coalition [FTC], 2017). Brazil, China, India, and South Africa all fully supported and amplified these calls, partly because each of them was in their own way and in pursuance of their own particular interests positioning themselves as champions of the interests of the developing world (Vieira & Alden, 2011; Cooper & Farooq, 2016), and partly because even though they gained more influence and were granted equal standing at the OECD as members of the G20, they still frequently found themselves outnumbered during the negotiations. While the Western powers refused to even entertain giving up their control over international tax matters by empowering the UN at the expense of the OECD, they understood that certain concessions would have to be made, and hoped that addressing offshore tax avoidance by way of a more serious reform of the international tax system, which they themselves had wanted by that point, would be sufficient to at least temporarily quell this unrest from the bottom.

Early discussions among the members of the G20 and the OECD of what such a reform would entail took place already in 2012, but it was only in 2013 that the OECD formulated a concrete outline and action plan for what came to be known as the Base Erosion and Profit Shifting (BEPS) project. The BEPS project was to consist of 15 deliverables referred to as "Actions," and the work was expected to take a little over two years (OECD, 2013). By September 2014, which marked the midpoint of the development phase of the project as well as the release date for several of the deliverables in an interim form, three things were already clear. First, while engagement with developing countries had improved, it remained superficial, falling far short of having them participate on the project on an equal footing with members of the G20 and the OECD. Second, dashing hopes of the non-OECD members of the G20 and the rest of the G77, none of the three basic principles of the international tax system were up for renegotiation as part of the project. And third, to the irritation of even many OECD members, especially those from the EU, due to intense pressure by the US under the Obama administration, which was determined to protect its Big Tech sector, other than the exploratory report that was being produced, all substantive work on the digital economy was to be postponed to an unspecified future date. As the BEPS project drew closer to completion, it also became clear that several of its deliverables would be watered down further when compared to their originally proposed versions. With the BEPS project circumscribed in these key respects, the non-OECD members of the G20 and the rest of the G77 proceeded with their calls for the establishment of a UN intergovernmental tax body. The calls formally came to a head in July 2015 at the Third International Conference on Financing for Development in Addis Ababa, but the proposal was blocked by members of the OECD, particularly the US, UK, and Japan, only a few months before the completion of the BEPS project (Anyangwe, 2015). The BEPS project was officially approved in October 2015, although some additional work, most notably on the Action 15 Multilateral Instrument (henceforth the BEPS MLI), on which the implementation of all of the treaty-related deliverables depended, would only be completed well into 2016. Arguably the most significant breakthrough of the BEPS project was the Action 13 Country-by-Country Reporting standard (henceforth the BEPS CbCR standard), which had its earliest exchanges among signatories take place in 2018, although just like with the digital economy, the US intervened here as well, insisting that the reports were not to be made public. Despite being more of a last-ditch attempt to preserve the three basic principles than a genuine reform of the international tax system, the BEPS project is an important stepping stone toward more ambitious future outcomes, and represents important progress in the fight against offshore tax avoidance (see Box 3.3).

Box 3.3: G20/OECD – Base Erosion and Profit Shifting (BEPS) Project

The BEPS project is the G20/OECD's first major attempt to tackle offshore tax avoidance by MNEs and constitutes the most substantial reform of the international tax system in almost a century (OECD, 2015). The result is a comprehensive package of measures that aims to restore confidence in the existing set of international tax rules and principles by ensuring that profits are taxed where economic activities take place and value is created. The outputs come in the form of 15 Actions that range from reports, assessments, and analyses, to soft law legal instruments of varying strength, depending on the level of support they have among the G20/OECD memberships. There are minimum standards, on which a relatively broad consensus has been reached, and all members have committed to implement them. There are changes to existing standards, which will be updated accordingly, but since they have not been endorsed by all members, they will not be introduced by all of them. And finally, there are recommendations and best practices, on which only the general tax policy direction has been agreed to, but the differences that remain are relatively widespread and substantial, so countries are likewise free to choose whether or not to follow them.

Action 1: Addressing the Tax Challenges of the Digital Economy – An exploratory report that highlights many of the key features of the digital economy that exacerbate offshore tax avoidance, but most of these challenges have been found to be too complex and contentious to be directly addressed within the limited time frame of the BEPS project, and have thus been postponed.
Output: Report with recommendations

Action 2: Neutralizing the Effects of Hybrid Mismatch Arrangements – A set of rules designed to prevent offshore tax avoidance through the use of hybrid mismatches, for example by generating multiple deductions for a single expense, deductions in one country without corresponding taxation in another, or multiple foreign tax credits for one amount of foreign tax paid.
Output: Recommendations with changes to the OECD MTC

Action 3: Designing Effective Controlled Foreign Company Rules – A set of rules designed to prevent offshore tax avoidance through the artificial shifting of income to subsidiaries in lower-tax jurisdictions.
Output: Recommendations and best practices

Action 4: Limiting Base Erosion Involving Interest Deductions and Other Financial Payments – A set of rules designed to prevent offshore tax avoidance through the manipulation of third party and intra-group debt financing, for example by artificially multiplying and shifting debt to higher-tax jurisdictions, generating excess interest deductions, or funding the production of tax exempt or deferred income.
Output: Recommendations and best practices

Action 5: Countering Harmful Tax Practices More Effectively, Taking into Account Transparency and Substance – A stronger set of standards requiring that the benefits of preferential regimes can only be granted upon demonstration of substantial activity, along with a new framework for improving transparency and exchange of information between jurisdictions in connection with certain tax rulings.
Output: Minimum standards

Action 6: Preventing the Granting of Treaty Benefits in Inappropriate Circumstances – A set of articles and anti-abuse provisions like the limitation-on-benefits (LOB) rule and the principal purposes test (PPT) rule, designed to prevent offshore tax avoidance through treaty shopping and other forms of treaty abuse.
Output: Minimum standards with changes to the OECD MTC

Action 7: Preventing the Artificial Avoidance of Permanent Establishment Status – A new definition of permanent establishment designed to prevent offshore tax avoidance through the abuse of commissionaire arrangements, the artificial fragmentation of business activities between closely related parties, and other similar strategies used to erode the taxable bases of source jurisdictions.
Output: Changes to the OECD MTC

Actions 8–10: Aligning Transfer Pricing Outcomes with Value Creation – A set of guidelines empowering tax authorities to focus more on economic substance over legal form in their transfer pricing evaluations, designed to prevent offshore tax avoidance through transfer pricing manipulation involving intangibles, risk allocation, intra-group services, and other areas where artificial transactions have become common.
Output: Changes to the OECD TPGs

Action 11: Measuring and Monitoring BEPS – An assessment of existing and new data sources, estimation methodologies, analytical tools, and indicators aimed at improving analyses of the scale and impact of offshore tax avoidance, and the effectiveness of the countermeasures deployed against it.
Output: Report with recommendations

Action 12: Mandatory Disclosure Rules – A set of rules requiring promoters, intermediaries, and MNEs to disclose upfront to tax authorities their promotion, facilitation, and use of offshore tax avoidance schemes that meet certain specific features or hallmarks.
Output: Recommendations and best practices

Action 13: Transfer Pricing Documentation and Country-by-Country Reporting – A transparency milestone requiring large MNEs to articulate their transfer pricing positions more clearly, enabling tax authorities to assess transfer pricing risks and deploy audit resources more effectively.
Output: Minimum standards with changes to the OECD TPGs

Action 14: Making Dispute Resolution Mechanisms More Effective – Commitment to minimize the risks of uncertainty and double taxation by strengthening the effectiveness of the mutual agreement procedure (MAP), with many OECD members also committing to mandatory binding arbitration.
Output: Minimum standards and best practices with changes to the OECD MTC

Action 15: Developing a Multilateral Instrument to Modify Bilateral Tax Treaties – A feasibility analysis and basic roadmap for the development of a mechanism that would expedite the implementation of the new treaty-related measures (BEPS Actions 2, 6, 7, and 14) into existing bilateral tax treaties.
Output: Report with recommendations

The CRS and the BEPS project are the most important products of the overall post-global financial crisis reform effort thus far. Through them, the G20 and the OECD aim to establish new global minimum standards and norms that, even though they are technically non-binding, will strengthen over time. The underlying idea is to use the politics of shame to impel countries to adhere to these new standards and norms, and thus better police offshore transactions. Recalcitrant jurisdictions will be subject to greater scrutiny, blacklisting, and potentially even further defensive measures should they refuse to cooperate, leading to a loss of investor confidence. The logic is that the pressure from these efforts will be sufficiently high that the demand for and supply of offshore services will fall, and OFCs, facing higher regulatory pressures and weakened demand, will assume a diminished place in the global economy.

However, the key and often neglected point is that the most important of these supposedly global standards still require extensive engagement at the national level for them to be effectively implemented. After all, taxation remains one of the most important sovereign rights, and this is not about to change anytime soon. For instance, while the CRS is often colloquially referred to as GATCA among industry insiders, as in the "global" version of FATCA, it is actually nowhere near as global as it may seem at first glance. For what is supposed to be a global automatic exchange of tax information standard, the most logical and reasonable assumption would be that by signing on to the standard, any new jurisdiction would begin exchanging information with all the other signatories, but this is not the case. Instead, all signatories still have to go through an arduous bilateral negotiations phase which essentially determines their exchange relationships, as in which specific signatories they send information to, and which specific signatories they receive information from. Similar arrangements also apply with regard to the BEPS CbCR standard, where the bilateral negotiations phase is essentially the same, as well as the BEPS MLI, although there it is not only about which of their tax treaty partners the jurisdictions decide to engage, but also about which specific articles of their DTAs they are willing to modify, and how, since several of the BEPS project's deliverables, including many of the treaty-related ones, have given signatories a considerable space for flexibility within which they would still be deemed compliant.

According to the OECD (2021c, 2021d), as of April 2021, a total of 110 jurisdictions have signed up to the CRS, 89 to the BEPS CbCR standard, and 95 to the BEPS MLI, and this includes most of the world's OFCs. Given how recent the global standards are, these are impressive results that have exceeded the initial expectations of many skeptics, but looking at the number of signatories alone conceals not only much of the reality on the ground, but also the sheer extent of what has yet to be achieved. When the crucial bilateral dimension of the standards is taken into consideration, the results are nowhere near as impressive. The OECD (2021c, 2021d) also reports that as of March 2021, over 4,200 bilateral exchange relationships have been activated under the CRS, over 2,900 under the BEPS CbCR standard, and over 1,680 DTAs have been bilaterally agreed to be modified under the BEPS MLI. Once again, this is impressive, but consider that for the coverage to be full, the 110 signatories of the CRS would need to activate 5,995 bilateral exchange relationships, the 89 signatories of the BEPS CbCR standard 3,916 of them, and the 95 signatories of the BEPS MLI have listed over 2,800 DTAs between them. This means that the current coverage among the signatories stands at roughly 70% for the CRS, 74% for the BEPS CbCR standard, and 60% for the BEPS MLI. If we move beyond the signatories, there are currently well over 230 jurisdictions with sufficient sovereignty to make their own tax laws and be able to negotiate and enter into at least some international treaties, which means that full global coverage would require activating more than 26,335 bilateral exchange relationships for both the CRS and the BEPS CbCR standard, and modifying more than 3,000 DTAs. Taking this as the baseline, the current global coverage stands at roughly 16% for the CRS, 11% for the BEPS CbCR standard, and 56% for the BEPS MLI, although with regard to the latter, it is worth reiterating that it is not just a matter of the number of DTAs that were covered but also how exactly they were modified. From this point of view, there is clearly a great deal of work still left to be done, both in terms of new signatories and in terms of the implementation process once new jurisdictions have decided to sign on.

In terms of new signatories, one of the complicating factors in getting more jurisdictions to adopt the new global standards and norms is that for much of the periphery and the semiperiphery, there is no feeling of ownership toward them. The standards were not designed to reflect their views or address their particular needs in the same way that they were for the memberships of the G20 and even more so of the OECD. More than a question of ownership, for some members of the G77, especially following the July 2015 vetoes against the establishment of a UN intergovernmental tax body in Addis Ababa, it may even be a question of resentment. At the November 2015 G20 summit in Antalya, members of the G20, especially the OECD ones, attempted to smooth over what happened at Addis Ababa while motivating more jurisdictions to sign up to the new global standards and norms by calling on the OECD "to develop an inclusive framework by early 2016 with the involvement of interested non-G20 countries and jurisdictions which commit to implement the BEPS project, including developing economies, on an equal footing" (G20, 2015). With this diplomatic gambit, the OECD members of the G20 hoped to kill two birds with one stone but the result appears to have been a mixed success. On the one hand, the Inclusive Framework on BEPS, established in June 2016, has attracted 139 members as of February 2021, and because one of the prerequisites for joining is to commit to the BEPS package, it can also be credited with contributing to the total number of signatories to the BEPS CbCR standard and the BEPS MLI. On the other hand, the G77 and many of its members, including those that have joined the Inclusive Framework on BEPS, have never let up in calling for the establishment of a UN intergovernmental tax body (FTC, 2017), and also, many jurisdictions have not exactly been impressed by finally having been invited to participate on international tax matters alongside the G20 and the OECD on an equal footing only more than a month after the BEPS project was officially released, but only if they committed to it. For example, the Philippines have thus far not only opted out of signing on to any of the new global standards and norms but also declined the invitation to join the Inclusive Framework on BEPS. According to the former commissioner of the Bureau of Internal Revenue of the Philippines and former member of the UN Committee of Experts on International Cooperation in Tax Matters, Kim Jacinto-Henares, since neither the identification of the problems nor the solutions discussed there were found to be "applicable to what a developing country is facing," the Philippines had decided that joining was not worth the membership fee and the frequent travel and accommodation costs (ICTD, 2021b).

In terms of the implementation process, due to the sheer comprehensiveness of the BEPS project, a strong consensus was not reached even among the members of the G20 and the OECD with regard to several of the deliverables. These particular deliverables have only been released as recommendations and best practices for signatories to consider implementing if they wish to do so. However, when it comes to the CRS, and the particular BEPS deliverables that have been released as minimum standards and must therefore be met by all signatories, which also includes the BEPS CbCR standard and the BEPS MLI, as per long-standing practice at the OECD, the implementation process is monitored through a system of periodic peer reviews to ensure full compliance. As always, there are certain exceptions. For example, the US has been deemed as CRS-compliant because of FATCA, even though FATCA is generally considered to be weaker than the CRS. Another example is mandatory binding arbitration, which is a part of the BEPS Action 14 minimum standard on Dispute Resolution Mechanisms, but because India and several other non-OECD members of the G20, along with many developing countries, have strongly opposed the measure, it is possible for signatories to opt out of it and still be considered to have met their obligations. These and other exceptions notwithstanding, the peer reviews are a major element governing the implementation of the new global standards and norms. In one interpretation, peer reviews are powerful probing exercises that strain and stress OFCs. As the team members responsible for negotiating DTAs on behalf of Mauritius described it to us during an interview in 2016, the peer review process begins with a written report comprising more than 100 detailed questions. Then, it turns to examining the accounting records of beneficial owners and the legislative framework. Next, it turns to examine how a jurisdiction exchanges tax information with other jurisdictions. Lastly, those jurisdictions are surveyed to report on their experiences in dealing with the jurisdiction in question. The output is a peer review rating that is publicly reported. The more pessimistic interpretation, expressed by one member of the broad epistemic community of tax experts, is that "the peer reviews are a joke, with Switzerland, for example, possibly serving as the next reviewer of Mauritius," adding that "there are unwritten understandings among many jurisdictions to go easy on each other during the peer reviews" (anonymous interview, Mauritius, 2019). Another astute observer, Sol Picciotto (2019, p. 23), has been similarly scathing:

> The evaluation is somewhat like a meeting of Alcoholics Anonymous, since it is done collectively by representatives of countries most of which have their own incentive regimes. While one might hope that they would encourage each other to be more virtuous and genuinely give up harmful practices, it is perhaps more likely that they will interpret the rules leniently, and learn from each other how to revise their regimes to merely mitigate the worst features.

Even if this is true, it is still possible to argue that since the peer reviews are periodic, and the pairings of jurisdictions doing the reviews and those being reviewed constantly change, it is only a matter of time before every jurisdiction encounters a serious reviewer. From this standpoint, the problem with the peer review system is at worst more that of delayed compliance rather than outright mock compliance, which is what jurisdictions have often been found to exhibit when confronted with new international standards, resulting in substantial implementation and enforcement shortfalls (Walter, 2008). However, even delayed compliance within the peer review system would still represent a huge implementation gap and should not be taken lightly. After all, periodic in this context does not mean annual, or even anything close to annual, and it is also not uncommon for scheduled peer reviews to be deferred. The peer review system often makes for a protracted undertaking and many jurisdictions have been found dragging their feet. As Woodward (2016) has amply demonstrated on the example of TIEAs based on the EOIR standard, OFCs have been pursuing mock compliance strategies within the new global tax transparency regime from the very beginning. The results of the recently published first round of peer reviews assessing the implementation of the CRS, which the OECD (2020, p. 22) called "very encouraging," were actually not all that encouraging. From the 100 jurisdictions that were assessed, only 54 were determined to have adequately put in place the required legal frameworks. Another 34 were determined to have put them in place but in ways that still need improvement, 10 needing significant improvement, and 2 not even having begun introducing them. This is more than 6 years since the CRS was officially approved and more than 3 years since the first exchanges took place. Whether the OECD has taken adequate note of this reality at least internally remains to be seen.

For these reasons and more, the skeptics, be they independent tax experts (BMG, 2015), tax justice-oriented CSOs (ActionAid, 2015), trade unions (TUAC, 2016a), or others, are unconvinced that the OECD's logic can significantly disrupt the operations of the offshore world. "The problem is that too many countries need to cooperate for the regime to be effective," write Avi-Yonah and Xu (2016, p. 4). In the case of the CRS, they continue, "every tax haven has to sign on because otherwise all the funds can be routed through the non-cooperating haven," and "we are far from there," while in the case of the BEPS project, it "only addresses artificial profit shifting, not tax competition." The point about tax competition is frequently brought up by the skeptics, and it is a crucial one, because it touches on the increasingly widely shared belief that unless we move beyond the three basic principles of the international tax system, the offshore world is here to stay, and so are all of its excesses, no matter how hard the international community may try to mitigate them. Despite all these shortcomings, one should not downplay the recent steps taken by the international community against offshore tax evasion and avoidance. After all, it bears repeating that these are the most consequential changes to the global tax architecture since the League of Nations process in the 1920s, so the progress has been historic, and as insufficient as it may have thus far been, it has finally begun to take place, which is no small thing (Christensen & Hearson, 2019a). Aside from this, there are at least two other reasons for some guarded optimism.

The first reason is that this historic progress has also been taking place outside of the main thrust advanced by the G20 and the OECD. Indeed, one of the most significant transformations that has occurred in the aftermath of the global financial crisis is that tax issues have been democratized to an unprecedented degree, and it is difficult to imagine how this particular genie could ever be put back in the bottle. This applies not only to the admittedly offensively long and in many ways still unfinished journey of the semiperiphery and the periphery to be granted equal standing alongside the G20 and the OECD in international tax matters but also to the growing access and influence of the civil society in what used to be the exclusive domain of various tax experts, especially those from the core. This democratization represents progress in its own right, but more importantly, it has also led to further tangible progress against the offshore world.

Take, for instance, the still steadily growing and increasingly diverse tax justice community, which in less than two decades has grown to include dozens of dedicated tax justice CSOs, most major development CSOs, trade unions, academics, networks of investigative journalists like the ICIJ, whistleblowers, and even racial, gender, and climate activists, who have come around to seeing just how deeply tax issues are intertwined with each of those causes. While the most influential elements of the tax justice community are still mostly tied to personnel, organizations, and funding sources based in the core of the global economy, their operations have spread across much of the semiperiphery and the periphery, joined up with CSOs and social movements there, and thus succeeded in significantly extending the reach of the tax justice cause. Today, it is no exaggeration to refer to the tax justice community as a major force, whether it is operating at the national, regional, or global level.

As evidence, consider the progress made on the four key policy solutions that made up their tax justice agenda, not long ago considered to be naïve and impossible. Since then, automatic exchange of tax information and country-by-country reporting have become global standards, despite, as discussed, the caveat with which the word "global" must be taken in this context. And while the outputs of the BEPS CbCR standard are, thanks to the intervention by the US, not yet publicly available, even this appears to be heading in the right direction from the tax justice perspective. In the EU for example, country-by-country reports have already been publicly available in the extractive and financial services sectors, and a political agreement has recently been reached to extend this transparency to the rest of the economy as well (TUAC, 2016b; Council of the EU, 2021a). Among industry insiders in much of the rest of the world, public country-by-country reporting is no longer considered to be a matter of if, but when. As for beneficial ownership registers, despite not having been anywhere near as much of a priority for the G20 and the OECD as automatic exchange of tax information and country-by-country reporting, they are well on their way to becoming a global standard as well. Thanks largely to the work of the tax justice community, especially the bombshell investigations by the ICIJ based on extensive data leaks and hacks, beneficial ownership registers have by now spread to more than 80 jurisdictions, with the UK, Ukraine, the EU, and a few others even making them public (Knobel et al., 2020). The US, a long-time holdout, has finally relented only in 2021, but has refused to make its beneficial ownership register public. Finally, as the most ambitious of the four key policy solutions, worldwide unitary taxation with formulary apportionment has naturally been the most elusive one, but surprisingly, some early progress has been made here as well. Ever the trailblazer, in October 2016, the European Commission relaunched the CCCTB in an updated format that sets out a more incremental implementation process, although opposition to it remains significant (EC, 2016). More surprisingly, a move in this direction was also made by India, which in April 2019 released a public consultation document proposing a major amendment that would, if adopted, essentially introduce a form of unitary taxation with formulary apportionment in the country. Some experts, like Avi-Yonah and Kir (2019, p. 2), believe that India's proposal may be the first real "break in the dam" of the three basic principles, because unlike the CCCTB, India's proposal "has a good chance of becoming law" already after what were then the upcoming 2019 general elections. However, despite the landslide victory of Narendra Modi's party, this has not happened yet, and at least for the time being, the Indian proposal appears to be more of a pressure tactic deployed against the OECD than something that was seriously considered by the Indian government, which brings us to the second reason for some guarded optimism.

The second reason is that regardless of what one may think about any of the progress made thus far, the main thrust of the overall reform effort advanced by the G20 and the OECD is itself nowhere near over. While the US technically succeeded in buying more time for its Big Tech sector by obstructing the digital economy agenda during the BEPS project, due to the brazenness of the Big Tech sector, the relief was relatively short lived. The sheer number of new tax avoidance scandals involving the Big Tech household names, whose digitalized business models have enabled them to run circles around existing international tax rules nearly as much after the BEPS project as they did before it, have led to several countries taking the matter into their own hands and unilaterally introducing different kinds of digital services taxes targeting the Big Tech giants rather than waiting for the G20 and the OECD to get around to it. Embarrassingly, the first mover was the UK, which despite being a staunch US ally and a member of both the G20 and the OECD, did not even wait for the BEPS project to be over before introducing, in April 2015, the diverted profits tax, colloquially also known as the Google tax. This was followed by Australia's introduction of similar legislation in January 2016, by India's introduction of its equalization levy in

June 2016, and several other announcements piling on soon after, ramping up pressure on the US, and thus clearing the path for the G20 and the OECD to officially begin addressing the tax challenges arising from the digitalization of the economy properly. The work on this new phase of the overall reform effort, which came to be known as BEPS 2.0, is still ongoing, but the proposals clearly indicate that even the least-ambitious version of what is currently on the table would represent a small but historic step beyond each of the three basic principles of the international tax system, something that was considered by most as unthinkable only a decade ago (see Box 3.4).

Box 3.4: G20/OECD – Addressing the Tax Challenges Arising from the Digitalization of the Economy (BEPS 2.0)

The current efforts to address the tax challenges arising from the digitalization of the economy formally began in 2017 as a follow-up to the preliminary work completed under BEPS Action 1, and although the negotiations are still ongoing, they are worth paying attention to because the proposed blueprints that have been discussed and released for public consultation are potentially groundbreaking (OECD, 2021a, 2021b). The crux of the matter has been the increasing futility of applying a set of international tax rules and principles originally developed for traditional business models operating in a brick-and-mortar economic environment based on physical presence to new business models operating in a progressively more digitalized and dematerialized economic environment based on scale without mass, reliance on intangible assets, and the centrality of data, or in other words, on a significantly more virtual presence. This unfolding global technological transformation has opened up numerous unique opportunities for offshore tax avoidance that the more digitalized MNEs have been able to seize and exploit, not only undermining the tax equity among traditional and digital business models but also further exacerbating the long-running conflict between jurisdictions of source and jurisdictions of residence over a more equitable allocation of taxing rights. The current efforts, commonly also referred to as BEPS 2.0, have been built on a broad mandate to come up with a comprehensive consensus-based solution that would adequately deal with all of the identified issues. The resulting program of work has been organized around two pillars.

Pillar 1: The Reallocation of Taxing Rights – The blueprint for this pillar aims to address the issue of highly digitalized MNEs being heavily involved in the economic lives of jurisdictions through a large and sustained economic presence with access to their pools of customers but without necessarily having any significant physical presence there, leaving these jurisdictions with no or only minimal rights to tax such MNEs. The proposed solution is to allocate more taxing rights to source jurisdictions, allowing them to tax MNEs once their sales in these markets exceed a certain threshold even if they are not physically present in those markets. This would be a significant development on its own given how untouchable the primacy of residence over source has historically been for the OECD and many of its members but what is arguably even more significant is the basis on which this new allocation is to be determined. Under the so-called "Unified Approach" on Pillar 1, which represents the latest baseline for a future agreement, one portion of the newly reallocated profits would be determined according to current international tax rules, meaning in line with the separate entity and arm's length principles, but the other portion would be arrived at through a formula and based on the consolidated financial accounts of MNEs. This is not the first tacit acknowledgement by the OECD that the separate entity and arm's length principles are no longer fit for purpose but it would be its first small but concrete step toward worldwide unitary taxation with formulary apportionment.

Pillar 2: Global Anti-Base Erosion Mechanism – The blueprint for this pillar aims to comprehensively address all of the remaining issues related to offshore tax avoidance by MNEs that have not yet been addressed by the BEPS project. The proposed solution is to introduce a global minimum corporate income tax rate that would reduce the incentive for profit shifting and establish a floor for tax competition among jurisdictions. Under this approach, jurisdictions would still be free to determine their own corporate tax rates, including whether to impose a corporate income tax at all, but it would allow other jurisdictions to tax income that would otherwise be subject to a lower level of taxation than the internationally agreed minimum tax rate. As for the exact rate that could possibly be the basis for such an international agreement, the scenarios presented by the OECD in a number of its public documents on Pillar 2 have worked with a fixed percentage ranging between 7.5% and 17.5%, although the final agreement will likely end up being closer to the 10.5% minimum tax rate imposed under the Global Intangible Low-Taxed Income (GILTI) regime in the US (anonymous interview with a high-level OECD official, 2019). Either way, the intention is that the rate should be significantly higher than the low or zero tax rates touted by many OFCs but lower than the tax rates found in most regular jurisdictions.

The negotiations, despite being conducted under the Inclusive Framework on BEPS, and thus being the most representative yet with its membership consisting of 139 jurisdictions, have nevertheless been accused of being dominated by the US and several other members of the OECD at the behest of their corporate interests, which have been lobbying to water down the proposals. It is in this context that we should understand India's groundbreaking April 2019 proposal to unilaterally introduce a form of unitary taxation with formulary apportionment. With this proposal, India essentially threatened that should BEPS 2.0 fail or not go far enough, it was once again willing to go it alone, which would likely have triggered an avalanche of similar unilateral moves, a scenario dreaded by the US and its Big Tech sector, as it would result not only in an unpredictable rise in taxes but also in an upsurge of tax disputes over double taxation. Aside from the Indian threat, although for similar reasons, France and several other members of the EU proposed a new batch of digital services taxes, in June 2020 leading the Trump administration to suspend the BEPS 2.0 negotiations, threatening to retaliate against any such unilateral measures. Partly as a result of this US withdrawal, and partly as a result of the COVID-19 pandemic, the BEPS 2.0 negotiations were de facto postponed until after the upcoming 2020 presidential elections. Marking a dramatic break from the obstructionist stance of both the Obama administration and the Trump administration, the new Biden administration, despite heavy Republican opposition, came out in support of the BEPS 2.0 agenda. In July 2021, 132 members of the Inclusive Framework have come to an agreement on the specifics of the two pillars of BEPS 2.0. The OECD projects that under Pillar 1, over US$100 billion in profits could be reallocated from residence jurisdictions to source jurisdictions every year, and that the global minimum corporate income tax under Pillar 2, set at a rate of 15%, which is lower than many wanted, but higher than most predicted, could generate as much as US$150 billion in additional global tax revenues every year (OECD, 2021e). The seven members of the Inclusive Framework that have thus far refused to sign on to the deal are Ireland, Hungary, Estonia, Sri Lanka, Barbados, and interestingly also Kenya and Nigeria.

As promising as much of this progress looks, this is the realm of international relations, where the overriding question must be the level of adherence to existing global rules. We should adopt a realistic perspective and look critically at any claim that the global offshore economy has been drastically transformed, or even more categorically, that it has been dealt anything close to a deadly blow. The following two statements point to the strong possibility that offshore networks will persist in the face of further reform efforts. First, as the deputy director of the ICIJ, Marina Walker Guevara (as quoted in Shane, 2016) asserts, "the offshore system is incredibly resilient, with a ton of smart lawyers and accountants to find new ways to hide money." Second, as noted by Zucman (2017), "every time tax havens are forced to close a loophole, a new one is exploited." If investors were to have it their way, the offshore world would carry on in its present form. Some economists, in fact, argue that offshore nodes are so integral to the global economy that "should investors no longer be able to use certain investment hubs, total FDI is likely to decrease through FDI destruction and diversion" (Hers et al., 2018, p. ii). The counterargument that immediately springs to mind is that if an investment is only profitable and thus worth undertaking because of tax and regulatory arbitrage, it was probably not a very sound investment to begin with.

If it is profitable even without such incentives, then it will still likely be made. And if the underlying issue has always been something like disproportionate political or legal risks in the jurisdiction hosting the investment, then it is still better for both parties to address those risks directly rather than attempting to cover them up with such incentives. Of course, that might not be persuasive to all political elites, especially if significant amounts of jobs or transfers of technology are also in the mix, or if the timing coincides with any upcoming elections. Should the 15% global minimum corporate income tax really become a part of international tax law, as it appears it will, tax competition will be reduced, but not eliminated completely, which means that the offshore world will continue to thrive, albeit within tighter confines than before.

International pressure is, not surprisingly, uneven. While the G20 and the OECD have set in force substantial change, the transition from a set of minimum, non-binding standards to credible implementation and enforcement across the world requires a high level of domestic commitment. Whether it is the CRS, the BEPS CbCR standard, or the BEPS MLI, the specifics still need to be negotiated bilaterally. The BEPS MLI, which serves as the primary vehicle for the implementation of all of the treaty-related deliverables, is especially problematic, because as efficient as it may be, it was designed to grant jurisdictions considerable flexibility to register a relatively wide range of reservations and opt-outs. Many treaties will undoubtedly be revamped, but many may not be for a very long time to come. This means that a great deal of variability will still remain in the existing network of DTAs, and it will continue to be exploited. Consider for example the two main anti-abuse provisions designed to address treaty shopping, the limitation-on-benefits (LOB) rule and the principal purposes test (PPT) rule. The LOB rule basically specifies the conditions under which an entity can be granted treaty benefits and it has proven to be an effective measure in preventing many forms of treaty abuse. The PPT rule is a much broader measure used to determine whether a given transaction or arrangement has been made in accordance with the intended aims of the treaty provisions or principally for the purpose of securing a treaty benefit, in which case the treaty benefit may be denied. It can be very useful as a supplement to the LOB rule, since it covers more ground, but by itself, it can often be difficult to uphold in courts. Logically, the most effective way for jurisdictions to prevent treaty shopping would be to include both the LOB rule and the PPT rule into their tax treaties. However, jurisdictions are also considered to be compliant with the BEPS project if they only include the PPT rule or if they only include the LOB rule supplemented by a mechanism that would deal with conduit financing arrangements not already dealt with in tax treaties. While including even just one of these measures represents improvement over the status quo ante, it is difficult to imagine what a more obvious invitation for engaging in mock compliance would look like. Applying this logic to OFCs looking even harder for any competitive edge in this new era or to African countries engaged in tax policy reform while still trying to attract FDI, and the future appears uncertain, to say the least.

Will African countries follow a similar trajectory to India or will they change their stances on tax policy earlier in their developmental trajectories? The key variables are governmental capacity and political commitment, both of which are typically required to achieve any meaningful results. However, many emerging and developing markets in Africa either receive or at least strive to receive large amounts of FDI and are likely to continue accommodating offshore capital in the belief that such a position is necessary to attract FDI, particularly given domestic capital deficits. While the scale of offshore financial growth may not ever match the high point of the 1990s and 2000s, offshore financial services continue to exist, and many emerging and developing markets, somewhat less held back by new regulations than in more developed economies, will look to OFCs to facilitate their capital flows. African countries fall in this category, encompassing capital recipients, as well as capital intermediaries, such as Mauritius. Thurbon and Weiss (2016) have convincingly argued that there is space in the global economy for independent national policies despite an apparent global consensus. In their scenario, the independent national policies were represented by the concept of the developmental state, and the apparent global consensus by the neoliberal development project. In our scenario, the potential outcome could, in a way, turn out to be the reverse, but the logic would be the same. There is still ample room for OFCs and pro-investment regimes, probably more likely to be found in emerging and developing markets, to diverge from, and thus partially undermine this new global reform consensus.

The multiple hierarchies of the offshore world and consolidated survivor OFCs

How global pressures and national elites interact in the contemporary environment is crucially important. This book aims to give the reader the conceptual and empirical basis of the conclusion that the offshore system has experienced change but that this change is not all-encompassing. The findings point to a middle ground in the study of the global political economy, specifically to what Streeck and Thelen (2005, pp. 4–9) have, in a broader context, referred to as "transformation without disruption," which is defined by processes of incremental as well as abrupt change that for the foreseeable time result in continuity, but may in due course, as a result of further incremental or abrupt changes, perhaps even ones that these processes may themselves give rise to, eventually "add up to major historical discontinuities." This pertains as much to the offshore world itself as it does to the multiple existing hierarchies it has exacerbated since its rise, and which constitute its unevenness.

The tremendous spread, growth, and wealth concentration that have over the decades come to define the offshore world have naturally been felt differently by different actors in different parts of the world. This is not surprising. After all, the offshore world has essentially evolved into its own vast parallel legal universe designed specifically to allow the privileged few that can afford access to it to select the tax and regulatory regime that suits them the most, regardless of where and how they acquired their income and wealth in the first place. It is the quintessential microcosm of the capitalist system, and just like its capitalist macrocosm, which is of course itself a space of immense unearned privilege fed by perpetual exploitation, it is highly uneven by nature. However, what may come as a surprise is that as historic as the post-crisis reform effort has been, rather than necessarily leading to any significant mitigation of the multiple existing hierarchies historically exacerbated by the offshore world, in most cases the new global standards and norms merely reconfigure these hierarchies, and in some cases even contribute to their further exacerbation. We observe and demonstrate this impact on four particular clusters of existing hierarchies historically exacerbated by the offshore world:

- Hierarchies between taxpayers;
- Hierarchies between professional intermediaries;
- Hierarchies between countries; and
- Hierarchies between OFCs.

Hierarchies between taxpayers, whether individual or corporate, have mostly been based on the wealth, and to a much lesser but still significant extent, also the profile of the individuals or entities in question. As demonstrated earlier in the chapter, offshore clientele is almost exclusively composed of the wealthiest individuals, and large, profitable MNEs. The logic behind this is effectively summarized by the veteran tax journalist, David Cay Johnston (2014), who in this case specifically references the US context, but most of the points are just as applicable to the rest of the world:

> For the vast majority of people with regular W-2 jobs, income taxes are taken out before you get your check. Congress does not trust you, so it demands its cut up front and requires your employer, bank and stockbroker to verify what they paid you. But if you are a multinational, the government takes your word on how much you owe, subject only to the increasingly rare audits by the IRS. . . . For multinationals, the taxes on each year's profits do not come due immediately, but often years or decades later. If a company goes broke before the taxes come due, they might never be paid, as happened with Enron, which, subpoenaed documents show, regarded its tax department as a 'profit center'. In effect, if you are a multinational corporation, the federal government turns your tax bill into an interest-free loan. Not every company gets this deal. Mom-and-pop companies and purely domestic enterprises that do not require large capital investments for factories, trucks and other costly equipment generally have to pay their taxes annually.

The two main wealth-based hierarchies are immediately apparent. One is between the majority of people whose main sources of income are salaries or wages, and the wealthy few whose main sources of income are dividends, interest, royalties, capital gains, or other less easily controlled and more mobile payments. The other is between smaller or purely domestically operating enterprises, and large MNEs, which by operating in multiple markets also have significantly more opportunities to engage in offshore tax avoidance.

The key mechanisms by which the offshore world exacerbates these two hierarchies are access and complexity. This is because access to the offshore world, if it is to have the intended effect on one's tax bills, has a relatively steep price of admission. The more one pays, the less risk one carries of being discovered and being exposed to litigation, at least under normal circumstances. Most individual taxpayers, regardless of where they are from, even if they have more sources of income than just salaries or wages, simply do not have enough income to warrant spending a portion of it to risk engaging in offshore tax evasion or avoidance with whatever finances they still had left after paying the fees of professional intermediaries. They may still try but they will only be able to afford low-end services that would be discovered with relative ease compared to a wealthier counterpart, who is looking to evade or avoid a much higher amount and as such can also afford high-end services involving a secretive web of several different types of bank accounts, trusts, and companies, none of which are registered under their beneficial owner's name, in several different jurisdictions, and thus significantly reduce any risks. The same goes for smaller or domestic-only enterprises, which either do not have enough income for the risk to be worth the reward, or, especially in the latter case, they might, but if their operations are purely domestic, and suddenly they begin establishing subsidiaries in OFCs, it might attract unwanted attention. This brings us to complexity, an important subset of which is secrecy, because that is the main reason why tax authorities focus their resources considerably more on regular individual taxpayers than on wealthy ones, and on smaller or domestic-only enterprises than on large MNEs. While it is widely known that there is more tax revenue to be recouped from wealthy individuals and large MNEs, because of the complexity and secrecy that high-end offshore services are able to introduce into their structures, such international audits and investigations, usually involving several different and often uncooperative OFCs, are significantly more costly and time-consuming. Even if misconduct is discovered, wealthy individuals and MNEs tend to have ample resources to defend against challenges or outright prosecutions, or if need be to lower the penalties by settling, which adds to the overall cost and time that needs to be spent. Comparatively, audits and investigations of regular individual taxpayers and smaller or domestic-only enterprises tend to be significantly less costly and time-consuming, which means there can be significantly more of them. Statistically, this results in a much higher proportion of successful challenges and prosecutions, which not only serves as an important deterrent but through the sheer number of penalties paid may even lead to the recouping of a comparable or even higher amount of tax revenue than if the resources were instead spent on chasing after the more complex and secretive structures of better protected wealthy individuals and large MNEs.

When it comes to wealthy individuals and MNEs, their profile understandably matters as well. This applies to famous people in general, who tend to face a lot more public, media, and other scrutiny, but especially to political elites and their family members or close associates, who as politically exposed persons (PEPs) face higher scrutiny in their financial dealings even from financial institutions, which are obligated to perform enhanced due diligence checks on them that normally do not apply to other wealthy clients. A similar logic as in the case of famous non-PEPs also applies to well-known, especially public-facing MNEs with broad customer bases, which is also why it is the likes of Google, Amazon, Apple, and Starbucks that have been dominating the headlines, and not the hundreds if not thousands of smaller, less well-known, or less public-facing MNEs with small, specialized, or purely corporate customer bases that have been engaging in offshore tax avoidance in the same or comparable ways. With greater visibility comes greater media exposure and that in turn forces tax authorities to launch probes they otherwise would not have bothered launching, and unless the MNEs in question are monopolies or parts of oligopolies, which they often are, it may sometimes even lead to consumer boycotts. Still, while profile certainly is a factor affecting hierarchies between taxpayers, it is minuscule in comparison with wealth, which can actually diminish its influence further.

The new global standards and norms will affect these two hierarchies as well, but perhaps not in the way that many expected. In terms of the hierarchy between regular and wealthy individual taxpayers, most of the impact will come as a consequence of the CRS, and of the proliferation of beneficial ownership registers. Both of them focus on tackling offshore tax evasion, which is much more common among individuals as it is among MNEs. Should these two standards ever become universal, their impact on offshore tax evasion could be expected to be roughly proportional, but that is not the case today and will not be for a long time. The vast majority of the jurisdictions that have implemented these standards and successfully negotiated exchange relationships are the more developed countries of the core and the emerging semiperiphery. OFCs are relatively well represented among those that have been implementing the CRS but not so much among those implementing beneficial ownership registers, and the more developing countries of the lower semiperiphery and the periphery are almost entirely absent from both. This means that the impact on offshore tax evasion will not only be minimal but will for the foreseeable time almost exclusively benefit the core and the emerging semiperiphery.

The minimal impact will essentially be based on the increase of the price of admission to the offshore world. With much of the core and the emerging semiperiphery covered by these new global standards and norms, professional intermediaries will face increased compliance costs. They will also have to find new loopholes to exploit, and in any case will have to shift any sensitive deposits to jurisdictions that fall outside of this coverage. This will not only take time but likely also more complicated structures if these new and comparatively more serious risks are to be kept at bay, and all of that will combine to raise prices, probably permanently. At the higher end of the individual offshore clientele, this will hardly be noticed, but the combination of increased prices and risks will slice off a small percentage of individual offshore users at the lower end. For these users, the reward will no longer be significant enough to be worth it and they will either find a way to extricate themselves from the situation, such as through a tax amnesty program, or simply get caught. The reason why this will mostly benefit the core and the emerging semiperiphery is not only because they are protected the most by the new global standards and norms but also because the lower end of individual offshore users that will suffer the brunt of the impact is significantly more likely to be composed of their taxpayers. This is because the countries of the core and the emerging semiperiphery are by definition wealthier, and often even more equal than those of the lower semiperiphery and the periphery, and as such tend to have a much higher proportion of taxpayers engaging in offshore tax evasion, a logic which is also supported by robust data (Cobham et al., 2020). As a result, the gap between regular and wealthy individual taxpayers is, ceteris paribus, likely to continue widening even faster than before.

In terms of the hierarchy between smaller or domestic-only enterprises and large MNEs, most of the impact will come as a consequence of the BEPS project and BEPS 2.0, both of which focus on offshore tax avoidance by MNEs. Because the world is estimated to annually lose more in direct tax revenues to offshore tax avoidance than it does to offshore tax evasion, and also because the former is a significantly more complex phenomenon than the latter, the BEPS project and BEPS 2.0 are comparatively more ambitious and more multifaceted than the CRS and beneficial ownership registers. The effect of these global standards and norms on this hierarchy will thus be more complicated, but the result is likely to be very similar. BEPS 2.0 is still an unknown with regard to any details of its implementation, but when it comes to the original BEPS project's BEPS CbCR standard and the BEPS MLI, the implementation and successful negotiation of exchange relationships and treaty modifications is again overwhelmingly concentrated within the core and the emerging semiperiphery, which means that the benefits will again almost exclusively be felt there. Just as in the case of the previous hierarchy, the general increase in prices and risks will likely also lead some small percentage of MNEs to cut their ties with the offshore world, either again because the reward will no longer be significant enough to be worth it, or because of a calculated rebranding strategy, or perhaps even because of genuine corporate social responsibility or sustainability concerns. However, unlike in the case of the previous hierarchy, where it will be the lower end of individual offshore users that suffer the brunt of the impact, the BEPS CbCR standard and the BEPS 2.0's 15% global minimum corporate income tax are specifically aimed at MNEs with annual consolidated group revenue equal to or exceeding €750 million (or US$850 million), which means that the lower end of corporate offshore users will overall end up comparatively better off than the higher end of corporate offshore users. Of course, this slight leveling of the playing field among corporate offshore users will only have a limited bearing on the position of smaller or domestic-only enterprises, because in most jurisdictions, the corporate income tax rate is still much higher than 15%. As a result, the gap between smaller or domestic-only enterprises and large MNEs is, ceteris paribus, likely to continue widening, although if the rollout of the BEPS 2.0's 15% global minimum corporate income tax is successful, probably slower than before.

Hierarchies between professional intermediaries have also mostly been based on wealth. However, in this case, that wealth is even more inextricably tied to nationality than in the case of the taxpayer hierarchies. Whether it is the accounting, legal, finance, banking, or other related sectors, they are all dominated by core firms and banks (Taylor & Derudder, 2016). The most profitable offshore tax evasion and avoidance schemes are devised by, or with the direct assistance of these core firms and banks, and then carried out and maintained by semiperipheral and peripheral offshore services providers. This is why, to use the earlier examples, it was Deloitte that was pitching Mauritius to major global banks and law firms, and why it was KPMG that advised Ubongo Group on how to go about its restructuring, while Codan, the Mauritius affiliate of a comparatively much smaller regional firm, was the one handling all of the work on the ground in Mauritius. Of course, this is not to say that semiperipheral and peripheral offshore services providers do not do their own work and outreach, or even that some firms and banks from the emerging semiperiphery are not catching up with those from the core, at least as far as size goes, but the control still rests securely within the core. On that much, the available data is unequivocal (Schumann, 2017; De Groen, 2017; ICIJ, 2021a, 2021b). After all, most of the thoroughfares of the global financial and offshore infrastructure are still controlled by the core, especially the US, the UK, and a few continental European powers, and operated by their firms and banks. Even schemes without any direct involvement of core firms still involve cross-border financial flows and most likely also core currencies, which means that they are almost completely dependent on core banks and the regulatory authorities that oversee their conduct.

This dominance also means that the distribution of profits and risks is skewed to favor core firms and banks at the expense of their semiperipheral and peripheral competitors. While profits disproportionately flow to the top, the risks tend to remain at the bottom. When major core firms or banks are engulfed in a scandal, even if they are repeat offenders, which at this point nearly all of them are, they tend to get off with non-prosecution agreements or deferred prosecution agreements and fines that in most cases barely threaten their profitability in the given year, let alone their ability to continue operating. When something similar happens to a firm or a bank from outside of the core, the results are frequently very different. For example, Mossack Fonseca, the Panamanian law firm and offshore services provider at the center of the Panama Papers was forced to shut down under the weight of local and international criminal prosecutions as well as irreparable reputational damage less than two years after the revelations about it went public, even though as much as 90% of its clientele comprised other professional intermediaries, including most major core firms and banks (Mossack Fonseca, 2016; Bernstein, 2017). There are of course some exceptions to this, such as when the criminal activity is so extensive and all-encompassing that it embarrasses a core power and undermines trust in its institutions, but at the same time the perpetrator is not deemed as too-big-to-fail, or when firms or banks from a weaker core power repeatedly irritate the preeminent core power. The first scenario is best exemplified by the Enron scandal, which resulted in not only the shutdown of Enron itself but also the firm responsible for its audits, Arthur Andersen, which is exactly how what used to be known as the "Big Five" accounting firms became today's "Big Four" accounting firms. The second scenario is best exemplified by the US crackdown against Swiss banking secrecy following the UBS tax evasion scandal. These exceptions notwithstanding, the privileges enjoyed by core professional intermediaries are massive and in no small part contribute to the resulting hierarchy.

As in the case of individual and corporate taxpayers, the profile of different professional intermediaries plays a role as well, except in this case, the specific sector in which they operate is at least as important as visibility. For example, large banks and financial institutions are generally considered to have the highest strategic importance because of their role in the global financial system, closely followed by large accounting firms, especially because of their function as auditors, while law firms, even large ones, are clearly behind them on the hierarchy. This also tends to correspond with visibility. In the core, most people interact with large banks and financial institutions in their daily lives through their bank accounts, mortgages, pension funds, insurance products, and more, making them highly visible. Scandals involving them could potentially affect much of the general population directly. Large accounting firms, despite employing a lot of people, are clearly behind, since they mostly focus on corporate clients, and even the largest law firms are practically unknown to the general public, because they rarely have any reason to directly interact.

This sectoral stratification became even clearer in the aftermath of the global financial crisis, where banks and financial institutions naturally faced the most scrutiny and were the targets of most reregulation efforts in a way that the other sectors of professional intermediaries were not (Rixen, 2013). While most of these reregulation efforts pertained to financial stability rather than offshore financial crime or tax and regulatory arbitrage, one of their side effects was that they led to slightly stronger internal oversight mechanisms as well as anti-money laundering (AML), combating the financing of terrorism (CFT), know your client (KYC), and other rules. In other words, as a consequence of the global financial crisis, banks and financial institutions have become slightly more cautious about servicing the structuring and banking requests of PEPs. For example, the Luanda Leaks shone a light on how the Angolan billionaire PEP Isabel dos Santos, daughter of the long-time former President of Angola, José Eduardo dos Santos, used offshore structures to benefit her companies and personal wealth. The leaks demonstrated the contrasting actions of banks and accounting firms. Whereas most core banks stepped away from dos Santos not long after the global financial crisis, the accounting and law firms stayed far longer, continuing to advise, set up shell companies, and move money, with the PwC singled out for playing the most active role (Hallman et al., 2020). In one highly problematic memo, PwC advised dos Santos on how to structure a brewery deal via Malta, noting that such a move would raise red flags if discovered, but that "the risk of detection is low" (Fitzgibbon, 2020a). Of course, this is not at all to say that banks and financial institutions have cleaned up their act. After all, the Luanda Leaks were in the very same year followed by the FinCEN Files, which were all about core banks continuing to either passively or actively facilitate money laundering that runs into the trillions, but the general point about profile, or specifically sectoral scrutiny and visibility as factors affecting hierarchies between professional intermediaries stands.

When it comes to the potential effects of the new global standards and norms on these hierarchies, we have already mentioned higher compliance costs, especially for banks and financial institutions as a consequence of having become the main actors in the servicing of the CRS, although most of these costs will likely be transferred to offshore users. Therefore, the impact should be minimal. The only other direct impact could result from the BEPS Action 12 Mandatory Disclosure Rules, but this deliverable has not reached the level of a minimum standard, so even jurisdictions that have signed on to the BEPS project are under no obligation to implement it, and to say that its voluntary uptake has thus far been weak would still arguably be an overstatement. As for the remaining deliverables, none of them target professional intermediaries, and as excitedly pointed out to us by one US tax lawyer, by essentially making the international tax system even more complicated than before, the new global standards and rules are actually generating more business for all these professions (anonymous interview, Portugal, 2016). Until the conduct of professional intermediaries becomes targeted more effectively, the hierarchies between them are, ceteris paribus, bound not only to persist but to actually get steeper.

Hierarchies between countries are of course considerably more complex and numerous than those between taxpayers and professional intermediaries, but they are also the most self-evident and thus need no further elaboration here. Regardless of whether one's preferred terminology is the core, the semiperiphery, and the periphery, or developed and developing countries, or any other such classifications, the hierarchies are always already in the name. As for the specific mechanisms through which the offshore world has exacerbated these hierarchies, these have been covered at some length here as well, as outgrowths of colonial relations designed to serve certain vested interests, which thanks to several historical and more current developments grew and contributed to the inequality that increasingly defines the global economy. This reality is succinctly summarized by the veteran CSO campaigner, Judith Cavanagh (2014):

> For me to sit in London and point the finger at African leaders without addressing the actions of my own country's leaders would be hypocritical. It would also overlook the wider context: that global structures, policies and practices, often under the jurisdiction of Northern countries, fuel corruption in Africa. To give one example: the UK, through its Crown Dependencies and Overseas Territories, is responsible for ten tax havens – more than any other country. The secrecy and lack of accountability in tax haven structures enable both corporations and wealthy elites to channel their money out of Africa to be held offshore.

These frank remarks capture how Western powers have played a central role in establishing the global financial and offshore infrastructure, and through it actively fostered divergent outcomes.

The data on these divergent outcomes is startling. Earlier in the chapter, we reported that the world loses an estimated US$427 billion in direct tax revenues every year, with US$182 billion (43%) attributable to offshore tax evasion by wealthy individuals and US$245 billion (57%) to offshore tax avoidance by MNEs. However, the authors of that study also disaggregated their data between "higher income" countries and "lower income" countries, with the former defined as high-income and upper-middle-income countries based on the World Bank classification, which roughly corresponds to the core and the emerging semiperiphery, and the latter defined as lower-middle-income and low-income countries based on the World Bank classification, which roughly corresponds to the lower semiperiphery and the periphery (Cobham et al., 2020, p. 4). Of the US$182 billion annually lost to offshore tax evasion by wealthy individuals, US$180 billion (99%) is evaded from higher income countries and US$2 billion (1%) from lower income countries, representing roughly 1.3% and 0.2% of their total collected tax revenues, respectively. Of the US$245 billion annually lost to offshore tax avoidance by MNEs, US$202 billion (82%) is evaded from higher income countries and US$43 billion (18%) from lower income countries, representing roughly 1.3% and 5.5% of their total collected tax revenues, respectively. What this disaggregation shows is that while higher income countries lose a lot more tax than lower income countries in absolute terms, approximately US$382 billion (89%) compared to US$45 billion (11%) in total collected tax revenues, lower income countries lose a lot more tax than higher income countries in relative terms, approximately 5.7% compared to 2.6% in total collected tax revenues. Moreover, the data also reveals that higher income countries are responsible for facilitating over 98% of all these global tax losses, while lower income countries only for less than 2%. There are several reasons behind these patterns, and several important implications that stem from them. We will proceed by getting the most obvious ones out of the way first.

Once again, wealth is among the most important variables. After all, one of the main reasons why offshore tax evasion and avoidance are so much more devastating for lower income countries than they are for higher income countries is that the latter, being wealthier and thus also being able to afford more effective institutions, are able to collect a much higher percentage of their GDP despite losing so much more of their tax revenues in absolute terms. Lower income countries are not able to do this, partly because comparatively much higher proportions of their populations do not meet the income thresholds to justify taxation and partly because they lack the capacities for domestic resource mobilization to be able to reach the remainders of their populations that do have sufficient incomes to be taxed (see Table 3.1).

This makes the tax mixes of lower income countries very different from those of higher income countries. Lower income countries are not only significantly more reliant on goods and services taxes, which are regressive but relatively easier to effectively implement, but also on corporate income taxes, which explains why it is specifically offshore tax avoidance by MNEs that hits their tax revenues so much harder than it does higher income countries (see Table 3.2, 3.3, 3.4, and 3.5).

Table 3.1 Total Tax Revenue as Percentage of GDP in OECD Member Countries, Non-OECD Asian Countries, Non-OECD Latin American and Caribbean Countries, and African Countries* – 2004–2018 (Unweighted Averages)

	2004	*2006*	*2008*	*2010*	*2012*	*2014*	*2016*	*2018*
OECD Members	32.5%	33.1%	32.6%	31.9%	32.7%	33.2%	33.5%	33.9%
Non-OECD Asia	–	18.0%	17.4%	16.8%	17.2%	16.6%	15.4%	15.9%
Non-OECD Latin America and the Caribbean	19.4%	20.9%	21.5%	21.1%	21.9%	22.5%	22.8%	23.2%
Africa	14.2%	14.4%	15.5%	15.1%	15.8%	16.4%	16.4%	16.5%

* The OECD.Stat Revenue Statistics data set features all 37 of the current (as of April 2021) OECD member countries: Australia, Austria, Belgium, Canada, Chile, Colombia, Czech Republic, Denmark, Estonia, Finland, France, Germany, Greece, Hungary, Iceland, Ireland, Israel, Italy, Japan, Korea, Latvia, Lithuania, Luxembourg, Mexico, Netherlands, New Zealand, Norway, Poland, Portugal, Slovakia, Slovenia, Spain, Sweden, Switzerland, Turkey, United Kingdom, and United States; the following 9 Non-OECD Asian countries: Bhutan, China, Indonesia, Kazakhstan, Malaysia, Mongolia, Philippines, Singapore, and Thailand; the following 24 Non-OECD Latin American and Caribbean countries: Antigua and Barbuda, Argentina, Bahamas, Barbados, Belize, Bolivia, Brazil, Costa Rica, Cuba, Dominican Republic, Ecuador, El Salvador, Guatemala, Guyana, Honduras, Jamaica, Nicaragua, Panama, Paraguay, Peru, Saint Lucia, Trinidad and Tobago, Uruguay, and Venezuela; and the following 30 African countries: Botswana, Burkina Faso, Cameroon, Cabo Verde, Chad, Congo (Democratic Republic of the), Congo (Republic of the), Côte d'Ivoire, Egypt, Equatorial Guinea, Eswatini, Ghana, Kenya, Lesotho, Madagascar, Malawi, Mali, Mauritania, Mauritius, Morocco, Namibia, Niger, Nigeria, Rwanda, Senegal, Seychelles, South Africa, Togo, Tunisia, and Uganda. **Due to the exceptional nature of the one-off stability contributions which in 2016 resulted in Iceland receiving unusually high tax revenues, Iceland has been excluded from the calculation of the 2016 "OECD Members" average, but all of the other "OECD Members" averages are based on the results from all 37 OECD member countries. Due to missing data, the reported averages for the remaining three country groupings are not always based on the results from all countries in their respective groupings, but always on the results from at least 7 of the 9 Non-OECD Asian countries, from at least 22 of the 24 Non-OECD Latin American and Caribbean countries, and at least 23 of the 30 African countries in this data set.**

Source: (OECD.Stat, 2021).

Table 3.2 Major Tax Categories as Percentage of Total Tax Revenue and as Percentage of GDP in OECD Member Countries* – 2004–2018 (Unweighted Averages)

		2004	*2006*	*2008*	*2010*	*2012*	*2014*	*2016*	*2018*
Individual Income, Profits, and Capital Gains Taxes	**%Rev.**	22.9%	22.7%	23.5%	22.5%	22.9%	23.2%	23.0%	23.5%
	(%GDP)	(7.8%)	(7.9%)	(7.9%)	(7.4%)	(7.7%)	(8.0%)	(8.0%)	(8.1%)
Corporate Income, Profits, and Capital Gains Taxes	**%Rev.**	9.7%	11.2%	10.5%	8.9%	9.4%	9.2%	9.4%	10.0%
	(%GDP)	(3.0%)	(3.6%)	(3.3%)	(2.7%)	(2.9%)	(2.8%)	(2.9%)	(3.1%)
Social Security Contributions	**%Rev.**	25.4%	24.6%	25.1%	26.4%	26.1%	25.9%	25.7%	25.7%
	(%GDP)	(8.4%)	(8.3%)	(8.4%)	(8.7%)	(8.8%)	(8.8%)	(9.0%)	(9.0%)
Property Taxes	**%Rev.**	5.6%	5.6%	5.4%	5.5%	5.5%	5.7%	5.8%	5.6%
	(%GDP)	(1.7%)	(1.8%)	(1.7%)	(1.7%)	(1.8%)	(1.9%)	(1.9%)	(1.9%)
Goods and Services Taxes	**%Rev.**	33.9%	33.0%	32.5%	33.8%	33.4%	33.2%	33.0%	32.7%
	(%GDP)	(10.8%)	(10.7%)	(10.4%)	(10.6%)	(10.8%)	(10.8%)	(11.0%)	(10.9%)

Note: **%Rev.** = Tax category as percentage of total tax revenue; **(%GDP)** = Tax category as percentage of GDP. Percentages do not add up due to the exclusion of minor tax categories.

* The OECD.Stat Revenue Statistics data set features all 37 of the current (as of April 2021) OECD member countries: Australia, Austria, Belgium, Canada, Chile, Colombia, Czech Republic, Denmark, Estonia, Finland, France, Germany, Greece, Hungary, Iceland, Ireland, Israel, Italy, Japan, Korea, Latvia, Lithuania, Luxembourg, Mexico, Netherlands, New Zealand, Norway, Poland, Portugal, Slovakia, Slovenia, Spain, Sweden, Switzerland, Turkey, United Kingdom, and United States. **Due to the exceptional nature of the one-off stability contributions which in 2016 resulted in Iceland receiving unusually high tax revenues in the "Property Taxes" tax category, Iceland has been excluded from the calculation of both of the 2016 "Property Taxes" averages, but all of the other reported averages are based on the results from all 37 OECD member countries.**

Source: (OECD.Stat, 2021).

Table 3.3 Major Tax Categories as Percentage of Total Tax Revenue and as Percentage of GDP in Non-OECD Asian Countries[*] – 2004–2018 (Unweighted Averages)

		2004	*2006*	*2008*	*2010*	*2012*	*2014*	*2016*	*2018*
Individual Income, Profits, and Capital Gains Taxes	**%Rev.** **(%GDP)**	–	10.9% (1.8%)	9.7% (1.6%)	10.1% (1.5%)	11.7% (1.8%)	12.1% (1.8%)	12.0% (1.8%)	11.5% (1.8%)
Corporate Income, Profits, and Capital Gains Taxes	**%Rev.** **(%GDP)**	–	36.2% (6.7%)	39.9% (6.6%)	36.2% (5.6%)	32.0% (5.2%)	31.4% (4.9%)	29.4% (4.3%)	30.7% (4.5%)
Social Security Contributions	**%Rev.** **(%GDP)**	–	–	4.6% (1.0%)	5.3% (1.0%)	5.6% (1.1%)	6.1% (1.1%)	6.5% (1.1%)	5.9% (1.2%)
Property Taxes	**%Rev.** **(%GDP)**	–	4.0% (0.6%)	3.0% (0.6%)	4.0% (0.7%)	3.5% (0.6%)	3.2% (0.6%)	3.2% (0.6%)	3.2% (0.6%)
Goods and Services Taxes	**%Rev.** **(%GDP)**	–	39.5% (7.2%)	39.0% (7.3%)	41.4% (7.6%)	43.0% (8.1%)	42.8% (7.7%)	43.7% (7.1%)	43.3% (7.3%)

Note: **%Rev.** = Tax category as percentage of total tax revenue; **(%GDP)** = Tax category as percentage of GDP. Percentages do not add up due to the exclusion of minor tax categories.

[*] The OECD.Stat Revenue Statistics data set features the following 9 Non-OECD Asian countries: Bhutan, China, Indonesia, Kazakhstan, Malaysia, Mongolia, Philippines, Singapore, and Thailand. **Due to missing data, the reported averages are not always based on the results from all 9 Non-OECD Asian countries in this data set, but always on the results from at least 7 of them.**

Source: (OECD.Stat, 2021).

Table 3.4 Major Tax Categories as Percentage of Total Tax Revenue and as Percentage of GDP in Non-OECD Latin American and Caribbean Countries[*] – 2004–2018 (Unweighted Averages)

		2004	*2006*	*2008*	*2010*	*2012*	*2014*	*2016*	*2018*
Individual Income, Profits, and Capital Gains Taxes	**%Rev.**	7.4%	7.4%	7.8%	7.8%	8.1%	8.4%	8.8%	8.8%
	(%GDP)	(1.6%)	(1.6%)	(1.7%)	(1.7%)	(1.8%)	(2.0%)	(2.1%)	(2.2%)
Corporate Income, Profits, and Capital Gains Taxes	**%Rev.**	12.9%	15.6%	16.3%	15.3%	15.6%	15.2%	14.0%	14.5%
	(%GDP)	(2.7%)	(3.5%)	(3.8%)	(3.5%)	(3.5%)	(3.5%)	(3.1%)	(3.4%)
Social Security Contributions	**%Rev.**	14.9%	14.4%	14.5%	15.9%	16.3%	17.2%	17.6%	17.8%
	(%GDP)	(2.9%)	(3.0%)	(3.1%)	(3.4%)	(3.6%)	(3.9%)	(4.0%)	(4.1%)
Property Taxes	**%Rev.**	4.6%	4.8%	4.8%	3.8%	3.7%	3.9%	3.6%	3.6%
	(%GDP)	(0.9%)	(0.9%)	(0.9%)	(0.8%)	(0.8%)	(0.8%)	(0.8%)	(0.8%)
Goods and Services Taxes	**%Rev.**	56.1%	53.4%	51.7%	52.4%	51.9%	50.8%	51.4%	51.1%
	(%GDP)	(10.6%)	(11.0%)	(10.9%)	(10.7%)	(11.1%)	(11.2%)	(11.5%)	(11.8%)

Note: **%Rev.** = Tax category as percentage of total tax revenue; **(%GDP)** = Tax category as percentage of GDP. Percentages do not add up due to the exclusion of minor tax categories.

[*] The OECD.Stat Revenue Statistics data set features the following 24 Non-OECD Latin American and Caribbean countries: Antigua and Barbuda, Argentina, Bahamas, Barbados, Belize, Bolivia, Brazil, Costa Rica, Cuba, Dominican Republic, Ecuador, El Salvador, Guatemala, Guyana, Honduras, Jamaica, Nicaragua, Panama, Paraguay, Peru, Saint Lucia, Trinidad and Tobago, Uruguay, and Venezuela. **Due to missing data, the reported averages are not always based on the results from all 24 Non-OECD Latin American and Caribbean countries in this data set, but always on the results from at least 22 of them.**

Source: (OECD.Stat, 2021).

Table 3.5 Major Tax Categories as Percentage of Total Tax Revenue and as Percentage of GDP in African Countries* – 2004–2018 (Unweighted Averages)

		2004	*2006*	*2008*	*2010*	*2012*	*2014*	*2016*	*2018*
Individual Income, Profits, and Capital Gains Taxes	**%Rev.**	–	15.5%	14.9%	15.4%	16.1%	16.5%	18.2%	17.5%
	(%GDP)		(2.4%)	(2.4%)	(2.4%)	(2.7%)	(2.9%)	(3.1%)	(3.1%)
Corporate Income, Profits, and Capital Gains Taxes	**%Rev.**	–	17.9%	19.7%	21.6%	22.3%	21.6%	17.8%	19.2%
	(%GDP)		(2.5%)	(2.9%)	(3.0%)	(3.3%)	(3.2%)	(2.7%)	(2.8%)
Social Security Contributions	**%Rev.**	–	–	–	7.1%	6.8%	7.3%	7.5%	7.2%
	(%GDP)				(1.3%)	(1.2%)	(1.3%)	(1.3%)	(1.3%)
Property Taxes	**%Rev.**	–	1.7%	1.8%	1.8%	1.7%	1.7%	1.7%	1.6%
	(%GDP)		(0.3%)	(0.4%)	(0.3%)	(0.4%)	(0.3%)	(0.3%)	(0.3%)
Goods and Services Taxes	**%Rev.**	60.0%	54.7%	54.1%	51.9%	50.4%	50.2%	52.2%	51.9%
	(%GDP)	(8.2%)	(7.6%)	(8.2%)	(7.8%)	(8.0%)	(8.3%)	(8.6%)	(8.7%)

Note: **%Rev.** = Tax category as percentage of total tax revenue; **(%GDP)** = Tax category as percentage of GDP. Percentages do not add up due to the exclusion of minor tax categories.

* The OECD.Stat Revenue Statistics data set features the following **30 African countries**: Botswana, Burkina Faso, Cameroon, Cabo Verde, Chad, Congo (Democratic Republic of the), Congo (Republic of the), Côte d'Ivoire, Egypt, Equatorial Guinea, Eswatini, Ghana, Kenya, Lesotho, Madagascar, Malawi, Mali, Mauritania, Mauritius, Morocco, Namibia, Niger, Nigeria, Rwanda, Senegal, Seychelles, South Africa, Togo, Tunisia, and Uganda. **Due to missing data, the reported averages are not always based on the results from all 30 African countries in this data set, but always on the results from at least 23 of them.**

Source: (OECD.Stat, 2021).

One of the most important implications stemming from these patterns is that whereas the tax losses of higher income countries are to a significant extent extractive internally, those of lower income countries are almost completely extractive externally. There is of course a great deal of diversity among higher income countries, just as there is among lower income countries, but the general point of this admittedly sweeping statement stands for two simple reasons. One, most wealthy individuals engaging in offshore tax evasion are logically either citizens or long-term residents in the countries whose taxes they are evading, and it appears that offshore tax evasion overwhelmingly affects higher income countries. Two, most large MNEs engaging in offshore tax avoidance are likewise either resident in higher income countries, or a significant proportion of their shares are owned by citizens of higher income countries, especially the US and several other leading members of the OECD, and to a lesser extent also China (Starrs, 2013). As such, offshore tax evasion in higher income countries, which accounts for almost all offshore tax evasion in the world, is overwhelmingly an inside job perpetrated by their own wealthy individuals with the assistance of OFCs, which are also overwhelmingly higher income countries. Offshore tax avoidance in higher income countries is an outright inside job only in the relatively few countries where large MNEs are either resident or where their shareholders come from, but even when it is not an outright inside job, it is still just MNEs from a few higher income countries cannibalizing other higher income countries, again with the assistance of OFCs, which are also overwhelmingly higher income countries. In lower income countries, offshore tax evasion is also an inside job perpetrated by their own wealthy individuals, but even though it only represents a relatively minor proportion of their total collected tax revenues, the fact that it happens with the assistance of higher income OFCs is already quite a stark contrast. However, the contrast gets even starker in the case of offshore tax avoidance, where lower income countries are essentially looted by MNEs from a few higher income countries, once again with the assistance of higher income OFCs. While offshore tax evasion and avoidance are extractive regardless of where and how they take place, that this extraction has such a distinctly external quality to it whenever lower income countries are involved should not be overlooked, because it represents one of the key mechanisms by which the offshore world exacerbates hierarchies between countries.

Many of the patterns contributing to hierarchies between countries have been reproduced within the new global standards and norms as well, and since we are dealing with entire countries here as opposed to specific groups of taxpayers or professional intermediaries, this applies to the full range of the new global standards and norms, with the impact emanating just as much from the CRS as it does from the BEPS project and BEPS 2.0. Much of this has already been covered. One example is the effective exclusion of most of the lower semiperiphery and the periphery from the negotiations of the CRS and the BEPS project, which naturally meant that these reforms were mostly tailored to the needs of the core and the emerging semiperiphery. Another example pertains to the implementation processes for the CRS and the BEPS CbCR standard. Certain aspects of this have already been discussed, but others require further elaboration from the perspective of countries. The chief executive of the TJN, Alex Cobham (2017), captures the main issues in the specific context of the BEPS CbCR standard, but the comment applies to the CRS as well:

> The problem is that instead of requiring a fully multilateral approach, the OECD has allowed bilateral relationships to the automatic exchange of CbCR. This makes it harder for more jurisdictions to exchange CbCR, and more costly to arrange – and in practice results in the exclusion of nearly all lower-income countries.

The first obstacle standing in the way of countries interested in joining the CRS relates to the costs and the technical capacities that are involved. Joining the CRS is not only a matter of signing on and negotiating exchange relationships. Countries must also demonstrate that they have put in place a robust legal, information technology, and administrative infrastructure before any information is allowed to be exchanged. In general, these requirements are quite reasonable. They are there to ensure not only that signatories are able to fully reciprocate in the information exchanges but also that they are able to safeguard the data and protect the confidentiality of taxpayer information. However, in practice, they represent a significant hurdle that most of the periphery is unlikely to be able to overcome anytime soon, which raises the question whether it would not be even more reasonable to at least temporarily lower some of these requirements in order to improve the coverage of the standards. Safeguarding data and protecting the confidentiality of taxpayer information is one thing, but is full reciprocity really all that important in these particular cases? Remember that it is higher income countries that are responsible for the vast majority of the global tax losses, which means that information from higher income countries is significantly more valuable to lower income countries than information from lower income countries is to higher income countries.

This brings us to the more nefarious interpretation pertaining to these requirements. In an earlier analysis by the TJN, Andres Knobel (2016) made the analogy to a dating game:

> Where countries *have* signed up to the multilateral [competent authority] agreement (MCAA), exchange is not guaranteed. Countries need first to prove to the OECD that their domestic laws and confidentiality provisions are compliant with a set of common standards. Countries receiving information also need to demonstrate to the sending country that they have satisfactory standards for the protection of personal data in place. As if this were not complicated enough, the worst obstacle . . . is in the final list of 'choices' that countries . . . have to submit: countries are allowed to choose with whom to exchange information among all other signatories of the MCAA, like in a dating system. This point is important. It means that the choice to engage in automatic exchanges is at the absolute discretion of each country, *even if* other countries meet all the legal and confidentiality provisions required by the OECD.

Knobel (2016) goes on to illustrate the point on the example of Switzerland with the following findings:

> Switzerland (which is starting exchanges in 2018) so far has 29 relationships only, all with EU countries. This is no surprise, since it has expressed from the beginning its intention to only exchange information with countries with close economic and political ties, and which represent promising relationships for the Swiss financial centre (i.e. they will only start exchanging information if *not* doing so would be damaging to them). Switzerland also requires countries willing to obtain information from them to offer their residents 'regularisation' or amnesties for undeclared accounts.

There are several reasons why developed countries exchange information with each other and with known OFCs but not with developing countries. For one, developed countries can pressure OFCs into at least partial compliance with new standards. In exceptional circumstances, this even applies to major powers pressuring OFCs in advanced economies, as already referenced in the case of Switzerland bowing to US pressure following the UBS tax evasion scandal, despite making no such concessions to other countries. This power differential is also on display between more advanced emerging markets and less powerful OFCs. India's reversal on its offshore stance toward Mauritius, discussed in more detail in the following chapter, is one example. In this vein, Hattingh (2017, p. 35) points out that "it is unclear whether the BEPS project will translate into net revenue gain for countries" suffering from "negotiation deficiency and information asymmetry," suggesting that "smaller countries will almost certainly lose out." They will lose out not only to wealthier Western economies but also to more advanced emerging markets that wield a relatively high degree of geopolitical power because of the size of their market. Tellingly, Daurer and Krever (2014) conclude that Asian countries have negotiated more taxing rights in DTAs than African countries, a dynamic which may very easily apply to the BEPS MLI as well once more developing countries sign on and more data becomes available. Another important reason is that it is simply not in the interest of many developed countries to exchange information with developing countries. Consider the hypothetical example of Bangladesh and Switzerland. Bangladeshi data are highly unlikely to be useful to Swiss authorities, because Swiss individuals and MNEs are unlikely to place assets in the Bangladeshi financial system, due to the concomitant political and economic risks. On the contrary, Swiss data may prove highly beneficial to Bangladesh because wealthy Bangladeshis may have taken advantage of the Swiss OFC to route both legitimate and suspect capital out of Bangladesh. Such information, were it to be made public, could be embarrassing to Switzerland and damage its financial sector.

To be fair, Switzerland has begun exchanging information with about as many other jurisdictions as some of the most active signatories of the CRS and the BEPS CbCR standard, but this is not actually saying much. After all, the signatories of the CRS, the BEPS CbCR standard, and even the BEPS MLI are still mostly members of the OECD and the G20, the rest of Europe, and then the known OFCs they coerced into joining. The near total absence of developing countries is especially glaring (see Table 3.6).

Table 3.6 Signatory Jurisdictions of the Common Reporting Standard, the BEPS Action 13 Country-by-Country Reporting Standard, and the BEPS Action 15 Multilateral Instrument (As of April 2021)

	Common Reporting Standard	*BEPS Action 13 Country-by-Country Reporting Standard*	*BEPS Action 15 Multilateral Instrument*
	110	**89**	**95**
OECD members, G20 members, and the rest of Europe	**(60)** Albania, Andorra, Argentina, Australia, Austria, Belgium, Brazil, Bulgaria, Canada, Chile, China, Colombia, Croatia, Cyprus, Czech Republic, Denmark, Estonia, Faroe Islands, Finland, France, Germany, Gibraltar, Greece, Greenland, Guernsey, Hungary, Iceland, India, Indonesia, Ireland, Isle of Man, Israel, Italy, Japan, Jersey, Korea, Latvia, Liechtenstein, Lithuania, Luxembourg, Malta, Mexico, Monaco, Netherlands, New Zealand, Norway, Poland, Portugal, Romania, Russia, San Marino, Saudi Arabia, Slovakia, Slovenia, South Africa, Spain, Sweden, Switzerland, Turkey, United Kingdom	**(58)** Andorra, Argentina, Australia, Austria, Belgium, Brazil, Bulgaria, Canada, Chile, China, Colombia, Croatia, Cyprus, Czech Republic, Denmark, Estonia, Finland, France, Georgia, Germany, Gibraltar, Greece, Guernsey, Hungary, Iceland, India, Indonesia, Ireland, Isle of Man, Israel, Italy, Japan, Jersey, Korea, Latvia, Liechtenstein, Lithuania, Luxembourg, Malta, Mexico, Monaco, Netherlands, New Zealand, Norway, Poland, Portugal, Romania, Russia, San Marino, Saudi Arabia, Slovakia, Slovenia, South Africa, Spain, Sweden, Switzerland, Turkey, United Kingdom	**(61)** Albania, Andorra, Argentina, Australia, Austria, Belgium, Bosnia and Herzegovina, Bulgaria, Canada, Chile, China, Colombia, Croatia, Cyprus, Czech Republic, Denmark, Estonia, Finland, France, Georgia, Germany, Greece, Guernsey, Hungary, Iceland, India, Indonesia, Ireland, Isle of Man, Israel, Italy, Japan, Jersey, Korea, Latvia, Liechtenstein, Lithuania, Luxembourg, Malta, Mexico, Monaco, Netherlands, New Zealand, North Macedonia, Norway, Poland, Portugal, Romania, Russia, San Marino, Saudi Arabia, Serbia, Slovakia, Slovenia, South Africa, Spain, Sweden, Switzerland, Turkey, Ukraine, United Kingdom

(*Continued*)

Table 3.6 (Continued)

	Common Reporting Standard	*BEPS Action 13 Country-by-Country Reporting Standard*	*BEPS Action 15 Multilateral Instrument*
Asia and the Pacific (Excluding OECD and G20 members)	**(21)** Azerbaijan, Bahrain, Brunei, Cook Islands, Hong Kong, Kazakhstan, Kuwait, Lebanon, Macau, Malaysia, Marshall Islands, Nauru, New Caledonia, Niue, Oman, Pakistan, Qatar, Samoa, Singapore, United Arab Emirates, Vanuatu	**(10)** Bahrain, Hong Kong, Kazakhstan, Macau, Malaysia, Oman, Pakistan, Qatar, Singapore, United Arab Emirates	**(14)** Armenia, Bahrain, Fiji, Hong Kong, Jordan, Kazakhstan, Kuwait, Malaysia, Oman, Pakistan, Papua New Guinea, Qatar, Singapore, United Arab Emirates
Latin America and the Caribbean (Excluding OECD and G20 members)	**(23)** Anguilla, Antigua and Barbuda, Aruba, Bahamas, Barbados, Belize, Bermuda, British Virgin Islands, Cayman Islands, Costa Rica, Curaçao, Dominica, Ecuador, Grenada, Montserrat, Panama, Peru, Saint Kitts and Nevis, Saint Lucia, Saint Vincent and the Grenadines, Sint Maarten, Turks and Caicos Islands, Uruguay	**(14)** Anguilla, Aruba, Bahamas, Belize, Bermuda, British Virgin Islands, Cayman Islands, Costa Rica, Curaçao, Haiti, Panama, Peru, Turks and Caicos Islands, Uruguay	**(8)** Barbados, Belize, Costa Rica, Curaçao, Jamaica, Panama, Peru, Uruguay
Africa (Excluding G20 member South Africa)	**(6)** Ghana, Liberia, Mauritius, Morocco, Nigeria, Seychelles	**(7)** Gabon, Mauritius, Morocco, Nigeria, Senegal, Seychelles, Tunisia	**(12)** Burkina Faso, Cameroon, Côte d'Ivoire, Egypt, Gabon, Kenya, Mauritius, Morocco, Nigeria, Senegal, Seychelles, Tunisia

Source: (OECD, 2021c; 2021d).

This is worrying on its own, but what is worse, the lists of activated exchange relationships for the CRS and the BEPS CbCR standard reveal that as of April 2021, signatories from developing countries have far fewer activated exchange relationships than those from developed countries. In many of these cases, far fewer actually means zero (OECD, 2021c, 2021d). The situation appears to be similar with regard to the BEPS MLI, with Oguttu (2018, p. 13) warning that the "selective or partial adoption of MLI provisions by developed countries is very concerning for developing countries," and that "this approach may inevitably create more gaps and mismatches between tax rules applied by different countries." Some progressive outcomes could perhaps come about with the implementation of BEPS 2.0 in the coming years, especially since Pillar 1 is projected to result in an annual reallocation of over US$100 billion in profits from jurisdictions of residence to jurisdictions of source. However, we should remain cautious about taking things at face value here as well. As impressive as the size of the projected annual reallocation may be, it is important to keep in mind that while virtually all developing countries are source jurisdictions, not all source jurisdictions are developing countries. Moreover, even the likes of the US, which is arguably the world's preeminent residence jurisdiction, is still a source jurisdiction for the thousands of MNEs that are not resident in the US. An evaluation of two earlier OECD proposals found that while the main losers of Pillar 1 would be OFCs, the main beneficiaries would by far be non-OFC higher income countries, with lower income countries either seeing only minor benefits or even some minor losses (Cobham, Faccio, & FitzGerald, 2019). Little is still known about the recent BEPS 2.0 agreement, let alone its implementation, so the results may not be as gloomy as they were in this evaluation of earlier proposals, but it is certainly not inconceivable that they will. For the time being, all available evidence suggests that the patterns of unevenness that have been reproduced within the new global standards and norms will, ceteris paribus, further exacerbate hierarchies between countries, leading to an even more unequal global economy than it has been up to this point.

Finally, hierarchies between OFCs naturally mirror those between countries, but since it is OFCs that are specifically targeted by the overall reform effort, it is here that we should see the most intense impacts. Similar to the way that world-systems analysis categorizes countries or zones as belonging to the core, the semiperiphery, and the periphery of the global economy, we identify three distinct categories of OFCs based on their offshore footprint, geopolitical significance, and vulnerability to the pressures of the contemporary reform effort. We call them core OFCs, consolidated survivor OFCs, and lowest common denominator OFCs.

Returning once more to the study by Cobham et al. (2020), of the estimated US$427 billion in direct tax revenues that the world loses every year, nearly US$159 billion (37%) is collectively enabled by the UK, responsible for US$42 billion (10%); the Netherlands, responsible for US$36 billion (9%); Luxembourg, responsible for US$28 billion (6%); the US, responsible for US$24 billion (5%); Ireland, responsible for US$16 billion (4%); and Switzerland, responsible for

US$13 billion (3%). These six jurisdictions represent what we refer to as core OFCs. Aside from their sizable offshore footprint, which is partly the result of their ability to offer some of the most sophisticated offshore services in the world, core OFCs also carry the most geopolitical significance. They have the highest degree of control over the global financial and offshore infrastructure, and are members of at least two of the most important and most influential bodies in charge of global economic governance, specifically the G7, the G20, the OECD, and the EU. This also makes them by far the least vulnerable to the contemporary reform effort. Of course, least vulnerable does not mean immune. The post-crisis reform momentum has in some ways been so unprecedentedly powerful that even core OFCs had to make certain adjustments, but these were relatively minor ones in comparison with other OFCs. After all, even though core OFCs are among the most prominent members of the bodies that have been leading the charge against the offshore world, there were many other prominent members that have had enough and needed to be appeased with at least some results.

Nevertheless, by being among the most prominent members of these leading bodies, core OFCs have enjoyed exceptional advantages unavailable to any other OFCs. The most important of these advantages have of course been their ability to postpone, water down, or in some cases outright veto proposals even against the wishes of the majority of the other members. The examples are countless. From the relatively few that have been covered here, there was Switzerland, Luxembourg, and especially the US undermining and ultimately scuttling the OECD's HTCI. There was the UK, Ireland, and the Netherlands serving as the primary obstacles to the CCCTB and numerous other EU proposals that likely would have been law by now and could have pushed the global boundaries much further than they had been up to this point (Hakelberg, 2016). There was the US intervening during the BEPS project in order to postpone work on the digital economy and to ensure that the BEPS CbCR standard was not to be made public. And as a final example, the US, the UK, and others blocking the proposal of the G77 to establish a UN intergovernmental tax body that would take over the responsibilities of the OECD, which, had it happened, would not only have reduced the influence of core OFCs but also have significantly radicalized the anti-offshore agenda.

Core OFCs also have the advantage of not having to worry about blacklists. While individual countries of course can and indeed have sometimes blacklisted core OFCs, neither the OECD nor the EU blacklist their own members. Should this against all odds change, core OFCs would still be left better off than other OFCs, because they would still have a say in the formulation of the criteria by which the blacklisting round was triggered. As such, it would be highly unlikely for them to fall afoul of any new standard in a way that would require any substantial changes on their part.

Last but not least, core OFCs are in a unique position to exploit in their favor any crackdowns against the offshore world that they were unable to prevent outright. The OECD's HTCI once again serves as an example, since it specifically targeted non-OECD OFCs. Some authors have also made the case that the same logic has been present throughout the contemporary reform effort as well, especially through the actions of the US (Hakelberg & Schaub, 2018; Hakelberg, 2020). The primary example is the continued refusal by the US to sign on to the CRS, even though FATCA is overall a weaker standard and its information exchanges are not fully reciprocal. By keeping FATCA and thus effectively undercutting the global standard established by the CRS, the US is able to reduce offshore tax evasion by its own citizens, while solidifying the position of its own OFCs, such as Delaware, Nevada, Wyoming, South Dakota, and others, which have become even more competitive as far as havens for international dirty money go (Bullough, 2019). Another example lending support to this theory came with the adoption of the new US beneficial ownership register. Not only was it adopted years after such registers became a standard throughout the developed world and beyond, but by refusing to make it public, the US is once again effectively undercutting the standard established by other, more progressive countries. As Hakelberg (2020) convincingly demonstrates, the US protecting its own tax base from offshore tax evasion while actively undermining the tax bases of other countries is not a matter of some happenstance, but of deliberate, long-standing policy. One final example of the exorbitant privilege of the US is that as far as the OECD is concerned, by having FATCA, the US is considered to be fully compliant with the CRS. This would be unimaginable even for other core OFCs, let alone those that are at the very bottom of the OFC pecking order.

On the opposite end of the spectrum from core OFCs are what we refer to as lowest common denominator OFCs. These OFCs are essentially the dinosaurs of the offshore world. They are the most obvious and brazen in permitting outright financial crime as well as the most aggressive forms of tax and regulatory arbitrage, usually by having little to no taxes or regulations to speak of. They generally have a smaller offshore footprint and only offer the most elementary of offshore services. In most cases, their main offering is absolute privacy in setting up offshore companies and trusts. Two examples of such unapologetic lowest common denominator OFCs are the Cook Islands and Nevis. The Cook Islands have been providing complete confidentiality to offshore clients for decades. As Harrington (2017, p. 50) observes, "to date, no effort to break a Cook Islands trust – despite numerous attempts by the US government, among other powerful states – has been successful." In a similar vein, Nevis is what Bullough (2018) calls a "bottom-feeder," specifying that:

> It specialises in letting its clients create corporations with greater anonymity than almost anywhere else on earth. Last year, information on 70,000 Nevisian companies was leaked as part of the Paradise Papers investigation, but that didn't help us find out who owns them: ownership information is so secret there that even the island's own corporate registry doesn't know. In other words, there was nothing substantial to leak.

Due to their small size, lowest common denominator OFCs generally carry virtually no geopolitical significance of their own. More importantly, because of the particularly toxic brand of their offshore model, which even many actors from within the offshore world have for years tried to disassociate themselves from, lowest common denominator OFCs generally cannot even rely on any powerful patron that might stand by them and look out for their interests when they draw the ire of one or more of the bodies in charge of global economic governance. As a consequence, lowest common denominator OFCs have been the most vulnerable targets of global reform efforts since the OECD's HTCI. While they have still weathered that storm relatively unscathed, the contemporary reform effort is different because it has succeeded in forcing them to submit to the new global standards. Their poor reputations and the unsophisticated nature of their offshore services has meant that these OFCs have never held much of an allure for MNEs, but they used to be able to profit handsomely from their individual offshore clientele. However, with their secrecy slowly but steadily dismantled, they are losing the only competitive advantage they had over other OFCs, and since they have never invested in upgrading their offshore services, which would admittedly in any case have been difficult with most major global banks steering well clear of them, their offshore sectors are unlikely to ever recover. Some of these lowest common denominator OFCs, such as Vanuatu (Bremner, 2017) and the Seychelles (Robertson, 2020), already appear to be destined to fall by the wayside, and many others are struggling as their clienteles flee to OFCs with better reputations and more sophisticated offshore services.

In between core OFCs and lowest common denominator OFCs is the vast space inhabited by what we refer to as consolidated survivor OFCs. This is the most diverse category, and we argue the most important to watch out for when attempting to understand the true impact of the contemporary reform effort, the future dynamics of the offshore world, and the likely contours of any potential future reform efforts. Unlike core OFCs, most of which have not really had to face any genuinely existential threat just yet, and lowest common denominator OFCs, most of which never really stood a chance against any determined concerted effort by the major global powers, consolidated survivor OFCs are those that could have easily been swept up by the post-crisis reform storm, but they succeeded in utilizing the relatively small window of opportunity they had to bend in the right direction and reinvent themselves by upgrading and reorienting their offshore services toward more permissible or less scrutinized avenues.

In terms of their offshore footprint, a few consolidated survivor OFCs outperform even many core OFCs. For example, of the estimated US$427 billion in direct tax revenues that the world loses every year, the Cayman Islands alone are responsible for US$70 billion (16%), far more than any other core OFC, Hong Kong for US$21 billion (5%), the BVI for US$16 billion (4%), Singapore for US$15 billion (4%), and Bermuda for US$14 billion (3%), each of which is more than Switzerland's contribution to annual global tax losses (Cobham et al., 2020). The offshore footprint of many other consolidated survivor OFCs is tiny in comparison. For example, Mauritius is responsible for 1.4 billion (0.3%) of the annual global tax losses and the United Arab Emirates (UAE) for 1.3 billion (0.3%). This may seem insignificant at the global level but it is highly significant at the regional and national levels, especially in India and much of Africa, where most of these particular losses have been incurred.

In any case, when it comes to consolidated survivor OFCs, it is not the quantitative aspects of their offshore footprints that matter the most but the qualitative ones. Consolidated survivor OFCs not only hold reputational advantages over lowest common denominator OFCs, but by offering a much wider range of more sophisticated offshore services, they have also managed to retain significant tax and regulatory advantages even after becoming fully compliant with the new global standards. As such, consolidated survivor OFCs remain highly sought-after, and many will likely even go on to improve on their previous positions, whether by absorbing some of the offshore clientele fleeing lowest common denominator OFCs, or by having established a foothold in what are expected to be the next centers of growth in the global economy, such as India and much of Africa. Besides this, there is another reason why the quantitative aspects of a jurisdiction's offshore footprint are less determinative of its status as a consolidated survivor OFC than the qualitative ones, and it goes back to the question of profile, or visibility, that we discussed in the context of some of the earlier hierarchies. Unlike in the case of some professional intermediaries, where being the largest may mean being too-big-to-fail, when it comes to OFCs, the size of their offshore footprint does not equate to the strength of their position. On the contrary, having the largest offshore footprint, like the Cayman Islands do, may in the long run very well turn out to be a curse, because it represents not only the sheer scale at which it undermines the tax bases of many far more powerful countries but also a direct competitive challenge to core OFCs. This raises not only the likelihood of being directly targeted by future reform efforts but also the likelihood of core OFCs themselves supporting or even leading such efforts, as long as they can retain some amount of control over the process so that they can effectively scapegoat a major OFC competitor from a lower category. Of course, targeting consolidated survivor OFCs is generally not as simple as targeting lowest common denominator OFCs because of the differences in their standing within the global economy.

In terms of their geopolitical significance, most consolidated survivor OFCs are not all that different from lowest common denominator OFCs as far as their size and influence goes, but there are a few key differences. One of them is that consolidated survivor OFCs have, already well before the global financial crisis, made the strategic decision to steer clear from the kind of elementary offshore services that most obviously and brazenly enable outright financial crime, and to actively strive to at least technically meet all new widely accepted and thus unavoidable global standards whenever they emerge. This alone has allowed these jurisdictions to work on and foster several knock-on effects. By boasting better reputations, they never became the kind of lowest common denominator pariahs that even major global banks and other professional intermediaries would shun or abandon, which in turn allowed them to upgrade into offering more sophisticated services that were considerably more difficult to effectively target by reform forces. When new global standards unavoidably emerged and required the phasing out of certain specific offshore services or schemes, it was much easier to adapt and reorient from this higher level of sophistication. With more sophisticated services, these jurisdictions were also able to expand their clienteles beyond the lower end of individual offshore users and attract major corporate clients through which they could indirectly exert some amount of influence. For example, when the European Commission launched its highly controversial state aid investigations targeting the "Double Irish with a Dutch Sandwich" offshore tax avoidance scheme used by many US MNEs, the US forcefully intervened, threatening to take "strong action" should the European Commission refuse to change its course (US Department of the Treasury, 2016). The US did not intervene because of its eagerness to jump to the defense of the OFCs involved, namely Ireland, the Netherlands, the UK, and Bermuda, but because it was looking out for the interests of its own MNEs and by a somewhat paradoxical extension also its own tax revenues. Regardless of the precise motivations of any of the actors involved, the point is that Bermuda was among the OFCs that have for years profited from the scheme, and when the scheme was finally challenged, Bermuda had several major powers on its side that indirectly fought also on its behalf. As a consequence of the EU pressure, the scheme was eventually phased out but neither the core OFCs nor Bermuda ever faced any repercussions because of it.

Another key difference between consolidated survivor OFCs and lowest common denominator OFCs is that the former often have a powerful patron at their back. A powerful patron can outright veto certain threats to OFCs under its patronage, significantly water them down, or postpone them. If neither is a possibility, or if the attempts fail, a patron can still be of use by blunting the impact of the threat on its OFCs, as Haberly and Wójcik (2015a) demonstrate on the case of the OECD's HTCI. Patrons can advocate on behalf of their OFCs, or at the very least can open a few more doors and ears than would otherwise have been possible, which is often sufficient for achieving more favorable outcomes.

The most prominent example of such a patron relationship is the UK vis-à-vis its Crown Dependencies and Overseas Territories, over all of which it has so much legal authority that they are essentially its extensions. Crown Dependencies have their own governments and make their own domestic legislation, but it still requires Royal Assent to become law, and if the UK chooses to, it may extend its own legislation to the Crown Dependencies (UK Ministry of Justice, 2013). Overseas Territories likewise have their own governments and legislatures but they are even less independent than the Crown Dependencies, because "the UK Parliament has unlimited power to legislate for the Territories," and if the UK chooses to, it can even impose direct rule on them, as it did with the Turks and Caicos Islands between 2009 and 2012 following a major political corruption scandal there (UK Foreign and Commonwealth Office, 2012, p. 14). It is not an exaggeration to say that the main reason why these OFCs are still around is that the UK wants them to be around. They are, after all, key nodes in its modern-day financial empire, and as such, it has protected them from foreign regulatory authorities on countless occasions. In 2013, for instance, the then UK Prime Minister, David Cameron, personally intervened to prevent offshore trusts – a specialty of the UK and its Crown Dependencies and Overseas Territories – from being fully included into the scope of an upcoming EU directive proposed as part of an EU-wide crackdown on offshore tax evasion (Brunsden et al., 2016). This intervention bought offshore trusts several more years of secrecy before they were eventually fully covered in an updated version of the directive. The UK has also heavily lobbied to keep its Crown Dependencies and Overseas Territories from EU blacklists, an effort which, with the exception of the Cayman Islands in 2020, has thus far been remarkably successful (Boffey, 2020; Council of the EU, 2021b).

The UK has arguably been the most active patron but it has not been alone. Reform efforts, past and present, are replete with such preferential hypocrisy. Even the EU, as progressive of an actor as it has striven to be, essentially serves as a patron to a few upper tier consolidated survivor OFCs, such as Malta and Cyprus, because of its policy of not blacklisting member states. While most patrons are logically core powers, a few can also be found among the emerging semiperiphery, as exemplified by China vis-à-vis its two Special Administrative Regions (SARs), Hong Kong and Macau. One highly publicized instance of China intervening on behalf of its OFCs took place on the eve of the contemporary reform effort at the April 2009 G20 summit in London. At the insistence of France, both Hong Kong and Macau were to be added to the summit's greylist, which was full of tax havens that have committed to the internationally agreed tax standard (referring to the post-crisis round of TIEAs based on the EOIR standard) but have not yet substantially implemented it. China strongly opposed having them listed among the tax havens and vociferously fought to keep them out of the greylist. The standoff got so serious that there was a real risk that the agreement on tackling offshore tax evasion would collapse, damaging the entire summit. At the last minute, the situation was resolved thanks to a compromise brokered by the US. Instead of being added to the greylist among the tax havens, Hong Kong and Macau would only appear in a footnote attached to the whitelisted China, stating that the SARs "have committed to implement the internationally agreed tax standard," which was the same wording as that of the greylist. Another part of the compromise was that the G20 would only "take note of," instead of "endorse," the lists in question (OECD, 2009; Hall et al., 2009; Luce, 2009).

In terms of vulnerability to the pressures of the contemporary reform effort, consolidated survivor OFCs have by definition been vulnerable (unlike core OFCs), but sufficiently resilient that they are likely to have made the cut for the foreseeable time (unlike lowest common denominator OFCs). Of course, just like the core, the semiperiphery, and the periphery should be thought of as a spectrum rather than some rigidly defined triad, so should core OFCs, consolidated survivor OFCs, and lowest common denominator OFCs. This has important implications for the future.

When it comes to core OFCs, the smaller and less diverse economies such as Luxembourg or Ireland, which are more dependent on their offshore sectors, are generally more vulnerable to the direct impacts of reform efforts than the larger and more diverse ones such as the US, the UK, the Netherlands, or Switzerland, which would be able to thrive even if their offshore sectors were significantly scaled down. However, the latter group tends to be more vulnerable to the indirect impacts of reform efforts, such as various initiatives against their own offshore sectors, organized by increasingly influential tax justice communities and their political allies. Such initiatives have not only become daily realities in each of the latter four core OFCs to varying degrees but actually even had some results, as exemplified by FATCA in the US, and the first public beneficial ownership register in the UK. Indeed, it is exactly this pressure that has also driven much of the activity at the EU level, and it is likely to keep intensifying, although the forces accommodative to offshore finance remain formidable as well.

While lowest common denominator OFCs are certainly not all the same either, we do not expect any dramatic differences in outcomes between them. The most successful among them may be muddling through for many years to come, but their old models have been made unsustainable, and new ones are unlikely to suddenly spring up there.

The category of consolidated survivor OFCs is the most diverse and the most important to watch out for, because it is here that we will, in the coming years, see the most intense competition and subsequent polarization into higher tier OFCs that will retain their designation as consolidated survivor OFCs, and lower tier OFCs that will find themselves on the chopping block next, just as lowest common denominator OFCs have found themselves on it this time. Some of the key criteria for success that will continue to play a decisive role have already been mentioned, such as the ability and willingness to innovate and continue upgrading services to attract a more diverse clientele, or close ties with a powerful country that can serve as a patron, however, with the environment becoming more competitive, this alone is unlikely to be enough. Success will be even more than before based on a complex equation involving a host of economic, political, social, cultural, legal, infrastructural, and geographical variables, and not just within the OFCs themselves, but in the world outside of them, as that is where their clients are, as well as the forces that are resistant to the offshore world. Some of these variables are to a greater or lesser degree changeable; others, like geographical location, are simply given and rely on pure contingency to work out in the favor of a particular OFC. Indeed, sheer luck should not be downplayed either, such as vis-à-vis scandals, leaks, and hacks, which are not going anywhere and will too likely keep intensifying, especially because since the spread of the CRS, the BEPS CbCR standard, and beneficial ownership registers, there is a lot more data to work with. Which OFC will be targeted by the scandals, leaks, and hacks next? Which major powers will be affected, and potentially embarrassed, the most? What is the balance of power between the forces of accommodation and the forces of resistance within said major powers? These are all key questions, and their answers, unknowable as they may be at this point, will contribute to determining future outcomes.

For the time being, it is clear that just as in the case of hierarchies between taxpayers, professional intermediaries, and countries, hierarchies between OFCs are, ceteris paribus, set to grow steeper as well. Of course, even though we have separated these hierarchies here so as to highlight the intricacies within them, in reality, all of these hierarchies overlap and are deeply intertwined, ultimately feeding into what we are referring to as the uneven offshore world. As stated at the outset, just like the capitalist system as a whole, the offshore world has itself been highly uneven by nature, indeed to such an extent that it has since the 1970s emerged as one of the main sources of unevenness in the global economy. As such, it should follow that a major reform effort designed to reign in the worst excesses of the offshore world would logically result in a reduction of unevenness in the global economy. However, based on the arguments laid out in this section, our conclusion is different.

We argue that the new global standards and norms hardly herald a truly global taxation project committed to developing a level playing field. The offshore world is being forced to undergo a major reconfiguration, but at this point in time, it does not seem that this will result in a substantial reduction of its size in the one way that matters the most, which is the overall volume of financial flows that it intermediates. The new global standards and norms will likely price out or deter the lowest end of offshore users, and eliminate or at least significantly curb the offshore activities of lowest common denominator OFCs, but the benefits from both of these outcomes will almost exclusively be reaped by higher income countries. In a rather perverse twist, higher income countries, including the OFCs that are responsible for most of the global tax losses, will not only be protected significantly more than the lower income countries they victimize the most through their offshore activities, but they will actually see the position of their OFCs improve because of all the clients they will absorb following the gradual elimination of lowest common denominator OFCs. It is also possible that this difference in coverage by the new global standards and norms will drive even more offshore activity toward lower income countries, especially the emerging ones, further intensifying offshore exploitation there. The ultimate result will thus be an even more differentiated global economy than before.

However, it is important to stress that by pointing out this crucial aspect of post-reform reality, we are not at all suggesting that the contemporary reform effort and its achievements are as such negative or somehow reactionary developments. While it may seem like a paradox to state that the contemporary reform effort is merely an exercise in picking the lowest hanging fruit and will end up exacerbating existing inequalities, and yet at the same time that it is an important historic step in the right direction, both can be, and in our view indeed are true. We are convinced that overall, the post-reform status quo is qualitatively superior to its pre-reform status quo ante, mainly because of the following two reasons. First, even with their flaws, the transparency milestones represented by the CRS, the BEPS CbCR standard, the various other CbCR standards, such as the EU's publicly available ones in the extractive and financial services sectors, and finally the beneficial ownership registers, especially the publicly available ones, will provide us with more information about the inner workings of the offshore world and its true impact than we have ever had, significantly strengthening the forces resistant to offshore finance. And second, again as flawed as they may be, the BEPS project and BEPS 2.0 contain within them the first real steps beyond the three basic principles of the international tax system. So, while it is true that the short to medium term impact of the contemporary reform effort will be the exacerbation of the existing patterns of unevenness, it is also paving the way for a more radical reform down the line, one which will be much better positioned to deliver more equitable outcomes than the contemporary one has been. As little of a consolation as this may be to the countries and peoples that will suffer in the meantime, as the saying goes, we should not let the perfect be the enemy of the good. At the same time, we should never be satisfied with this kind of good and should continue striving for the perfect.

In summary, an alignment of accommodative forces at the global, regional, and national levels has until recently drove the political economy of the offshore world and shaped its upward trajectory. This began to change in the 1990s, with the emergence of a new alignment of forces that have risen to resist the continuing expansion of the offshore world. The resistance finally began to pay dividends in the aftermath of the global financial crisis, when objections to the freewheeling nature of global finance, combined with widespread outrage at the offshore financial dealings of some of the wealthiest individuals and MNEs, prompted the authorities to act. The main thrust of the ongoing reform effort has been led by the G20 and the OECD, and has already resulted in a major rewriting of the international tax system. These changes are embodied within the CRS, the BEPS project, and BEPS 2.0, the three main initiatives which represent the new global standards and norms. These agreements generally follow the logic of incrementalism. They begin with the setting of minimum standards, which, with success, can subsequently be raised again. However, the implementation of these new global standards and norms must ultimately still take place at the national level, and so has a considerable amount of other activity that needs to be taken into account. Some of this activity has in no small part contributed to the very existence of these new global standards and norms, some of it has been focused on strengthening them even more, but some of it has also been aimed at undermining them. Indeed, just as it took an alignment of accommodative forces at the global, regional, and national levels to shape the upward trajectory of the offshore world, we argue that it will take an equivalent alignment of resistant forces at all three levels to do away with it, or at least to bring it under control. In line with the logic of world-systems analysis, we argue that in order to understand the complexities of the contemporary reform effort and accurately assess the potential for change in this new era for the political economy of the offshore world, a global and regional level of analysis must be complemented with a national level of analysis. In the following two chapters, such analyses are carried out, respectively, on the relationships between Mauritius and India and between Mauritius and Africa.

4 A case study of the Mauritius–India offshore relationship

India's experience illustrates that resistant national action, as opposed to accommodative national action, is possible in the realm of global taxation. India serves as an example of a country that is restricting the use of offshore financial vehicles and contributing to international tax policy reform. India has stood on the frontlines of the post-crisis G20/OECD reform effort, serving as a leading advocate and presenting new proposals to further advance the campaign. Nonetheless, observers of India's recent conduct should bear in mind that its present policy stance represents the culmination of a far longer process marked predominantly by accommodation. This chapter presents that journey, which is a three-part story of a rapid escalation in offshore usage via Mauritius that began in the 1990s, was followed by a long period of civil society contestation, before ending with newfound attention to domestic and international tax reforms.

When India sought foreign investment during the 1990s, offshore practitioners took advantage of the essentially dormant India–Mauritius DTA, which enabled investors to escape capital gains taxes in both India and Mauritius. From 2000 to 2016, 34% of all FDI and 27% of all foreign portfolio investment (FPI) into India came from Mauritius (DPIIT, 2021; Securities and Exchange Board of India [SEBI], 2021). The 1990s are widely acknowledged to have been boom years in the use of Mauritian structures to invest portfolio capital in India, so Mauritius's share was almost certainly above 27%, although data collected by the Indian authorities covering the 1990s were unavailable at the time of writing. Moreover, nearly all foreign investment (97%) that flowed into India from Mauritius between 2004 and 2014 was routed from a third country via Mauritius (Jaiswal, 2017, p. 22), and Mauritius was not the only such route. OFCs have featured prominently as the primary channels for foreign investment entering India over the last two decades, with Singapore, the Netherlands, Cyprus, the UAE, and the Cayman Islands being, respectively, the second, fourth, eighth, ninth, and tenth largest country investors from 2000 to 2020 cumulatively (DPIIT, 2021).[1]

In May 2016, the governments of India and Mauritius revised the DTA, with India recovering the right to tax the capital gains of Mauritius-based companies according to its own domestic tax rates. During the ensuing transition phase that lasted until March 2019, capital gains were levied at half of India's capital gains rate. In April 2019, India's normal capital gains rate came into effect.

DOI: 10.4324/9781003161011-4

Table 4.1 India Inward FDI Stock – Top 5 Sources – 2010–2019 (Billions of USD)

2010	*2011*	*2012*	*2013*	*2014*	*2015*	*2016*	*2017*	*2018*	*2019*
Maurit. 56.92 (27%)	**Maurit.** 56.37 (27%)	**Maurit.** 61.30 (27%)	**Maurit.** 63.78 (26%)	**Maurit.** 68.64 (22%)	**Maurit.** 65.02 (20%)	**Maurit.** 70.45 (20%)	**Maurit.** 79.84 (17%)	**US** 83.87 (18%)	**US** 78.03 (17%)
UK 39.37 (19%)	**UK** 35.18 (17%)	**UK** 35.98 (16%)	**UK** 39.45 (16%)	**US** 52.63 (17%)	**US** 52.86 (17%)	**US** 57.10 (16%)	**US** 73.27 (16%)	**UK** 71.07 (15%)	**UK** 73.65 (16%)
US 35.80 (17%)	**US** 32.00 (15%)	**US** 35.56 (16%)	**US** 39.07 (16%)	**UK** 48.04 (15%)	**UK** 45.93 (14%)	**UK** 52.14 (15%)	**UK** 68.68 (15%)	**Maurit.** 70.68 (15%)	**Maurit.** 65.43 (14%)
Japan 13.89 (7%)	**Singap.** 14.46 (7%)	**Singap.** 18.16 (8%)	**Singap.** 23.62 (9%)	**Singap.** 29.94 (10%)	**Singap.** 33.46 (10%)	**Singap.** 39.01 (11%)	**Singap.** 52.52 (11%)	**Singap.** 53.63 (12%)	**Singap.** 57.46 (13%)
Germa. 13.45 (6%)	**Japan** 14.00 (7%)	**Japan** 15.59 (7%)	**Japan** 17.73 (7%)	**Germa.** 24.71 (8%)	**Japan** 24.40 (8%)	**Japan** 33.06 (9%)	**Japan** 48.81 (11%)	**Japan** 41.20 (9%)	**Nether.** 43.91 (10%)
Total 212.73 (100%)	**Total** 210.61 (100%)	**Total** 229.20 (100%)	**Total** 249.87 (100%)	**Total** 312.85 (100%)	**Total** 320.29 (100%)	**Total** 352.76 (100%)	**Total** 458.78 (100%)	**Total** 458.60 (100%)	**Total** 456.82 (100%)

Note: Percentages may not add up due to rounding.

Source: (IMF, 2021).

Table 4.2 India Outward FDI Stock – Top 5 Hosts – 2010–2019 (Billions of USD)

2010	*2011*	*2012*	*2013*	*2014*	*2015*	*2016*	*2017*	*2018*	*2019*
Singap. 20.07 (28%)	**Singap.** 21.15 (27%)	**Singap.** 21.64 (23%)	**Singap.** 20.56 (23%)	**Singap.** 20.91 (23%)	**Singap.** 18.72 (21%)	**Singap.** 15.66 (22%)	**Singap.** 14.40 (17%)	**Singap.** 15.28 (18%)	**Singap.** 17.85 (19%)
Maurit. 11.05 (15%)	**Maurit.** 15.33 (20%)	**Maurit.** 12.39 (13%)	**Maurit.** 12.48 (14%)	**Maurit.** 13.63 (15%)	**Maurit.** 16.48 (18%)	**Maurit.** 10.18 (14%)	**Nether.** 12.46 (15%)	**Nether.** 13.02 (16%)	**Nether.** 13.25 (14%)
Nether. 10.34 (15%)	**Nether.** 10.67 (14%)	**Nether.** 11.33 (12%)	**Nether.** 11.89 (13%)	**Nether.** 11.78 (13%)	**Nether.** 12.27 (14%)	**Nether.** 10.18 (14%)	**US** 11.97 (14%)	**US** 11.81 (14%)	**US** 13.04 (14%)
US 5.53 (8%)	**US** 5.92 (8%)	**Zambia** 10.33 (11%)	**UAE** 9.69 (11%)	**US** 10.18 (11%)	**US** 9.27 (10%)	**US** 9.16 (13%)	**Maurit.** 10.14 (12%)	**Maurit.** 9.94 (12%)	**Maurit.** 10.76 (12%)
UAE 3.38 (5%)	**UAE** 3.80 (5%)	**US** 7.25 (8%)	**US** 7.25 (8%)	**Bahrain** 4.57 (5%)	**UAE** 5.22 (6%)	**UAE** 6.30 (9%)	**UAE** 5.82 (7%)	**UAE** 4.95 (6%)	**UK** 6.41 (7%)
Total 71.32 (100%)	**Total** 78.54 (100%)	**Total** 93.41 (100%)	**Total** 90.16 (100%)	**Total** 89.01 (100%)	**Total** 90.78 (100%)	**Total** 72.51 (100%)	**Total** 82.80 (100%)	**Total** 82.89 (100%)	**Total** 92.05 (100%)

Note: Percentages may not add up due to rounding.

Source: (IMF, 2021).

India threatened one of the deepest and longest standing offshore relationships in the Global South by removing the exemption of capital gains on funds routed through Mauritius. Today, investors have to pay tax on the capital gains earned from investments in India, rather than being able to avoid this tax completely, as was the case in the period before 2016. Since the revision of the DTA, the position of Mauritius vis-à-vis India has been steadily weakening, with several of its OFC competitors gradually making its losses their gains (see Table 4.1 and 4.2).

For over two decades, a supportive constellation of factors comprising economic conditions, domestic elites, and weak international pressures underlay the continuity of Mauritius as an OFC for India. However, as a result of shifting structural conditions and the behavior of domestic elites, this equilibrium broke down. Factors at the structural level (the changing capital position of the Indian economy and changing international pressure on the offshore system) and at the level of agents (changing political elites in India and Mauritius) are integrated into this chapter to explain India's rewritten relationship with Mauritius.

The origins of Mauritius as an OFC for India

This case embodies the neoliberal globalization that was at its height in the 1990s and 2000s, when investors could choose how and where to structure their deals in the global economy with relative ease. India was integrated into this global offshore system after its economic opening in 1993–1994. India's offshore relationship with Mauritius only flourished because there was a pro-investment framework already in place. India and Mauritius had signed a DTA in 1982. A central figure in the civil society effort to undo the India–Mauritius financial relationship, Shiva Kant Jha (2012), contends that "in all probability, the terms of the Indo – Mauritius DTA were devised for the benefits of those Indians who wanted to use Mauritius as a route for investing in India their tainted wealth amassed outside the country." Jha was a former senior tax official who became a fierce critic of India's dealings with Mauritius and launched legal action in response. While Jha presented his interpretation about the corrupt intent behind the DTA without evidence, our interviews suggest a different history. Mauritius became an offshore finance provider to India as a result of accidental factors on both sides.

To begin with, no Indian or Mauritian interviewee could explain with certainty why a capital gains exemption was included in the 1982 India–Mauritius DTA. For Indian policymakers, the more common thinking appeared to be that Indian companies might trade and invest with a country with a substantial historical connection to India. No one imagined that Mauritius, a minor economy with a small population, would be the source of significant investment flows into India, which was a closed economy at the time that seemed unlikely to change. It is highly doubtful that senior Indian officials in 1980 expected Indian companies to invest abroad in large numbers. Consequently, these officials adopted the default OECD MTC for its tax treaties, which allocates more taxing rights to jurisdictions of residence and promotes inward foreign investment flows. By doing so, India relinquished the right to collect certain categories of taxes that would normally be payable by non-resident entities.

During the 1980s Mauritius faced deteriorating markets for sugar and textiles, and in the early 1990s it began introducing an offshore industry initiative in the hopes of stimulating new forms of capital accumulation. Rama Sithanen, the Finance Minister of Mauritius at the time, recounted his thinking as follows:

> The offshore wasn't an obvious choice. The World Bank thought we had no case to venture into the offshore sector. I said: 'You keep telling us to diversify; how are we supposed to do that?' They did not have a convincing answer and we went ahead with the offshore sector (interview with Rama Sithanen, Mauritius, 2016).

In the private sector, Sushil Khushiram, a management consultant that likewise went on to become the Finance Minister of Mauritius, worked assiduously with Sithanen to advance the Mauritius offshore financial services plan. Both Khushiram and Sithanen, nowadays considered as the founding figures of the Mauritius OFC, envisioned it as providing a broader and more diversified range of services, including a wealth management hub servicing global HNWIs (interview with Sushil Khushiram, Mauritius, 2019). Mauritian policymakers never seriously considered India to be a target market, and pitched the OFC as one that would primarily serve South African individuals and institutions, which were large users of offshore structures at the time (multiple interviews, Mauritius, 2014 and 2016).

The role of chance is often underplayed in studies of global economic change. It was only after practitioners began to realize that the India–Mauritius DTA contained beneficial provisions that India's relationship with Mauritius shifted dramatically. After India opened up its economy in the early 1990s and sought foreign investment, private actors strategically exploited the provisions of the already decade-old but largely dormant India–Mauritius DTA to shepherd global capital flows into India via Mauritius. It was then that India became by far the largest market for Mauritius business structures. In that same period, India levied capital gains taxes as high as 55%. As one of the most crucial business actors at the time later reflected, "even if you open doors, who will invest if taxes are that high?" (telephone interview with Nishith Desai, 2017). This notion especially applied to US investors, who were drawn to the India story but were disadvantaged by the 1990 India–US tax treaty, because it granted India the right to tax capital gains.

In 1993, two young Indian professionals were contemplating methods to channel foreign capital into India: Nishith Desai, a lawyer running his own firm, and Bobby Parikh, a member of the Arthur Andersen team in Mumbai. Both reached the conclusion that Mauritius could solve India's capital needs. Desai and Parikh were the first practitioners to meet with the Mauritian offshore authority as well as the first to obtain Mauritian tax residence certificates for their clients. Parikh negotiated the first certificate, but the deal subsequently fell through.

Desai then negotiated the first functioning certificate and recalls that he wrote it by hand (telephone interview with Nishith Desai, 2017). By securing a Mauritius tax residence certificate, foreign businesses qualified for the DTA, which stipulated that capital gains were to be taxed by the country of residence, in this case Mauritius with its zero capital gains tax. Building on the foundation established by Desai and Parikh, the Mauritius OFC captured the international spotlight in late 1993 when Mauritius hosted a major Euromoney conference and pitched its OFC to international investors.

Throughout the 1990s and 2000s, both Desai and Parikh played sizable roles in registering Mauritius-resident companies seeking to do business in India. These encompassed emerging market and Western multinational capital, as well as non-resident Indians investing into India, the latter group often engaging in round-tripping (Srinivasan, 2005).[2] The Mauritius offshore route was not without conflict. Mauritius acquired a negative image in India for tax avoidance. One of the fundamental issues of contention was whether a foreign company routing its money through Mauritius to make an investment in India should be considered as a Mauritian company. As part of the perceived foreign investment trade-off, senior Indian officials and business elites maintained that the answer should be yes. Disagreeing with this interpretation, in early 2000, the aforementioned Indian revenue inspector, Shiva Kant Jha, launched the first of what became a series of attacks on these entities registered in Mauritius. The inspector deemed the administration offices in Mauritius as representing a shell company structure and refused to grant these Mauritian companies treaty status under the DTA. A furor ensued in India, forcing high-level officials from the Department of Revenue to step in and issue a circular protecting Mauritius-resident companies from such inspector-level challenges.

Tax officials were displeased. Decrying the circular, Shiva Kant Jha and the Azadi Bachao Andolan social movement initiated legal proceedings against the Indian government. The legal case proved successful at the New Delhi court and the government's circular was struck down. Rather than repealing the circular, the government appealed to the Supreme Court. As part of extensive hearings, India's top lawyers argued before the Supreme Court on whether it was within the rights of the government to treat Mauritian offshore vehicles as enterprises that could do business in India with all of the benefits of the India–Mauritius DTA (Union of India v. Azadi Bachao Andolan, 2003). The Supreme Court sided with the government and the circular was reinstated, thus protecting all entities with a valid Mauritius tax certificate and reviving Mauritius-mediated investment flows into India, with the added moral and legal weight of a Supreme Court ruling. And yet, the forces of accommodation would soon begin to lose ground.

The Vodafone case

The Vodafone case represents another key illustration in the history of offshore usage in India, and the fierce resistance it can provoke. In 2007, the Dutch subsidiary of the UK telecom giant Vodafone acquired Indian telecom assets worth over

US$11 billion from another multinational player, structuring the deal through offshore holding companies based in Mauritius and the Cayman Islands, using the India–Mauritius DTA to avoid over US$2 billion in capital gains taxes payable to India. In 2009, the Indian tax authority served a demand notice to Vodafone ordering it to pay the taxes. Vodafone challenged the demand notice in the Bombay High Court, which in 2010 ruled in favor of the Indian tax authority. Subsequently, Vodafone challenged the Bombay High Court's ruling in the Supreme Court, which in 2012 delivered a landmark ruling that Vodafone's interpretation was correct and that the company did not have to pay any of the disputed taxes. Unlike its more accommodative predecessor, this time the Indian government responded with fury, not only revising its legislation on holding company use, but also passing a highly controversial retrospective tax law allowing the Indian tax authority to make retroactive claims on overseas corporate deals, in this case immediately requiring Vodafone and several other companies to pay back the withholding and capital gains taxes deemed to have been avoided. After a failed attempt to settle the dispute out of court, in 2014, Vodafone used the India–Netherlands BIT to initiate arbitration against India. In 2020, the Hague-based arbitration court ruled in favor of Vodafone, leading India to challenge the ruling in a more senior court based in Singapore, the verdict of which is yet to be delivered. However, in August 2021, India proposed scrapping the controversial retrospective tax law and refunding the disputed amounts if Vodafone and the other affected companies withdraw litigation and agree to no longer claim damages, signaling that the nearly 15-year old case may be coming to an end (Aryan, 2020; Ahmed & Kumar, 2021).

The Vodafone case is crucial for at least two reasons. First, it had a similar impact in India as the Philip Morris case had around the world. It hardened Indian views toward BITs and DTAs, as well as toward Mauritius and other OFCs. The implications were far-reaching. Not only did this hardened stance resulted in India's refusal to renew the India–Netherlands BIT upon its expiration in 2016 as part of a larger plan to rework all of its existing BITs, but it also directly contributed to its determination to renegotiate several of its DTAs, above all the India–Mauritius DTA. Second, even though it appears that in this particular instance, India had exhausted its options and has been forced to yield to global capital, the Vodafone case nevertheless demonstrates in no uncertain terms the lengths that this emerging power is willing to go to take on even very powerful actors in order to safeguard its tax base and lead the way toward more equitable outcomes for source jurisdictions.

The historical importance of economic factors

A combination of domestic and global variables explains how the Indian government accommodated Mauritian offshore structures for more than two decades before coercing Mauritius to renegotiate the DTA. Economic dynamics played a decisive role in the long-standing Indian acquiescence to Mauritian offshore structures. Mauritius acted as a conduit of capital to India – a huge economy desperately short on capital – and elites in both countries granted legitimacy to this arrangement. India's long-term capital deficit underpinned the durability of the India–Mauritius DTA. Current account and fiscal deficits combined with negligible bond markets empower actors that support offshore capital, as seen in India during the 1990s and 2000s, and in many African countries today. A capital surplus, in contrast, lessens the need for foreign investment, but can spur greater interest among capitalists in outward investment via offshore channels. Despite the perceived accomplishments of India's economic liberalization program, India still had limited foreign reserves and limited bond markets in the ensuing two decades. In this context, Mauritius channeled capital from surplus economies to deficit economies in the global economy at low cost – first to India and now to many African countries. The CEO of a major management company (MC) – the term for Mauritian enterprises that register offshore structures for global clients – remarked that he considered Mauritius as a "gateway" for global economic flows (interview with Ben Lim, Mauritius, 2014).[3] Indian investment boosters like Nishith Desai (Desai & Sanghavi, 2008, p. 98) have also been adamant about the economic benefits of the Mauritian gateway:

> Instead of resenting the loss of tax revenue on capital gains in India, we should celebrate the increased gains in other direct taxes such as corporate, dividend and employment taxes, and indirect taxes due to increased economic activity brought about by FDI facilitated by the India – Mauritius Treaty.

Over a long period of time, the role of Mauritius as a gateway was largely accepted at elite levels of Indian society. Indicating the centrality of Mauritius, India's financial markets fell each time there was discussion of reviewing the India–Mauritius DTA.[4]

The historical importance of political factors

Political factors also sustained the continuity of India–Mauritius financial ties during much of the 1993–2016 period. One important factor was the role of supportive political elites who were willing to fight for the Mauritius route all the way to the Supreme Court. There were divided voices on this issue, with even the Finance Ministry unable to reach a unanimous opinion; in general, the Department of Revenue was ardently in opposition to the Mauritius channel while the Department of Economic Affairs upheld the route (multiple interviews, New Delhi, 2017). The Vodafone case further complicated and intensified this division, but all told, more government decision-makers aligned behind Mauritius than against it, and that also included Manmohan Singh, whose backing of the Mauritius route, first as the Finance Minister and then as the Prime Minister, was critical throughout the years. These patterns confirm Kohli's (2007, p. 112) conclusion that "the development model pursued in India since about 1980 is a pro-business model that rests on a fairly narrow ruling alliance of the political and the economic elite." This coalition may have been narrow, but it held a commanding influence.

Over two decades, the prevailing ideology of Indian political and business elites was that foreign investment was an essential component of national economic development and that accommodating foreign investors was a legitimate policy imperative, given the presence of capital deficits within India. Indian politicians considered themselves to be pragmatic by voicing support for Mauritius as a conduit of capital into the country. This support often led to intimate ties between business and political elites, and at key junctures business elites had direct influence on policy outcomes. Our interviews revealed that a key figure from the financial world was summoned to meet with the Finance Secretary and the head of the SEBI right after the Indian revenue inspector's challenge of Mauritius offshore structures during the year 2000. This business figure prepared the first draft of the circular that would be binding on all field authorities and then offered media guidance. In the Supreme Court case, multinational capital entities formed an association with the Mauritian offshore industry, and this association, the Global Business Institute (GBI), filed an appeal alongside the Indian government to the Supreme Court. The GBI cooperated closely with key Indian lawyers on the government side, especially Nishith Desai, to prepare the case (telephone interview with Nishith Desai, 2017). These actions demonstrate that Mauritius's function as a gateway was largely accepted at elite levels in India over a long period of time.

National sovereignty stood at the heart of the Supreme Court's ruling, illustrating the role of domestic political factors in Mauritius's financial history with India. First, the court ruled that when a country signs a DTA with another country, those tax provisions override the Indian Income Tax Act. The court declared that tax policy was the government's domain and the government was within its rights to use a tax treaty to promote investment. The court also stressed the sovereignty of Mauritius and its right to determine which firms qualify as domiciled in Mauritius. The court made clear that the decision to tighten the treaty's rules would have to be taken by the governments of India and Mauritius.

International institutions exerted no significant pressure on India and Mauritius for most of the two decades after the first Mauritius offshore vehicles were designed. Many international discussions took place, but there was little substantive change in how the global offshore system functioned. One telling indication of this is found in the Panama Papers and the Paradise Papers, which furnished evidence of individuals and firms capitalizing on offshore services in the period after the release and official approval of the CRS and the BEPS project in a manner that did not look very different at all from the situation before that. At the bilateral level, the offshore sector pressured the Mauritian government not to meet with its Indian counterparts when India proposed bilateral discussions on the DTA in 2006 (multiple interviews with offshore practitioners and former policymakers, Mauritius, 2014 and 2016). Ultimately, a joint India–Mauritius working group was formed and India was willing to consider the imposition of a 3% to 5% capital gains tax, but the Mauritius side steadfastly refused (anonymous interview, Mauritius, 2014). One of the two former Mauritian Finance Ministers we spoke to pointed out that Mauritius made more changes to its tax framework with

India than did Singapore, not only turning the certification application into an annual process, but also permitting Indian government auditors to reside in Mauritius and adding a basic information-sharing clause to the DTA (interview with Rama Sithanen, Mauritius, 2016). Fundamentally, however, Mauritius refused to amend its zero capital gains tax policy for India, and it was this element above all that drove demand for Mauritian offshore companies. In summary, the two decades following Desai and Parikh's moves to exploit the advantageous provisions of the India–Mauritius DTA were marked by accommodation on both sides, despite persistent opposition from India's tax authorities and civil society forces. The durability of the pro-Mauritius elite coalition and its pro-foreign investment worldview held relatively strong until cracks emerged in the 2014–2016 period.

Explaining the reversal of the India–Mauritius policy

India's lengthy financial relationship with Mauritius, through which it received tens of billions of dollars of offshore capital flows via the island nation, triggered a political response. The tax treaty with Mauritius was challenged by India's tax authorities and civil society forces, eventually even reaching India's highest court, and in 2016 the tax advantage of the Mauritius route was eliminated. In assessing this outcome, it is useful to begin by asking what factors have changed relatively little, and thus hold less explanatory power. First, one could argue that this outcome resulted from the Indian tax authorities doggedly pursuing what they had seen to be an unfair tax treaty. Indian tax authorities sought to revise the country's tax treaty with Mauritius largely because India had struggled to collect taxes. However, the pressure exerted by this arm of the Indian state has been consistent over time. In fact, the failure to generate change in the India–Mauritius relationship left Indian officials exasperated. One well-placed Mauritian offshore figure, the then head of Global Finance Mauritius (the body representing the financial services industry of Mauritius), recalled a 2012 lunch he held with senior officials from the Indian Department of Income Tax, and the shock he felt at both the deep resentment these officials harbored toward Mauritius and its offshore model, and the tenor with which they expressed it (interview with Nikhil Treeboohun, Mauritius, 2016).

Second, civil society forces have long questioned India's financial networks with Mauritius. The best example is the social movement Azadi Bachao Andolan, the leaders of which have argued that Mauritius is a grave threat to India's fiscal health and launched legal action against the Indian government. This group is influenced by a lengthy Indian tradition of opposing market expansion (Jenkins, 2003). Moreover, CSOs such as the Centre for Budget and Governance Accountability (CBGA) published articles critical of India's relationship with Mauritius, rallied other organizations to call for the renegotiation of the tax treaty, and released easily comprehensible data that supported their criticism of the Mauritius OFC (e.g., the People's Budget Initiative). Some Indian politicians joined this chorus and India's press reported these criticisms with zeal over the years. Indian newspapers regularly featured stories on these voices asserting what they saw as the harm caused to India by the Mauritius DTA.

Civil society is not irrelevant and the efforts of civil society actors provided a foundation upon which the Indian Prime Minister Narendra Modi could act, although its advocacy and research had not previously generated a tipping point. Nonetheless, these factors were essentially constant over time, with no noticeable increase in pressure in the period leading up to Modi's decision to amend the Mauritius DTA. Hence, we need to look to other factors to explain the policy shift. The long-standing equilibrium between India and Mauritius ruptured due to a shift in India's economic position, changing political elites and ideas in both countries, and a significantly different international environment following the global financial crisis. International and domestic pressures that developed subsequent to the global financial crisis provided a new structural context that empowered Indian political elites who favored a tax reform agenda. Under the Modi government, India negotiated new international tax rules and converted these rules into domestic legislation.

The growth of the Indian economy left India better positioned to change policy direction. The country's consistent annual growth of 7% made it easier to close the capital gains loophole with Mauritius without the concerns of economic damage to India that there had been in the past. A number of specific economic indicators stand out. First, foreign exchange reserves rose. In earlier periods, India's precarious balance of payments was particularly hazardous, as it had low foreign exchange reserves. Despite India's growth, it was not until 2010 that foreign exchange reserves reached sizable proportions. Between 1990 and 2000, the reserves had increased from US$3 billion to only US$38 billion, but by 2010, they had multiplied to US$287 billion, increasing to US$364 billion by 2016 and to US$577 billion by March 2021 (Reserve Bank of India [RBI], 2021). Second, the reputation of India's domestic economy recovered to the extent that India now sits atop many investor surveys – see, for example, the conclusion of one major EY (2015, p. 5) survey, in which respondents ranked India as "the most attractive investment destination in the world." However, India continues to run trade deficits, which contribute to its long-standing current account deficit. With local capital markets and India's private sector unable to fully bridge this divide, India's large infrastructural needs make foreign capital inflows necessary. The difference now is that special and often disadvantageous deals with jurisdictions like Mauritius are no longer indispensable to filling the capital deficit.

New political features also came into play. Media reports of leaks about the offshore financial dealings of individuals and companies gave the general public a clearer view of the functioning of the notoriously opaque offshore system, and the outcry affected national leaders in several countries. Journalists exposed how the largest MNEs, such as Google, Amazon, Apple, Starbucks, and many others shifted billions in profits around the global economy to significantly reduce or even eliminate their tax bills (Drucker, 2010; Griffiths, 2012; Duhigg & Kocieniewski, 2012; Bergin, 2012). To take one example from Africa, the Paradise Papers revealed how Mauritian shell companies were used as intermediaries to shift revenues away from Namibia's fishing industry (Meisel & Grossman, 2017). Long being on the margins of society, the tax justice community took center stage in public discourse. The OECD, which had previously been relatively unconcerned about tax exemptions, such as the India–Mauritius arrangement, subsequently undertook more discussions on the operation of the global offshore system. These negotiations culminated with the CRS in 2014, concerning the oversight of individual assets in different national economies, and the BEPS project in 2015, concerning the regulation of MNEs.

When one speaks to the Indian tax policy community today, nearly everyone recites some variant of the following line: "We are a signatory to the BEPS agreement" (interviews with 20 public and private sector tax policy specialists, New Delhi and Mumbai, 2017). The depth and speed of India's response to the BEPS project have gone well beyond those of most countries. First, India began the process of renegotiating its tax treaties before the OECD guidelines were in place, particularly BEPS Action 6 and the BEPS MLI. Second, India has passed into law what are known as general anti-avoidance rules (GAARs), which empower tax officials to look closely inside an enterprise's operating data to carry out a test of its residency. Other countries found this too challenging and GAARs were not even listed as a recommendation under the BEPS project. India recognizes tax reform as a global issue but, more importantly, it has used the BEPS process as a domestic impetus to push policy changes favored by the Modi regime. There is little history in India of external pressure forcing economic change (Mukherji, 2013), and this instance is no different. The OECD has not forced India's hand to revise its global tax policy. Rather, the pattern that is evident in Indian political economy is that policy change is preceded by substantial technocratic preparation that enables the state to act authoritatively when political decisions are made (Mukherji, 2013). Interviews in New Delhi confirmed that Finance Ministry officials engaged in extensive internal planning on possible responses to the evolving OECD processes.

New elites in India and Mauritius, influenced by structural change, precipitated the India–Mauritius DTA renegotiation and the closing of the capital gains loophole. The seriousness of India's commitment to international tax processes is partially a function of its new leadership. Although Prime Minister Modi has always been seen as a pro-business leader, he has increasingly turned to the language of class struggle, claiming that he is willing to upset the business class with policies designed to benefit the poor. As a popular leader with a strong conviction of the need for tax reform, Prime Minister Modi strengthened the country's tax authorities, unlike previous regimes that mostly accommodated the preferences of the business class. He was also unencumbered by any legacy related to the India–Mauritius DTA, unlike members of previous Congress governments. The newfound pressure placed on India's tax treaty partners has been one tangible result. The political environment has also facilitated Prime Minister Modi's more aggressive stance on taxation domestically and internationally. Nearly 2,000 Indian names, including those of politicians, were part of the 2015 Swiss Leaks. The Panama Papers and the Paradise Papers did not directly influence the DTA negotiations with Mauritius, as they were released afterward. Nonetheless, these leaks, which named members of the Indian political and entertainment classes, galvanized India into additional domestic and global tax activity.

There was also an ideational component to India's policy shift on OFCs. The lens through which Prime Minister Modi and allied Indian officials perceive India's place in the global economy colors India as a highly attractive market. Whereas Rixen (2013, p. 436) was correct to note that the prevailing logic in many countries is that "governments fear losing internationally mobile financial activity to competitor states," today's Indian political elites think differently. These officials are confident that India can command foreign investment directly. Unlike previous government officials, there is no sense of alarm that tackling the Mauritian offshore investment channel will undermine the willingness of foreign investors to place capital in India. Some of this confidence is derived from a comparative standpoint: Indian elites believe that India is already the most investor-friendly country among the BRICS economies given the general retreat from market-opening behavior that has been displayed by Brazil, China, Russia, and South Africa (multiple interviews, New Delhi, 2017), and thus foreign investors should be willing to invest directly into India.

In Mauritius, the key difference was the new Ministry of Financial Services and Good Governance that was created in late 2014, led by a new Minister (Roshi Bhadain) who acted with autonomy from the offshore industry. The Mauritius offshore sector was marginalized and was not even consulted before Mauritius started negotiations with India. The Mauritian government was therefore consulting with Indian practitioners but not its own industry. One of India's top chartered accountants told us that he was consulted by the Mauritian government and strongly recommended that Mauritius push hard during negotiations to obtain tax advantages on debt transactions (interview with TP Ostwal, Mumbai, 2017). Certainly, Mauritius's new approach does not result from a homegrown opposition campaign. There is no strong civil society coalition in Mauritius that is opposed to the offshore sector. This is reinforced by our own failure to find any such interviewees during three different fieldwork trips.

Lacking foresight, Mauritius invested little in public relations (PR). One former Mauritian decision-maker reflected on how Mauritius is seen within India: "The Indian perception was that Mauritius does nothing. Indians said to me, 'You have no strategy and you've reaped all the benefits.' " (anonymous interview, Mauritius, 2014). This is partly the result of the failure of Mauritius to appreciate the value of network building and lobbying. The Finance Minister of Mauritius went on national television in India in the 2000s and said India should learn to appreciate the benefits of the DTA, a public statement that Indian officials felt was inappropriate (anonymous interview, New Delhi, 2017). Subsequently, Mauritius hired an Indian PR firm for one year to make its case in India, but decided against any further communication strategy after this period (anonymous interview, Mauritius, 2017). A cynical offshore practitioner (anonymous interview, Mauritius, 2017) contrasted the island nation to the Netherlands, explaining that:

> There was no sustained effort from Mauritius to respond to critics. The Netherlands responded to moral campaigns effectively. They made a public statement that they would review all treaties with Africa. It was a good political move, although nothing really changed in practice.

For these reasons, Mauritius was poorly positioned in the court of Indian public opinion.

Minister Bhadain acted from an ideational point of view as well. He was certain that new sources of foreign investment in Mauritius would materialize after the India–Mauritius DTA was renegotiated. He spoke optimistically to the media about the future of financial services and asserted that Mauritius would gain 10,000 jobs in the captive insurance field – a large figure for a small country like Mauritius. There was no accompanying logic to this claim, whether generally as to why Mauritius held any competitive advantage in captive insurance, or particularly in relation to the global leader, Bermuda. There is also a broader point here: Mauritius's goal of developing a more diversified financial sector is constrained by the presence of niches in the global offshore financial system and the professional networks that coalesce around these niches. For example, just as Bermuda is the domicile of choice for the captive insurance industry, the Cayman Islands plays the same role for the global hedge fund industry, and Ireland for the mutual fund sector. In each case, there is a deep network of associated services providers. The BVI is widely used in offshore financial transactions by Asian clients because a network of specialized services providers recommends BVI structures. It is difficult to replace these offshore financial niches. While Mauritius can offer cost savings in many areas of offshore finance, pre-existing niches and networks serve to reduce the likelihood that government-led initiatives in Mauritius will draw away significant market share from lead jurisdictions. Thus, although the government proceeded with tax incentives for captive insurance and invited industry experts from abroad to lead training exercises, it was highly doubtful that 10,000 Mauritian jobs would be created in the captive insurance industry. In hindsight, Minister Bhadain held an idealistic view about the ease of attracting new foreign business.

In summary, the long-standing relationship between India and Mauritius ruptured due to shifting domestic economic and structural conditions, revised international norms concerning the offshore financial system, and a new configuration of domestic elites in both countries. This is a fascinating case where, returning to Chapter 2, the dominant geoculture is challenged by new social and political forces in the Global South. These new domestic elites holding different ideas have emerged concomitantly with new international contexts. Chapter 5 turns to the experiences of African countries before returning in the chapter's conclusion to the question of whether India's actions constitute a decisive shift in the global political economy of development.

Notes

1 In 2019, the Netherlands surpassed the UK to become the fourth largest investor in India from 2000 to 2020 cumulatively (DPIIT, 2021). Future research could investigate whether the Netherlands, which has maintained its capital gains exemption for investments in India, holds only a short-term or a more lasting advantage for global deal-making in India. Some Indian commentators are concerned that the Netherlands will replace Mauritius as the principal offshore tax jurisdiction for investing in India (Jaiswal, 2018). However, two lawyers with a major law firm

advising clients on deals with Mauritius historically, AZB & Partners, told us that in their single experience with structuring an Indian transaction via the Netherlands, they found Dutch law too complicated and have advised clients against this route since (interview with Aditya Jha and Ganesh Rao, Mumbai, 2017).

2 Round-tripping refers to a method by which domestic capital artificially flees its country of origin and then flows back disguised as FDI, whether for the purpose of money laundering, circumvention of regulations, access to more favorable tax rates and tax incentives, or other advantages.

3 Gateway is a term also used in the academic literature by geographers (Taylor & Derudder, 2016; Scholvin et al., 2019).

4 In both 2001 and 2006, the Indian stock market fell over 10% in one day and trading was suspended due to fears over the future of the India–Mauritius DTA. There were also significant stock market drops in 2007, 2010, 2011, and 2012.

5 A case study of the Mauritius–Africa offshore relationship

The analysis thus far demonstrates that change in the governance of offshore finance is likely to be a product of synergies between new domestic actors with distinct ideas and new global conditions. A country's capital position and pressures from international regimes represent two important structural conditions. The ideational frames of political elites in different periods also matter, especially when elite norms concerning the value of foreign investment gain new currency through new political alliances and new global conditions. In the Indian case, international and domestic forces prompted by the global financial crisis provided a new structural dynamic that strengthened the hand of political elites who favored a tax reform agenda. Indian Prime Minister Modi's government took a leadership role in international negotiations to revamp the international financial architecture and promote the incorporation of new tax principles into domestic legislation. This represents ideational change led by top national political leaders, bolstered by changed international contexts.

In the last five years, India has convincingly exhibited its independence in global financial affairs. Going forward, whether the African continent mimics India will indicate the transferability of this approach. In this context, the future viability of Mauritius's self-proclaimed status as the financial gateway to Africa is being tested by the signing and implementation of OECD tax instruments, particularly treaty shopping provisions. Will the BEPS MLI – by way of the PPT rule, or possible future bilaterally negotiated LOB rules – put an end to treaty shopping via Mauritius for investment into African economies? Earlier, we quoted the OECD's top tax official, Pascal Saint-Amans, who declared the end of tax treaty abuse (The Economist, 2018). The evaluation in this chapter shows less certainty over this outcome. A national level of analysis reveals that countries have maneuvered around treaty abuse standards rather than strictly following the new OECD guidelines. The sharp policy break in the Mauritius–India offshore relationship stands out in comparison to other less affected offshore financial linkages in today's global economy. India's history of defensive multilateralism and its economic leverage are virtually unique among emerging markets. Africa is different, at least for now. Although the space in the global system for unhindered offshore capital movements has unquestionably shrunk, many African regimes look set to

DOI: 10.4324/9781003161011-5

continue allowing the use of Mauritian offshore financial structures, rather than following India's lead and taking punitive steps against such routes.

Key historical points

As of September 2020, Mauritius has signed 46 DTAs with a strong emphasis on African countries. Well over one-third of the DTAs in force, more than half of the DTAs awaiting ratification and signature, and over one-third of the DTAs that are being negotiated are with African countries (see Table 5.1).

DTAs between Mauritius and African parties came into force in two waves: the first from 1992 to 2005 and the second from 2011 to 2020, with a spike from 2011 to 2013. Just as in the India case, the foremost advantage for investors contemplating striking deals in Africa is that investing via a Mauritian company lowers or eliminates capital gains taxes. In African countries that levy capital gains tax, the rate is typically 30% to 35%. Mauritius, in contrast, offers low or zero capital gains taxes. Even in cases in which an African country has decided against taxing capital gains, structuring deals through a Mauritius DTA provides insurance against paying such taxes should a country revise its tax regime. Other benefits complement the capital gains reduction, namely lower taxes on dividends, interest, and royalties than would be paid domestically (see Table 5.2).

When these advantages are added up, they can be substantial. For example, in the emerging market case of Rwanda, where Mauritian offshore structures are commonly used for business transactions, an investment carried out using a Mauritian vehicle would be subject to zero tax on dividends, interest, royalties, and of course capital gains. In contrast, the same investment placed directly into the Rwandan economy would be liable for 15% tax on dividends, interest, and royalties, and 30% on capital gains. This hypothetical deal would be made even more attractive to investors by the Mauritius–Rwanda BIT, which offers protection against nationalization or confiscation of assets. These pro-investment policies have spurred substantial activity by MNEs. There have been highly publicized cases of treaty shopping, the foremost being those of SABMiller (ActionAid, 2012) and Associated British Foods (ActionAid, 2013b). These high-profile cases involved complex offshore ties linking Mauritius with offshore structures in Ireland, Jersey, the Netherlands, and Switzerland. One of the lesser known but important sources of MNE demand for Mauritian offshore vehicles comes from South African firms seeking a better platform to do business in Africa. Bond (2017, p. 53) has sharply but compellingly argued the following:

> It is not only Western TNCs which looted this continent for centuries. The single biggest country-based source of FDI in Africa is internal, from South Africa. A dozen companies with Johannesburg Stock Exchange listings draw out excessive FDI profits: British American Tobacco, SABMiller breweries (which in 2016 was acquired by US-based Anheuser Busch), the MTN and Vodafone cellphone networks, Naspers newspapers, four banks (Standard,

Table 5.1 Mauritius Double Taxation Agreements (As of September 2020)

Mauritius DTAs		*With African Countries*	*With Other Countries*
DTAs in force	**46**	**(18)** Botswana, Cabo Verde, Congo (Republic of the), Egypt, Eswatini, Ghana, Lesotho, Madagascar, Mozambique, Namibia, Rwanda, Senegal **(Terminated)***, Seychelles **(Amended through Protocol)**, South Africa **(New)**, Tunisia, Uganda, Zambia **(Terminated)****, Zimbabwe	**(28)** Australia **(Partial)**, Bangladesh, Barbados **(Amended through Protocol)**, Belgium, China **(Amended through Protocol)**, Croatia, Cyprus **(Amended through Protocol)**, France **(Amended through Protocol)**, Germany **(New)**, Guernsey, India **(Amended through Protocol)**, Italy **(Amended through Protocol)**, Jersey, Kuwait, Luxembourg **(Amended through Protocol)**, Malaysia, Malta, Monaco, Nepal, Oman, Pakistan, Qatar, Singapore, Sri Lanka, Sweden **(New)**, Thailand, United Arab Emirates, United Kingdom **(Amended through Protocol)**
DTAs awaiting ratification	7	**(5)** Gabon, Comoros Islands, Kenya, Morocco, Nigeria	**(2)** Estonia, Russia
DTAs awaiting signature	**5**	**(4)** Angola, Côte d'Ivoire, Gambia, Malawi	**(1)** Gibraltar
DTAs being negotiated	**21**	**(8)** Algeria, Burkina Faso, Lesotho **(New)**, Mali, Senegal **(New)**, Sudan, Tanzania, Zambia **(New)**	**(13)** Canada, Czech Republic, Greece, Hong Kong, Iran, Montenegro, Portugal, Saudi Arabia, Saint Kitts and Nevis, Spain, Turkey, Vietnam, Yemen
Protocols to existing DTAs being negotiated	**4**	**(2)** Mozambique, Uganda	**(2)** Germany, Pakistan

* Following the termination of the DTA between Mauritius and Senegal, the treaty will be applicable for the last time, in the case of Mauritius, for the fiscal year ending on 30 June 2020, and in the case of Senegal, for the calendar year ending on 31 December 2020.

** Following the termination of the DTA between Mauritius and Zambia, the treaty will be applicable for the last time, in the case of Mauritius, for the fiscal year ending on 30 June 2021, and in the case of Zambia, for the calendar year ending on 31 December 2020.

Source: (MRA, 2020).

Table 5.2 The Tax Benefits of Mauritius Double Taxation Agreements With African Countries (As of September 2020)

	Withholding Tax on Dividends		*Withholding Tax on Interest*		*Withholding Tax on Royalties*		*Capital Gains Tax*	
	No DTA	*Under DTA*	*No DTA*	*Under DTA*	*No DTA*	*Under DTA*	*No DTA*	*Under DTA*
Botswana	7.5%	5/7.5%	15%	12%	15%	12.5%	22%	Exempt
Cabo Verde	0%	0/5%	20%	10%	20%	7.5%	22%	Exempt
Congo (Rep.)	15%	0/5%	20%	Exempt	20%	Exempt	20%	Exempt
Egypt	5/10%	5/10%	20%	10%	20%	12%	22.5%	Exempt
Eswatini	12.5/15%	7.5%	10%	5%	15%	7.5%	0%	Exempt
Ghana	8%	7%	8%	7%	15%	8%	25%	Exempt
Lesotho	25%	10%	25%	10%	25%	10%	25%	Exempt
Madagascar	10%	5/10%	20%	10%	10%	5%	20%	Exempt
Mozambique	20%	8/10/15%	20%	8%	20%	5%	32%	Exempt
Namibia	10/20%	5/10%	10%	10%	10%	5%	0%	Exempt
Rwanda	15%	10%	15%	10%	15%	10%	30%	Exempt
Senegal*	10%	Exempt	8/13/16%	Exempt	20%	Exempt	30%	Exempt
Seychelles	15%	Exempt	15%	Exempt	15%	Exempt	0%	Exempt
South Africa	20%	5/10%	15%	10%	15%	5%	22.4%	Exempt
Tunisia	10%	Exempt	10/20%	2.5%	15/25%	2.5%	25%	Exempt
Uganda	15%	10%	15%	10%	15%	10%	30%	Exempt
Zambia**	20%	5/15%	20%	10%	20%	5%	0%	Exempt
Zimbabwe	10/15%	10%	0%	Exempt	15%	15%	1/5/20%	Exempt

* Following the termination of the DTA between Mauritius and Senegal, the treaty will be applicable for the last time, in the case of Mauritius, for the fiscal year ending on 30 June 2020, and in the case of Senegal, for the calendar year ending on 31 December 2020.

** Following the termination of the DTA between Mauritius and Zambia, the treaty will be applicable for the last time, in the case of Mauritius, for the fiscal year ending on 30 June 2021, and in the case of Zambia, for the calendar year ending on 31 December 2020.

Source: (MRA, 2020; EY, 2020; PwC, 2021).

> Barclays, Nedbank and FirstRand), the Sasol oil company and the local residues of the Anglo American Corporation empire. The result is the systematic internal looting of Africa by South Africa, especially as the main retail chains – for example, Walmart-owned Massmart and its affiliates – use the larger market in the south to achieve economies of scale in production that then swamp and wipe out Africa's basic-needs manufacturing sector.

The Mauritian route is still, in principle, open. Any cursory search of offshore services providers would reveal the extent of providers that still promote Mauritius as a domicile for business deals around the world, especially in Africa. The argument explored in this chapter is that the route is not only theoretically open but also still commonly used, although the intensity of its use is tempered by new global pressures. There has undoubtedly been change in the African region in response to the new agenda of offshore tax reform, headlined by the following examples:

- Rwanda renegotiated its DTA with Mauritius, securing approval for a 10% withholding tax on Mauritian companies when no such tax existed before;
- South Africa renegotiated its DTA with Mauritius, curbing the tax abuses of the original;
- Senegal withdrew from its DTA with Mauritius;
- Zambia has requested a renegotiation of its DTA with Mauritius;
- Ghana petitioned many of its treaty partners to revise DTA specifications to be more in line with the UN model framework;
- Uganda has publicly criticized its DTA terms and challenged its DTA partners to revise these agreements; and
- Tanzania and South Africa have cancelled some of their BITs.

The examples cited here fall short of the more ambitious tax reform agenda envisioned by ActionAid (2014, p. 8) for African countries, which is as follows:

> These options include taking the UN model as a point of departure, and incorporating provisions from more progressive models that have been developed in the Andean region in Latin America to ensure optimal taxing rights in the country where profits are generated and productive activities take place.

Instead, we are witnessing a mixed pattern on the African continent in which questions are being raised about the dominant historical pattern of engagement with global capital, even though the larger pattern remains one of accommodation. The changes thus far have been moderate.

The role of international factors

This chapter finds that pressures derived from the post-crisis reform effort have proved less consequential for Africa than for India. This is in line with Hearson's

(2020, p. 3) argument that when it comes to the BEPS project, "uptake from developing countries was muted." The mediating factors include the flexibility enshrined in OECD processes, inadequate domestic capacity, emergent but still undeveloped social movements, and the lack of cross-regional coordination. The nature of the recent OECD agreements is such that each signatory has some degree of choice about how far it will take the standards of an agreement. There are also many opt-in and opt-out clauses that are non-binding. Mauritius, for example, has thus far turned down all major optional measures under the BEPS project. One of the more fundamental elements of the OECD playbook that often goes unacknowledged is that new OECD standards on taxation are essentially a guide for national policymakers. For example, there is no direct specification in the BEPS project of what corporate tax rates should be adopted, although the 15% global minimum corporate income tax negotiated as part of BEPS 2.0, for the first time ever provides at least a floor. Moreover, the coverage of different forms of taxation is far from exhaustive. As Oguttu (2016, p. 27) noted: "The BEPS project does not explore certain practical measures (such as withholding taxes) that may be more suitable for African countries in addressing BEPS."

Action 6 of the BEPS project, concerning the prevention of treaty abuse, recommends that DTAs should integrate the following: i) a statement on the intention to avoid opportunities for non-taxation or reduced taxation through tax evasion or avoidance; ii) a specific anti-abuse rule in the form of the LOB rule; and iii) a general anti-abuse rule in the form of the PPT rule. The mandatory minimum standard is stipulated to be either the LOB rule, or the PPT rule, or both. In the BEPS MLI, optional measures pertain to "Dividend Transfer Transactions," "Capital Gains from Alienation of Shares or Interests of Entities Deriving their Value Principally from Immovable Property," an "Anti-Abuse Rule for Permanent Establishments Situated in Third Jurisdictions," and the "Application of Tax Agreements to Restrict a Party's Right to Tax Its Own Residents."

The Mauritius–Africa DTA landscape has not been significantly affected by the BEPS MLI. Of the 18 African countries that have a DTA with Mauritius, only four are a party to the MLI (Egypt, the Seychelles, South Africa, and Tunisia). Of the additional 17 that are being ratified, are awaiting signature, or are under negotiation, only four are party to the MLI (Gabon, Nigeria, Côte d'Ivoire, and Burkina Faso). Algeria, Eswatini (Swaziland), and Kenya have expressed their intention to join the MLI but have not yet done so. In what was widely suspected to be a "delaying tactic" (Carter, 2017, p. 19), Mauritius initially excluded its African treaties from the BEPS project. However, in October 2018, Mauritius committed to the Action 6 provisions of the BEPS project for all of its African DTAs. With a peer review approaching, Mauritian decision-makers felt that it was too reputationally risky to be an outlier on the BEPS project and reversed their course (anonymous interview with a Mauritius Revenue Authority [MRA] official, Mauritius, 2019). Singapore's earlier about-face on Action 6 paralleled that of Mauritius. This increases the chance of OECD principles being embedded within OFCs, but caution is still in order.

Despite an extensive set of LOB models offered under the BEPS project, Mauritius has chosen the route of the PPT rule for now, as a kind of broadly subjective GAAR-like instrument that gives tax administrations discretion to decide whether to grant treaty benefits. Whereas the PPT rule is a subjective measure, the LOB rule is more objective: it specifies that certain conditions need to be met – in the parlance, that "substance" must be demonstrated – for the treaty benefits to be granted. In any future discussions of LOB rules, the bilateral level will be of central importance, with Mauritius and its existing or potential treaty partners entering into specific, likely difficult and lengthy bilateral negotiations to formulate what level of business activity would be sufficient for a Mauritian company to be accepted as being rooted in an economy. In the meantime, Hattingh (2017, p. 33) expressed concern about the choice to proceed with the PPT rule, arguing that "the PPT is a vague measure, perhaps by design," and that it "affords significant discretionary power to revenue administrators." The PPT rule also demands significant technical capabilities if it is to be implemented properly. This point is discussed in the next section.

As a result of the BEPS project and the changing global environment, Mauritius has recently instituted some changes under its new Finance Act, which specifies higher substance requirements in Mauritius. While ensuring that accounting records, audits, bank accounts, directors, and board meetings are located in Mauritius is a small step forward – and, of course, beneficial to the Mauritian economy – an informant explained that holding company structures can still be approved in Mauritius (anonymous telephone interview with a MC operator, 2019), which puts in question the whole notion of higher substance requirements. That is, holding companies are typically seen as part of the earlier, overly permissive offshore system. Picciotto (2019, pp. 25–26) argues that the changes under the Finance Act were "cleverly designed" to enable companies registered in Mauritius to continue to conduct business in the global economy with relative ease. In summary, OECD standards have reduced the room for offshore financial vehicles to operate in the global economy, but these standards are also constrained by their own nature and by the nature of international relations.

The role of domestic factors

The prevailing historical pattern around which supportive coalitions have formed is the pattern of accommodation. India chose to accommodate the global offshore system beginning in the 1990s. That same choice has now been taken by many African countries. Hearson (2018b, p. 237) offers an important insight into the decision-making setting in which elites in developing economies may find themselves:

> All in all, we cannot say with certainty that tax treaties have generated new investment into their developing country signatories, nor can we say that there is a compelling legal rationale to motivate the conclusion of tax treaties given their costs. . . . It is likely that tax treaty policy is made in conditions of considerable uncertainty about treaties' potential to promote inward investment.

Mutava (2019, p. 11) adds that tax treaty negotiations in Africa are, "due to political influence," often carried out "very speedily, not allowing enough time for consultation with relevant experts." In an interview with Mauritius's DTA negotiating team, they noted that they had just completed DTAs with the Gambia and Malawi in only one round (interview with the DTA team from the Ministry of Finance, Mauritius, 2016). In many cases, such a situation is the result of an ideological commitment among African countries to institute a pro-investment economic regime. In other cases, it may, as Mutava (2019, p. 11) argues, result from unprepared negotiating teams that lack not only expertise but also a clear national "tax treaty policy" and "negotiating strategy" that would provide guidance, outline minimum acceptable treaty terms, and ensure consistency and accountability throughout the process as well as after its conclusion. Although uncertainty may be present, it is also likely, as Hearson (2018b) notes, that two other factors are at play.

First, decision-makers recognize that other countries are accommodating offshore investors from OFCs such as Mauritius and fear that inaction will place them at a comparative disadvantage in the competition for FDI. Kenya's former Finance Minister, Henry Rotich, argued that the country's tax deal with Mauritius needs to be understood as part of a competitive landscape in which many other African countries have signed DTAs with Mauritius (Michira, 2014). Second, there are the prevailing ideological predispositions of political elites, notably the conviction that foreign investment is an economic imperative. Speaking in analogous terms to Indian political elites in the 1990s, Rotich (as quoted in Michira, 2014) defended the Kenya–Mauritius DTA with the following claim: "Through this treaty, we are encouraging direct capital investment which will bring with it hard currency and jobs for our local people."

If African countries were committed to contesting pro-investment norms in tax and investment agreements, they would empower their finance ministries during negotiations. Instead, African negotiators are typically drawn from revenue authorities (Hearson, 2020, p. 4). African countries are also counseled by Mauritian elites on how global investors perceive the relative shortcomings of their domestic systems. One former Finance Minister of Mauritius advises African decision-makers in these terms: "If you think you can attract investment and get capital gains tax and other taxes, then you should go for it. However, it's not that easy. You need to build trust and confidence first, and then create the conducive ecosystem" (interview with Rama Sithanen, Mauritius, 2014). African countries have tended to heed this advice, enabling a key role for Mauritian offshore financial services providers.

DTAs are still part of the global economy, and while the new OECD processes attempt to make it more difficult for countries to grant advantages to third parties through these treaties, such a change is dependent on the degree to which Mauritius and its African treaty partners enforce these standards. For the OECD processes to produce lasting change, domestic political will is required, along with domestic tax capacity and geopolitical skills. Durst (2019, pp. 94–96) is correct to remind us that political will is the crucial variable and that technical factors, while important, are secondary. Since political will has already been discussed in the preceding section, this section focuses on the administrative capacity required to fulfill the OECD agenda. Reflecting the concerns of many observers of Africa's engagement with the OECD reform process, Prichard and Moore (2018, p. 2) point out that "rules premised on the economic formality and administrative capacity of Western countries may prove excessively complex and difficult to implement in the more informal lower-capacity environment of low-income countries."

The existence of sophisticated MNEs and their ability to set up complex structures using highly paid intermediaries has been a significant feature propelling the development of the offshore economy. In one example, Oguttu (2017, p. 9) reports on how African countries have been concerned about the complex schemes designed by MNEs to deduct interest and avoid taxes, and on their inability to prevent these practices. Transfer pricing, a focal part of the BEPS project, must also be considered. Transfer pricing is an area that has generated substantial fees for the advisory business community (Picciotto, 2013, p.23), and is therefore a strategic focus of advisory firms. Developing countries, for their part, tend to lack the expertise and resources to determine and enforce transfer pricing standards. The BEPS project added over 150 pages to the last version of the transfer pricing guidelines, theoretically giving tax administrations more powers but making the guidelines even more complicated. This poses a challenge to smaller tax authorities that had already struggled with the last version of the guidelines. The South African Ministry of Finance noted that they had discussed the BEPS project with international tax experts who themselves "had difficulties in understanding the instruments" (PMG, 2017).

If international tax experts are confounded by the BEPS project, it is hard to imagine most African tax authorities mastering the new guidelines and creating effective systems to implement and enforce them. Moreover, there are innumerable analyses centered on using the court system to combat tax treaty abuse (e.g., Duff, 2018). These are sensible analyses but they are Western-centric and do not transfer well to other parts of the world with different legal traditions and legal developments. More broadly, it would be simplistic to commend Western countries for their action against offshore tax evasion and avoidance, considering the immense challenge of monitoring the offshore financial system and their own failures. The recently published exposé on the Malaysian sovereign wealth fund, 1MDB, which has become synonymous with one of the world's biggest corruption scandals (Wright & Hope, 2018), should be required reading for those interested in how Western financial institutions failed to stop billions of dollars of questionable offshore capital flows. This failure stemmed from flawed compliance processes and co-opted elites. If Western financial institutions are ill-equipped for the task, it is hard to envisage most African tax authorities effectively scrutinizing MNEs.

Despite all the concerns that are regularly raised about African tax administrations, Moore et al. (2018, p. 31) remind readers that the majority of the national tax systems in Africa "have functioned continuously since the end of colonial rule," and "perform relatively well," certainly better than they are often depicted. However, one of the major problems is that the complexity of tax regulation has increased dramatically. As Durst (2019, p. 7) argues, "today's international laws have evolved over decades to generate, rather than reduce, complexity and unpredictability of application, and . . . this tendency has greatly impaired efforts to enforce the law and reform it legislatively in countries around the world." Increasing complexity is a challenge for all countries, but is especially burdensome for developing countries and their ability to properly legislate and enforce new tax standards. How can countries respond to global tax complexity? A common response, as summarized and critiqued by Prichard and Moore (2018, p. 1), is to invest in various mechanisms that are based on an excessive reliance on "elaborate procedures (e.g. complex criteria for valuing individual buildings for property tax purposes), so-called best practice (e.g. the introduction of the most complex rules to combat transfer mispricing), and the latest technology (e.g. sophisticated IT systems)." Such approaches will always struggle to keep up with fast-changing rules and fast-changing corporate practices. The better approach, according to authors such as Prichard and Moore (2018) and Durst (2019), is to simplify tax rules.

PPT rules are a particular challenge for many African tax authorities. As Oguttu (2017, p. 22) effectively pointed out, PPTs are "difficult for tax administrations to administer . . . as they require proof of intent." To carry out a PPT, tax officials must assess the operations of an enterprise, which requires investigative skills and resources. This necessitates forensic analysis and auditing expertise on a scale that may not exist in these administrations (Oguttu, 2016). It also requires a lot of data, but taking the example of transfer pricing, ActionAid (2015, p. 16) found the following:

> Datasets of comparable transactions (or 'comparables') may be expensive for tax authorities to obtain or difficult to use. The Kenyan Revenue Authority bought an expensive comparables database and was largely unable to find relevant data in it. Rwanda's tax authority has previously declined to buy such databases, citing similar concerns.

The better option would be to press for LOB rules as part of future renegotiations. These LOB rules would entail an objective set of benchmarks to be met for the enterprise to be entitled to the tax benefits of the DTA. While Moore et al. (2018, p. 144) are correct to call for new tax policies in African countries, especially policies that would more effectively target MNEs and the "ease" with which they "avoid local corporate income taxes by shifting profits overseas," the analysis in this book suggests that it is uncertain whether these changes will be realized anytime in the foreseeable future.

There have been normative calls from interested outside parties for greater regional cooperation in Africa. In a study requested by the European Parliament's Committee on Development, Mascagni et al. (2014, p. 32) outlined four possible directions that Africa might take on a coordinated regional basis to protect itself from excessive competition among governments for private investment, and thereby protect its revenue base:

- A set of principles covering the criteria for the granting of tax exemptions for investors, the procedures through which those decisions will be taken, and, ideally, some upper boundaries on the amount of exemptions.
- A regional agreement to subject all contracts with foreign investors, especially in the extractive sector, to standard national tax regimes and therefore to forego special arrangements for certain types of investment.
- A regional agreement to move towards the levying of minimum withholding taxes on all dividend payments made by locally-incorporated subsidiaries of transnational groups. This may require the modification of double-taxation treaties.
- A regional agreement to adopt Brazilian-style presumptive minimum or normal profit margins or markups when assessing subsidiaries of transnationals for corporate income tax.

Few signs are evident of any such regional action beyond basic technical training and the sharing of best practices through the African Development Bank (AfDB) and the African Tax Administration Forum (ATAF). Offshore tax evasion and avoidance were added to the agendas of African Union (AU) summits, and an influential group led by the former President of South Africa, Thabo Mbeki, railed against IFFs (United Nations Economic Commission for Africa [UNECA], 2015). However, these discussions have translated into only modest national action, particularly in terms of any substantive push-back against tax treaties with Mauritius. Only with buy-in across the region will tax competition be mitigated. The national level is paramount; the regional level, at least in terms of coordination among policy-makers, is undeveloped. The best example of regional activity is located outside the formal political system. As discussed in the next section, CSO action has gathered pace across the region, despite starting from a low base.

The politics of contestation

Tax policy is gradually becoming more of a political issue in African countries, and social movements are a key reason for this. However, one example illustrates how oppositional forces in Africa have not yet mobilized campaigns that are sufficiently strong to have an effect on political and business elites who favor offshore structures. The case is Zambia. During the 2015 election campaign, the presidential candidates concurred on the need for tax reform and taxation was a top-tier campaign issue. However, once in power, the regime backtracked on campaign promises and the status quo held. The result was electoral change but not policy change, an outcome that might have been different with stronger civil society campaigns.

One factor is the generally poor domestic resource mobilization in African countries. In this context, bringing up tax in political campaigns means bringing up the uneasy specter of taxing the population, and because the vast majority of the people are not yet able to afford paying taxes, it is easy for opposition elites to manipulate the discourse in the name of "fairness," and retain the status quo.

Several years ago, Moore (2013, p. 1) pondered why tax issues are "so prominent on the public political agenda in most high-income countries, and so low profile in most developing countries," and came to the following conclusion:

> The public at large have little interest in tax policy. When politicians seek public support, they seldom talk of tax. Political parties typically take few positions on tax policy. Think-tanks produce few tax policy analyses. Legislative debates on government revenue are often cursory and badly informed.

The key point here is also the legacy of colonialism and the highly extractive tax regimes of the past, thanks to which taxation in general is viewed with suspicion in much of Africa. The magisterial work of the Guyanese historian and political activist, Walter Rodney (2018), deserves to be quoted at length here to understand why:

> One of the main purposes of the colonial taxation system was to provide requisite funds for administering the colony as a field of exploitation. European colonisers ensured that Africans paid for the upkeep of the governors and police who oppressed them and served as watchdogs for private capitalists. Indeed, taxes and customs duties were levied in the 19th century with the aim of allowing the colonial powers to recover the costs of the armed forces which they despatched to conquer Africa. In effect, therefore, the colonial governments never put a penny into the colonies. All expenses were met by exploiting the labour and natural resources of the continent; and for all practical purposes the expense of maintaining the colonial government machinery was a form of alienation of the products of African labour. . . . In those parts of the continent where land was still in African hands, colonial governments forced Africans to produce cash-crops no matter how low the prices were. The favourite technique was taxation. Money taxes were introduced on numerous items – cattle, land, houses and the people themselves. Money to pay taxes was got by growing cash-crops or working on European farms or in their mines.

Another factor is that civil society takes time to build up its capacity to contest dominant structures in the national political economy. Civil society contestation on offshore finance is less established in Africa than it is in India. There are indications, however, that social movements in Africa are gaining strength and influencing political elites. ActionAid has been a leader, applying its global model to African issues. ActionAid's global model entails conducting rigorous research, then presenting its findings to companies, and threatening harmful media coverage should corporate reform not be endorsed (Dyreng et al., 2016). Its efforts appear to have had a major effect on African policy-makers and societies and have shaped a negative impression of Mauritius in particular. ActionAid reports have exposed treaty shopping carried out by MNEs in Africa. Their reports on SABMiller in Ghana (ActionAid, 2012) and Associated British Foods in Zambia

(ActionAid, 2013b) have generated extensive national and international coverage including nearly 100 citations on Google Scholar. ActionAid has also taken African countries to task for signing investor-friendly tax treaties with Mauritius. Nigeria has been a focus but this social action has encompassed many more African countries.

When we interviewed Mauritius's DTA team in the Ministry of Finance in 2016 and held a separate roundtable with senior members of the MRA, both groups of officials commented that ActionAid's message had reached surprisingly deep into African political life. The DTA team explained that African officials and other actors had frequently spoken to them about ActionAid and its claims about unjust tax treaties. At the MRA roundtable, officials were more specific and relayed that the term "blood suckers" – deployed by ActionAid to refer to the role of OFCs, principally Mauritius – was now more commonly found in public discourse within African countries and had been brought up by African officials. Influential Mauritius elites are so ideologically committed to what they believe foreign investment accomplishes that they have written to ActionAid in stark terms, declaring that in trying to help African countries, ActionAid was making them poorer (interview with Nikhil Treebhoohun, Mauritius, 2016).

Tax Justice Network Africa represents another case. This CSO has gone beyond activist campaigns to launch its own legal actions. Most notably, its case against the Kenyan government contesting the terms of the Kenya–Mauritius DTA proceeded to the Supreme Court. It also threatened legal action against the Nigerian government. Tax Justice Network Africa has also moved beyond nationally focused chapters to regional campaigns. It launched the pan-African "Stop the Bleeding" campaign to target the tax behavior of multinational capital in Africa, which made use of creative and original slogans and also featured a campaign song. Although nominally, many of these CSOs are still local chapters of major foreign CSOs like ActionAid, Oxfam, or the Tax Justice Network, they can be viewed as relatively autonomous offshoots in which decision-making is national or regional rather than global and the organizational leaders are Africans and not foreigners. Mirroring patterns found among Western tax justice movements, African lawyers have become important members of and advisors to these CSOs.

Some African countries have adopted tougher postures against Mauritius than others, and these exceptional cases tend to be larger economies. Nigeria, Kenya, and South Africa are notable in this respect. In contrast, Rwanda is a representative example of a country that has prioritized prospective investment and capital flows over taxing rights. Mauritius is the largest investor in Rwanda, four times larger than the next largest source country (IMF, 2021). Nigeria, Kenya, and South Africa are countries with elevated governmental capacity and also countries where tax justice organizations are located. Nigerian authorities are perhaps the most assertive in opposing the conditions that Mauritius has commonly negotiated with African economies. A lawyer from a high-profile law firm who advises African firms and governments explained that in their interactions with key players in Nigeria during 2012, senior government officials admitted that they had erred in signing an overly investor-friendly DTA with Mauritius (anonymous interview,

Mauritius, 2019). Subsequently, with the BEPS project gathering momentum and with African tax justice campaigns increasing their profile, Nigerian officials decided that they would decline to ratify the tax treaty with Mauritius.

Kenya is a less straightforward case. It has witnessed significant contestation over its taxation strategy, with its DTA with Mauritius becoming the subject of Supreme Court hearings just as in India. Like the earlier India–Mauritius DTA, this bilateral treaty specifies that capital gains will be taxed in the home country, which means that Mauritius-registered companies pay no tax on capital gains. These companies also benefit from lower withholding taxes. The Supreme Court ruled that parliamentary procedure had been incorrectly followed. Although Tax Justice Network Africa felt some satisfaction with the tone of the ruling (Nguegan, 2019), the reality is that there was no rupture with Mauritius. The Kenya–Mauritius DTA was signed again, with almost identical wording.[1] That outcome is telling in terms of the continuity of hierarchies and accommodation as a predominant pattern in Africa, even in larger African economies with better equipped state apparatuses. The next chapter, building on the global context set out in Chapters 2 and 3, presents some guarded optimism on the potential for change in Africa on the basis of two factors: the increasing effectiveness of tax justice advocates and investigative journalists, and the growing proficiency of tax officials. But before that, a brief return to the Indian case.

Re-evaluating India's offshore change

It can now be seen that India's experience is somewhat anomalous in terms of its lessons for most other emerging markets. The conditions that were found in India are to a significant extent missing in other lower-middle-income countries, meaning that other countries may be unable or unwilling to follow India's lead. India was uniquely qualified to execute a new taxation strategy given its economic clout and its lengthy multilateral track record. Most emerging markets have a much less extensive experience with offshore transactions than India, and their political economies feature less resistance, less attractiveness to global investors, less exposure to multilateral negotiations, and less competent governmental administrations.

First, an enticing domestic market enables larger emerging markets to make demands on foreign investors, which confirms Walter's (1998) earlier argument that emerging markets often have leverage over international capital, rather than the other way around. Hence, a large emerging market like India is capable of exerting pressure on its tax treaty network. However, recall that it took over two decades for India to act on its large domestic market weight and the majority of emerging markets host much smaller domestic markets than India. Thus, these economies do not possess the same leverage as did India.

Second, even among sizable emerging markets, India has distinctive characteristics. It is a country that has a long history in the multilateral system of contesting liberalizing processes that are seen as unfavorable to developing countries (Blustein, 2009; Prashad, 2012).[2] It is a country skilled not only at defensive multilateralism but also at advancing its interests in international trade negotiations

(Hopewell, 2018). This history has produced a talent pool within the Indian government capable of negotiating bilateral and multilateral deals that few other emerging markets possess. These specializations in the Indian bureaucracy enabled India to act immediately when the Modi government signaled a change in its international tax policy.

Third, India is challenging some of the norms of global finance, whereas most other emerging markets tend to be rule followers. India's experiences have afforded it a better position to push back against the offshore economy. Consequently, India has been among the most active emerging market governments in international discussions at the OECD on reforming the current global tax structure – far more so than even China, for instance – and also in calling for the UN to take on a more central role in shaping global taxation. In particular, India played a decisive role in multilateral negotiations to review tax treaties, flagging over 50 reservations to the latest OECD MTC and its Commentaries (OECD, 2019). India also successfully led the opposition to the minimum standard on arbitration proposed by Western countries as part of the BEPS initiative, claiming that it held a Western expert bias and was unnecessarily secretive. In addition, India is the only country to have provided funding to the unofficial UN Committee of Experts on International Cooperation in Tax Matters through the UN Tax Fund to support greater developing country participation in international tax negotiations (Chowdhary, 2018). Furthermore, India is contributing to discussions on new international standards by publishing a BIT model that is considerably less investor-friendly. Lastly, India appears to be considering the unilateral introduction of a form of unitary taxation with formulary apportionment, a step that only a few other countries have signaled any willingness to take.

Despite the more contested environment for the Mauritius OFC in the African continent and despite the calls for a coordinated regional plan of action against the tax avoidance industry, this chapter has outlined the overarching trajectory of accommodation to Mauritius within the African political economy. Chapter 6 attempts to draw out some of the larger points of significance from the empirical developments outlined in Chapters 4 and 5. It features separate sections on India, Africa, and Mauritius.

Notes

1 As Picciotto (2019, pp. 11–12) explains, "the treaty signed in April 2019 has not been published by either country, though authoritative sources suggest that it is the same as that signed in 2012."

2 The quips of a former Indian Minister of Commerce and Industry, Kamal Nath (as quoted in Blustein, 2009, p. 185), reportedly delivered in 2004 at a World Trade Organization (WTO) meeting in Geneva, colorfully capture India's willingness to challenge the trade diplomacy of Western powers: "Next time can you bring a picture of an American farmer? I have never actually seen one. I have only seen US conglomerates masquerading as farmers."

6 The significance of the case studies for the political economies of India, Africa, and Mauritius

This chapter considers the significance of the relative deterioration of India's financial relationship with Mauritius in contrast to the relative continuity of Africa's offshore connections to Mauritius. It explores three principal arguments: i) that India has gone beyond closing the Mauritius loophole to a broader and deeper set of domestic tax reforms and a new role as a leading voice on global tax reform; ii) that the African region is far behind India in its commitment to the new tax agenda but there are emerging forces, led by tax justice advocates and investigative journalists, as well as increasingly better trained tax officials, that offer hope for a different future; and iii) that Mauritius, despite all its advantages, looks unlikely to become the Singapore or Switzerland of Africa.

The significance of Indian developments

On the fundamental conflict inherent in the offshore economy, Shaxson (2015) writes that: "It is, really, a fight between a globetrotting elite, in one corner, versus ordinary people in rich and poor countries – who all have a shared interest in tackling these problems." If that is the case, which individuals and groups are seeking reform of the system on behalf of ordinary people? The answer often starts with actors in Europe. For example, no other region has approached European levels of deliberation on tax reform. There is strong support among many of the EU institutions and member states for the CCCTB, a detailed proposal to erect a single system within the EU for companies to use to report their revenue and profits. Yet, the EU is hindered by the requirement of unanimity and the CCCTB, though showing signs of life, has been long delayed. Smaller countries – in particular Cyprus, Luxembourg, Ireland, Malta, and the Netherlands – object to EU reforms that will weaken their investment-friendly economic policies. The contradictions of Europe are apparent: it is a region featuring numerous countries that have designed tax-minimizing regimes within a larger political economy that boasts innumerable progressive elements and a desire to advance tax justice.

An additional factor is relevant to the implications of Europe's taxation approach. The EU has adopted a forceful global stance on taxation and European coercion has been a causal factor in the participation of some developing countries in the new global tax regime (Hearson, 2020). Rightly or wrongly, the use

DOI: 10.4324/9781003161011-6

of blacklists and the critical tone of EU foreign policy officials can upset OFCs. According to the account of one senior MRA official, Yamini Rangasamy, presented at the 2019 International Fiscal Association (IFA) conference in Mauritius that one of us attended, the EU treats small OFCs as vassals that it can command and address in an arrogant manner. Specifically, Rangasamy asserted that the EU is generally less prepared than the OECD, and yet tends to attach additional conditions to any newly agreed-to OECD guidelines in order to be seen as having higher standards. Continuing, Rangasamy lambasted the EU for its inability to stay on top of its ever-changing positions. Jurisdictions are often not notified of the changing criteria, and thus discover that they are non-compliant only once they find themselves on a greylist, or in exceptional circumstances, a blacklist.

Rangasamy's apprehensions were realized again in May 2020 when the EU labeled a number of countries, including Mauritius, as deficient in their AML/CFT policies, threatening to add them to its upcoming blacklist. There was a vehement response from Mauritius, first from its Ministry of Financial Services and Good Governance (2020) and then, more pointedly, from the Prime Minister's Office (2020). Matching the MRA official's description, the Prime Minister's communiqué noted that "Mauritius was . . . neither consulted nor heard, let alone informed that a new methodology had come into effect" (Prime Minister's Office, 2020). In addition, the communiqué criticized the EU for relying on the methodology of the FATF, but then misinterpreting the underlying data. During a series of damage control webinars organized in June 2020 by two Mauritian law firms, Axis and BLC Robert (2020) and DTOS (2020), three Mauritian private sector officials heatedly contested the EU process, and more importantly, the resulting damage, with clients having expressed concerns about the negative publicity and the possible effect on global banking facilities in the country. The two main concerns of being blacklisted by the EU were that financial institutions would have to conduct "enhanced due diligence" on transactions involving Mauritius, and that it would not be possible to route EU funds through Mauritius, possibly affecting new projects of development finance institutions (DFIs). In the end, Mauritius was able to avoid the EU blacklist but the episode demonstrates the power that larger markets can have over smaller OFCs.

If these views are held among a reasonably wide cross-section of elites in developing economies, there is likely to be space available for newer actors beyond traditional powers like the EU in the debate over how to undertake global tax reform. Moreover, the EU and the US are bitterly divided in their approaches on how to tax the rapidly expanding digital economy (Christensen & Hearson, 2019b), providing room for new powers to offer leadership. Brazil was a strong candidate to fill this vacuum. From the early 2000s to the early post-global financial crisis years, during the presidency of Luiz Inácio Lula da Silva, Brazil was more active than India in challenging the status quo in global finance and tax policy, especially as it pertained to US global leadership (Armijo & Echeverri-Gent, 2014). However, Brazil has been slowed by its economic crisis and domestic dysfunction and no longer serves as a leading force in those debates. In contrast,

India is establishing itself as the most important emerging power in global finance and tax policy. Even if there are doubts as to whether many other countries can match India's experience in reconstituting their relationships with OFCs, it stands out as a key example of change in the global economy, particularly in terms of its efforts to reshape the global tax regime to have a stronger emphasis on tax justice.

The scope of India's major tax initiatives is impressive. It has introduced stringent tax measures, which have clamped down on offshore practices such as shell companies, transfer pricing manipulation, and profit shifting. India is taking a hard line against offshore companies, harder than many advanced economies. There are no longer any major special deals for offshore companies and the Indian government imposes much stricter oversight on company formations. The Modi administration has passed a range of technical bills related to tax reform. These include stricter rules on where the place of effective management (POEM) and control of a company lies, how internal company transactions are carried out (i.e., transfer pricing), and how debt is shifted around jurisdictions to lower taxable income (i.e., thin capitalization). Moreover, India has proceeded with a tax on digital economy transactions, one of the few countries in the world to do so and going well beyond the original BEPS process, which did not explicitly endorse this type of taxation.

Internationally, India is filling a gap in the various G20/OECD processes, where the specific tax avoidance concerns of developing countries have otherwise thus far been given "limited regard" in deliberations (Vlcek, 2019, p. 355), and where "international tax policy formulation has almost exclusively been the purview of experts from developed countries" (Christians, 2009, p. 31). India is no longer a country that sees its role as only putting the brakes on the market access demanded by Western countries. It has become a country that adopts offensive positions in international trade negotiations, in addition to its more traditional defensive postures. We build on the work of Hopewell (2018) to refer to offensive positions as both interest-based action and principles-based action. Through its active role in the G20, OECD, and UN processes, India is advancing concrete initiatives and proposals to reshape the norms and rules of global finance.

One important development concerns India's attempt to move beyond stalled international attempts at unitary taxation with formulary apportionment. The current international tax regime enables companies to use separate accounting for their national subsidiaries, thereby facilitating an often questionable allocation of revenue and profits. Tax justice advocates call for the elimination of these systems and the rapid implementation of worldwide unitary taxation with formulary apportionment, wherein an MNE would be treated as a single entity and its revenue and profits would be allocated more fairly to countries across the world based on added value. This would represent a dramatic break from the current tax regime, and unsurprisingly, MNEs and other status quo actors have lobbied vociferously against this concept. As discussed, the EU continues to explore the potential of unitary taxation but faces significant dissent from some member states and most MNEs. India has joined the EU in closely studying how a unitary taxation system could be carried out within India. Firms with international operations would be required to report data for their full international operations. Given the history of EU decision-making, India's unitary taxation initiative arguably has higher prospects of materializing, and even if it does not, it is a credible threat that can serve as a powerful bargaining chip for India in its efforts to push the boundaries of global tax reform. India stands out for being at the cutting edge of these efforts, and for illustrating that an uneven global landscape also means that some formerly accommodative parts of the global economy have turned resistant.

The significance of African developments

There are several significant points to highlight from the developments presented in Chapter 5 concerning the African region. First, Mauritian structures have frequently been deployed in a manner that is detrimental to sustainable African development. The natural resources sector stands out. Surprisingly, two of the most influential offshore business leaders in Mauritius concur. At the 2019 IFA conference in Mauritius, these critical views were voiced by Richard Arlove, the CEO of one of the foremost Mauritian offshore services providers, Ocorian, and by Rama Sithanen, the former Finance Minister and current Chairman of Sanne Mauritius, another top-tier offshore services provider in the country. Arlove argued that Mauritians should recognize that taking certain taxing rights away from developing African countries, only to tax that applicable income at 0%, has contributed substantially to the backlash that Mauritius now encounters. Arlove went so far as to call out Mauritian actors for the greed they have supported in the extractive industries. Sithanen seconded this viewpoint but tried to make a distinction between what he termed the "underground" and the "overground." When it comes to deals involving the "underground" – such as mining and other similar activities, which are essentially about taking raw materials out from under the ground and away from the countries of origin without creating much value in them – Arlove may be correct in calling out Mauritian tax structures. However, when it comes to deals involving the "overground" – such as building a hotel – Sithanen contends that professional services from Mauritius can facilitate projects that contribute significant value to African economies.

Africa is not monolithic, and at the broadest level, there are two country-level groupings in terms of their ability to tax, with those countries that are unable to capture at least 15% of their GDP in the form of taxes being particularly badly positioned. The current state of taxation in low-income African countries is of concern, especially in sub-Saharan Africa, due to the policy frameworks they have put in place and their tax collection capacities. As Fundira (2015, p. 20) notes of these countries, "governments are failing to harness their potential revenues – especially compared with their counterparts in developed countries." Even positive stories on rising tax revenue collection are largely stories on macroeconomic trends that are unrelated to fundamental tax reform. For example, when Mascagni et al. (2014, p. 11) describe the progress that has been made in the last decade, they do so in the following terms:

> In most emerging and low income countries, government revenues are on an upward path and on average they are increasing more in the post-crisis level than originally expected, partly due to good cyclical conditions and partly, in some cases, due to rising commodity prices.

This interpretation resonates with Arlove and Sithanen's emphasis on Mauritius's role in the extractive sector but also finds confirmation in the broader analysis presented here.

While the analysis in this book demonstrates that OFC-facilitated tax avoidance is under greater pressure than before, many additional changes must occur before comprehensive offshore reform takes hold. If interested observers are expecting full adherence to new global norms on taxation, the analysis found in this book will disappoint. Nevertheless, there are discernible seeds of possible future change, as follows: i) tax justice advocates and investigative journalists are shining a brighter light on offshore financial practices in Africa; ii) tax officials across the region are becoming better negotiators; and iii) international organizations are asking harder questions about the global tax system.

First, tax justice advocates and investigative journalists have proven to be critical agents in elevating the tax justice agenda. Investigative journalists have utilized raw data released by whistleblowers, uncovered unknown linkages, and pursued leads that have resulted in new narratives concerning the global offshore financial system. The resulting stories have been the product of genuine global journalism, as the ICIJ process brought together journalists from across the world. The ICIJ epitomizes what Berglez and Gearing (2018) aptly call "global network journalism." Domestic coalitions can also be critical. Consider the 1MDB case in Malaysia, so effectively told by Wright and Hope (2018), in which a journalist in Malaysia worked with a whistleblower and rival domestic political elites to uncover the scandal. For large MNEs, public pressure emanating from journalists and CSOs concerning tax avoidance can inflict reputational damage, and, in the case of Starbucks, as examined in detail by Dyreng et al. (2016), even corporate change.

Reporters in India have participated in these emergent global networks, most notably through their investigative research on Indian connections to the Panama Papers. The quality and range of stories published in the Indian media stand out. The newspaper *India Express*, especially through its reporter Ritu Sarin, has distinguished itself with high-quality investigative journalism. The question, then, becomes whether a similar process will play out in Africa. Until recently, signs did not point in this direction. Now, however, one can guardedly say that African journalists are starting to hold offshore financial users to account.

African journalists are engaged with the ICIJ network more than ever, with the first-ever involvement of journalists from Namibia (*The Namibian*) and Nigeria (*The Premium Times*) in the analysis of the Paradise Papers. More recently, African journalists stood at the forefront of a global effort, involving over 50 journalists based in 18 countries, to investigate the Mauritius Leaks. The Luanda Leaks drew on the journalistic skills of reporters in Angola, Mauritius, Mozambique, Namibia, and South Africa. A recent case exemplifies the potential of investigative journalism in Africa. A joint investigation by Finance Uncovered and journalists in Ghana, Nigeria, and Uganda, laid bare how MTN, the South African telecommunications giant, used offshore structures in Mauritius and Dubai to shift over US$1 billion out of its operations in Ghana, Nigeria, Uganda, and Côte d'Ivoire, under the guise of management and technical services fee payments as well as royalty payments (Turner, 2015).

This outcome is partially the result of specialized training designed by tax justice groups and journalists in the West with experience in researching offshore structures. The Centre for Investigative Journalism (CIJ) and Finance Uncovered have been running courses in London for African journalists and researchers, which build on the lessons that they have already learned from their own activities to prepare them for further investigative journalism. Topics include how to untangle webs of subsidiaries via registers in different national jurisdictions and how to better comprehend company accounts by analyzing financial statements, especially on the revenue side. In 2015, one of us participated in this course and observed journalists from six African countries: Botswana, Malawi, Nigeria, Sierra Leone, South Africa, and Uganda. Moreover, the ICIJ is now launching training programs for West African journalists in tandem with Cenozo, the Burkina Faso-based Norbert Zongo Cell for Investigative Journalism.

The analysis in this book illustrates the continuing demand for offshore financial structures to carry out business in Africa. Clearly, media reporting has not been powerful enough on its own to upend Africa's offshore finance equilibrium. The next decade will reveal whether civil society, led by journalists and CSOs, can reshape the political context. Given recent trends, it seems probable that journalists will make it more difficult for MNEs, HNWIs and political regimes to execute the sort of deals they were accustomed to during the 1990s and 2000s. An eye should be kept out for reporting on the outflows of foreign investments that take place in the coming years from deals that were completed via Mauritian offshore financial vehicles. Many of these transactions may be highly profitable for foreign investors, and these profits, because of the underlying Mauritius corporate structures, may depart the African economy in question with little or no capital gains tax paid. Headlines such as Fitzgibbon's (2017) "Tax haven Mauritius' rise comes at the rest of Africa's expense" may become more commonplace, eliciting further societal and governmental grievances.

Second, developing countries, including those in Africa, have significantly improved their negotiating abilities over time. A learning process is at play, Hearson (2018b) argues, and the terms of treaties become less biased against developing country interests over time. To this perspective, we can add the work of Moore (2014b) and Moore et al. (2015) on strategic investments into the development of the capacities of African tax administrations, including via the ATAF. Substantial resources have been invested in this project, both by governments themselves and by regional and international organizations. The overriding question then becomes whether African negotiators will act on their improved knowledge and negotiating skill-sets. The first response is to note that the improvement in these tax administrations is coming from a low base. The second and more important issue is whether the ideological commitment to the perceived foreign investment trade-off will constrain these negotiators in the future, as much as it has in the preceding two decades. This remains an open question.

Third, a more progressive ideological realignment within the IFIs, especially among their technocratic cadres, is also playing a role in the shifting discourse on OFCs in general, and Mauritius in particular. One recent paper, titled "The costs and benefits of tax treaties with investment hubs: Findings from sub-Saharan Africa," and published by both the IMF (Beer & Loeprick, 2018a) and the World Bank (Beer & Loeprick, 2018b), stands out in exemplifying this shift. The title is somewhat misleading because the paper's authors found plentiful evidence of the costs, and no evidence of the benefits of signing tax treaties with so-called investment hubs, or what we refer to as OFCs in this book. Based on a sample of 41 African economies from 1985 to 2015, the authors offer a direct refutation of the theory that the trade-off between attracting FDI and foregoing tax revenues leads to net positive outcomes. On the contrary, the authors conclude that the signing of tax treaties with OFCs – principally Mauritius – induced little foreign investment in sub-Saharan Africa beyond that which would have materialized anyway, and at the same time caused these governments substantial tax revenue losses. OFCs like Mauritius, the authors argue, incentivize MNEs to engage in profit shifting. Although this document is only a working paper, its publication by economists from the two most prominent and influential IFIs may add fuel to the fire, leading to further skepticism about tax treaties, and emboldening those African officials who have been questioning the economic value of tax treaties in the region. Not surprisingly, the paper has caused alarm among Mauritian elites. At the 2019 IFA conference in Mauritius, it was referenced by multiple speakers in panels and on the sidelines, with many expressing concerns about the possible repercussions of the paper's findings and its wider dissemination within elite circles in Africa.

The significance of Mauritian developments

In the wake of its changed relationship with India and the mounting number of damaging scandals, leaks, and hacks involving its offshore sector, Mauritius has sought to achieve three aims, namely: i) to convince regulators and other relevant authorities that it is not a tax haven; ii) to shift its offshore services to the African market; and iii) to cultivate higher value-added financial industries.

Just as it is with many other OFCs, Mauritius's vehement rejection of the tax haven label is a recurrent theme. For example, the case has been made in the wake of the global financial crisis (Gowrea, 2009), and it has resurfaced again following the Mauritius Leaks, when a considerably less contrite Rama Sithanen (2019) penned an article outlining several arguments why it is allegedly "blatantly wrong, flatly erroneous and definitionally incorrect to characterise Mauritius as a tax haven."

Sithanen's main argument why Mauritius cannot and should not be thought of as a tax haven is that the jurisdiction is fully compliant with OECD standards and has not been blacklisted by any of the other global standard-setting institutions. Historically, this statement is false. As demonstrated in Chapter 3, Mauritius has been blacklisted or greylisted by the OECD, the FATF, the FSF, and the IMF, and has also frequently appeared on the lists of tax havens of numerous major national bodies such as the US Senate (Palan et al., 2010, pp. 41–45). In recent years, Mauritius has indeed made it a priority to meet all new global standards in a timely manner, but even this has not kept it completely safe from all blacklists, as evidenced by the recent blacklisting threat from the EU, even though in the end it did not materialize. The fact that Mauritius is always on the razor's edge of falling afoul of some blacklisting criteria is itself a strong indication of how most of the world views its offshore sector. More importantly, this focus on global standards and blacklists bypasses the main argument advanced by critics of the offshore world, which is that the global standards are generally weak, and the blacklists highly politicized, so not getting blacklisted represents only the lowest possible bar. Crossing this bar is no indication that a jurisdiction is free from being defined as a tax haven. After all, most of the blacklists produced by the OECD frequently feature fewer than five and often only one or two so-called uncooperative jurisdictions,[1] usually small and largely inconsequential lowest common denominator OFCs. If the existence of tax havens was to be based solely on OECD blacklists, there would only be a handful of them in the world and offshore tax evasion and avoidance would barely register as a problem at all. As such, academic and civil society sources are the more accurate gauges for which jurisdictions are tax havens and which are not, and the consensus that Mauritius is one is unequivocal. Aside from the wealth of evidence already presented in this book, Garcia-Bernardo et al. (2017, pp. 2–6) rank Mauritius as eleventh among the world's "sink-OFC," which they define as "countries that attract and retain foreign capital," mostly having "small domestic economies and large values of foreign assets, which are attracted through low or zero corporate taxes," and are "usually characterized as tax havens." Mauritius also ranks fifteenth on the Tax Justice Network's most recent Corporate Tax Haven Index (TJN, 2021), with TJN Africa (2019) referring to the jurisdiction, together with the UAE, as being "among the most corrosive corporate tax havens against African countries." This claim is also supported by additional data from Cobham et al. (2020, p. 74), whose study found Mauritius to be Africa's "worst offender" when it comes to the jurisdiction's contribution to global tax losses.

Sithanen also argues that with its maximum effective corporate income tax rate of 3%, Mauritius is better than many other OFCs that levy a zero corporate tax, and as for the infamous capital gains exemption enabled by its DTAs, treaty partners are free to renegotiate that clause just as South Africa and India have. Although all of this is technically true, this argument has much closer to an admission of guilt than it does to a convincing defense, because instead of demonstrating that Mauritius is not a tax haven, it merely points out that it is not the worst one out there, while attempting to shift all blame on the treaty partners. What this argument conveniently omits is the subtle and often not so subtle international pressure that was put on developing countries to enter into as many DTAs and BITs as possible if they hoped to attract FDI, as well as the various information, expertise, and capacity asymmetries that were and still are often involved in such treaty negotiations between OFCs and developing countries. After all, even in the cases of South Africa and India, which as emerging powers have both long been much better positioned in all respects than most developing countries, it took decades of negative experiences and costly tax avoidance scandals before widely recognizing just how damaging the original arrangements were and mustering enough political will to remedy the situation. It is also not a coincidence that these two major renegotiations finally took place only at a time when the post-crisis anti-offshore backlash was already in full swing, significantly facilitating the process. As such, the argument that developing countries did not have to enter into DTAs at all, or could have negotiated better terms, or could have easily demanded renegotiation at any point in time and gotten their way, let alone without suffering reputational damage among investors, is not only disingenuous and misleading, but very reminiscent of the way in which predatory issuers and resellers of toxic subprime loans tried to blame what were often financially illiterate borrowers for the resulting financial crash. In both scenarios, it has indeed first and foremost been the system as a whole that has been broken but that does not mean that those profiting from it should be absolved of responsibility, even if they are not the ones profiting from that system the most.

Finally, Sithanen argues that Mauritius has played a constructive role in the development of many countries, pointing out that "Mauritius is the preferred jurisdiction in Africa for ALL development finance institutions," such as the World Bank's International Finance Corporation, the AfDB, Norfund, and many others. Throughout this book, we demonstrated numerous ways in which OFCs are detrimental to development, and yet, it is true that the use of OFCs by DFIs has been extensive. According to Carter (2017), the main reason behind this paradoxical use of OFCs by DFIs is that the former provide the latter with a politically stable and secure platform for investment. This not only makes up for what are often significant shortcomings in the legal systems of many of the poorest and most capital-scarce developing countries most in need of investment but at the same time also offers investors so-called tax neutrality, meaning that investing through, for example, Mauritius does not incur more tax losses than if the investment was direct. From this standpoint, the provision of such a platform is a valuable service that could foster investment that might otherwise not have taken place. Of course, this service could also be provided by any number of non-OFC jurisdictions, but Mauritius and other OFCs tend to be cheaper. However, the provision of this service cannot serve as a legitimate defense of Mauritius and other OFCs used by DFIs, because it is in no way dependent on the secrecy and the various exploitative tax practices enabled and facilitated by these jurisdictions. OFCs could with relative ease eliminate these negative features of their offshore models, and still continue to provide DFIs with a politically stable and secure platform for investment based on a trusted legal system and tax neutrality. As such, the fact that Mauritius is the preferred jurisdiction of DFIs investing in Africa is not only immaterial to whether it is a tax haven or not but it also does nothing to weaken the case against its offshore model.

In fact, over the past decade, and especially as the post-crisis anti-offshore backlash intensified, governments and CSOs alike have increasingly begun to question the use of OFCs by DFIs, focusing on several problems with this arrangement that could threaten its long-term viability. For example, as early as 2008, the Norwegian government appointed a Commission tasked with investigating and reporting on Norfund's use of tax havens as investment platforms (NOU, 2009). The Commission concluded that "tax havens represent an important hindrance to growth and development in poor countries, and that they make it opportune for the political and economic elites in developing countries to harm the development prospects of their own countries," leading it to several recommendations, including that "Norfund should gradually cease to make new fund investments via tax havens over a three-year period" (NOU, 2009, pp. 13–14). The main justification for this resolute recommendation was the Commission's identification of three possible detrimental effects of Norfund's use of tax havens, namely: "the loss of tax revenues by developing countries," a point which was explicitly illustrated on Mauritius's DTA network and its negative impact on African countries; the "maintaining" of "tax havens by providing them with income and legitimacy which, in turn, contributes to lower growth in poor countries"; and the risk of contributing to "money laundering and tax evasion" (NOU, 2009, pp. 82–85). What is also of interest is that Mauritius was not only referred to as a tax haven throughout the report but has actually been singled out as "an example of a tax haven" (NOU, 2009, p. 85). The Norwegian government eventually decided not to heed the Commission's recommendation against a blanket ban on Norfund's future use of tax havens but it did revise its rules and safeguards on their use, and in accordance with the general findings of the Commission's report "has taken gradual measures to reduce investments through OFCs" (Norad, 2015, p. 47). A few years later, conclusions similar to those of the Norwegian government's Commission were also reached by the CSO Eurodad, whose investigation of three multilateral and 14 bilateral DFIs found significant deficiencies and lack of ambition in terms of their internal standards on the use of tax havens, as well as their level of due diligence and portfolio transparency (Vervynckt, 2014). As a result of these pressures, the ties that previously bound OFCs and DFIs are increasingly becoming strained, and in some cases even severed (Fouche, 2017, 2021).

Going forward, as global standards and norms continue to tighten, unless Mauritius radically transforms its offshore sector away from enabling and facilitating offshore tax evasion and avoidance, it is highly unlikely that it will be able to succeed in persuading many relevant actors that it is not a tax haven. And if staying under the radar is no longer an option for its offshore sector, it will have to make itself as indispensable to as many actors as it can. In this vein, the Mauritian government and offshore services providers envisage a focus shift toward the growing African market, as well as financial upgrading, which denotes a financial sector that provides strategic and technical support to global and local investors. Despite providing significant earnings for the economy, the level of sophistication of Mauritius's OFC is still relatively low. Consider one of the fields widely considered to be a success story: private equity. Most private equity funds only domicile their funds in Mauritius, while conducting most of their business functions outside of Mauritius. Singapore and Switzerland are considered role models for capturing a significant share of the market for high-end offshore financial services. Senior Mauritian business officials frequently spoke admiringly about Singapore as a model for Mauritius as an African super-hub at the 2019 IFA conference in Mauritius. Can small states such as Mauritius undergo a process of financial upgrading? Given the nature of global competition, it is doubtful that Mauritius will transform its financial sector, pointing to the challenges of financial development among small emerging markets.

There are two conceivable images of Mauritius's financial future, both of which we have witnessed in person. In one image, there remain a considerable number of offshore financial services providers based in the capital, Port Louis, with offices in old buildings crammed full of paper files and filing cabinets. This suggests Mauritius may never move beyond serving as a back office in the global economy that provides administrative services. In the second image, there are the glass buildings in the neighborhood of Ebene, as depicted in global media campaigns run by the Mauritius government. Mauritius in this case is no longer peripheral; instead, it is on the path to becoming more like Singapore or Switzerland.

The optimistic scenario is expounded by younger Mauritians, particularly lawyers, accountants, and other private sector practitioners below the age of 45, nearly all of whom work in the private sector and not in government or political office. These elites tout the numerous advantages that propel the Mauritius OFC, as follows:

- Mauritius's unique historical connections to both India and many African countries;
- An educated and qualified multilingual workforce;
- Proficiency in, and wealth of experience with, both common law and civil law;
- Access to the Privy Council;
- An advantageous time zone;
- Political stability; and
- Natural beauty.

Older business elites in Mauritius tend to be far less sanguine about the country's economic and business outlook. These practitioners typically come from a broader social-scientific background rather than only law or accounting, such as economics, international relations, and political science. Many of them also have work-histories that include elected or appointed public office. One of the dividing lines between the younger and older professional generations concerns the assessment of the regulatory and competitive threats on the horizon for Mauritius. Older elites express more concern about the new regulatory agenda and the effect it will have on Mauritius. These elites believe that Mauritius's historical advantages are threatened in this new environment, and that there is an intense need for Mauritius to innovate and find ways to stay ahead of the regulatory and competitive curve. There are different ideas of what direction Mauritius should take to survive the headwinds, but most of these older elites are concerned that Mauritius is not moving in that direction, or has been far too slow in doing so.

The more optimistic Ebene image of a reinvigorated financial services hub in Mauritius is founded on three aspirations, as follows: i) the continuing growth of African markets; ii) the advent of new financial industries; and iii) the renewal of Indian commerce sparked by the preferential treatment of Indian debt transactions. However, there are significant impediments to each of these three points.

The potential of the African market

First, in terms of the potential of the African market, a CEO of a Mauritian MC explained to us that when they conduct business in African countries, "they don't treat us like India, with suspicion. They look up to Mauritius and they want to become like Mauritius" (anonymous interview, Mauritius, 2014). This comment points to a reserve of goodwill that could lay the foundation for closer Mauritius–Africa financial ties. The African continent holds potential for Mauritius, but it is difficult to imagine that it will surpass India's economic contribution.

Indian deals transacted through a Mauritian business structure have tended to be substantially bigger than African deals. Using FSC (2020a; 2020b) data, we calculated the 2019 value of all of the investment made in India and in African countries through Mauritian companies, including direct investment and portfolio investment. Of this total investment, worth over US$774 billion, 54% was located in India and only 10% in Africa. This measurement of actual economic activity in Mauritius rebuts business and government rhetoric, reported in global media outlets such as *Reuters* (Blair, 2015) and the *Financial Times* (Houlder, 2016), that over half of the incorporated companies are focused on doing business in Africa. These figures represent an expression of interest rather than realized foreign investment flows, and these planned investments may not materialize. These investments may also be low in value. Consider that an Indian-focused private equity fund registered in Mauritius could reach well beyond US$500 million in capital, whereas that of most African-focused private equity funds would be less than US$100 million.

There will be winners in the Mauritian private sector if African economies expand further, especially in fields such as private equity. The private equity industry speaks positively about investing in Africa via Mauritius, with seemingly no intention of looking elsewhere to domicile funds (FSD Africa & EMPEA, 2015). A survey of senior private equity executives found that 97% of private equity funds that are domiciled in Mauritius were either satisfied or very satisfied with the jurisdiction, "despite the fact that the market has come under political criticism in recent years, and is viewed suspiciously by some civil society groups" (FSD Africa & EMPEA, 2015, p. 13). However, the overall pattern is that most Mauritian offshore financial services providers are unprepared for a post-India era. These MCs ran long-standing businesses servicing clients investing in India and collecting management fees in the process. Given the strong demand for Mauritian offshore financial vehicles since the mid-1990s, few MCs explored markets beyond India. As the former director of Mauritius's Financial Services Commission noted: "it was so easy to get the business . . . all you needed was a fax machine" (interview with Iqbal Rajahbalee, Mauritius, 2016). Clients would approach Mauritian MCs directly, without MCs even needing to properly invest in marketing programs.

Many debates on shaping the future of offshore services in Mauritius took place during the late 1990s. The lobby for low-cost incorporations was powerful, with the majority of MCs concerned that small MCs would be disadvantaged if there was active encouragement of investment funds and wealth management (multiple interviews, Mauritius, 2014 and 2016). As time went on, a number of MCs developed expertise in fund management and gained a share of the African and Indian hedge fund and private equity markets. Today, these top MCs are pushing into new markets. Most of the offshore financial industry, in contrast, was short-sighted in its ambitions, leaving it ill-prepared once the Indian tax loophole was gone and thus constraining the ability of the Mauritian government to translate policy intentions concerning financial upgrading into market outcomes.

Until now, there has been little in the way of long-term strategic thinking between government and business concerning the future of offshore finance in Mauritius. One of the founding figures of the Mauritian OFC lamented the lack of action by the political class and by offshore practitioners to respond proactively to growing criticisms of tax treaty shopping and unfair sharing of taxation rights (interview with Sushil Khushiram, Mauritius, 2019). Government and business officials hold considerably different interpretations of this outcome. In interviews, leading MCs in Mauritius stressed their investment in African offices and their constant travel to Africa to cultivate new business. When asked, few of these executives could point to government support to open doors in Africa. Several observed that they could not remember a targeted roadshow that Mauritius had organized in Africa, in contrast to many other OFCs. The most successful MCs in India and Africa, Sanne and Ocorian, respectively, have developed their own client base without any direct government involvement.

At the same time, government officials are deeply critical of MCs. One official stated that in the wake of the revised DTA with India, "we told MCs that you are going to get hit and the business sector said, you as the government should give us some ideas" (anonymous interview with a Financial Services Promotion Agency [FSPA] official, Mauritius, 2016). Another official commented that "they [MCs] are waiting for the Chinese to come to them when you have to go and get Chinese clients" (anonymous interview, Mauritius, 2016). One cited example concerned an occasion when Mauritius assembled a team to visit a major offshore summit in China and sent out invitations to MCs, but few Mauritian MCs joined the delegation (anonymous interview, Mauritius, 2016). Only a small number of MCs have had the vision and resources to participate widely in the field. The conclusion is that the top-tier MCs in Mauritius – companies such as Sanne, Ocorian, DTOS, and Intercontinental Trust – look set to continue successfully navigating the global economy, but the remainder of Mauritian MCs are in a weaker position. It is a top-heavy industry with the top 5 companies controlling much of the market and fewer than 25 of these companies holding over 90% of the market (anonymous interview with a government official, Mauritius, 2016).

The potential of new financial industries

Financial upgrading is no small task for a country like Mauritius. Mauritian operators have been collecting small management fees for providing administration services to companies that qualify for tax advantages under the India–Mauritius DTA. This work pales in comparison to the higher-end financial services provided in jurisdictions such as Singapore and Switzerland. Another complicating factor, as discussed in Chapter 4, is that market niches in the global offshore economy are enduring and tough to disrupt. There are niches in particular countries for offshore finance, and professional networks that coalesce around them. While Mauritius certainly has its strengths, any significant disruption of these established niches and networks in favor of Mauritius remains unlikely. These factors also call into question the extent to which government-led initiatives can catalyze new financial activity in Mauritius.

Mauritius intensified its pursuit of new financial industries in March 2016 when it created the Financial Services Promotion Agency (FSPA). The FSPA aims to rebrand Mauritius and produce a more diversified financial sector. The principal instrument is a tax incentive program. The longest tax breaks are designated for enterprises that set up regional headquarters in Mauritius, with shorter tax holidays offered to operations launched by firms in the areas of asset management, family offices, foundations, and investment banking. What the government's program fails to recognize is the significant obstacles created by global financial competition. There is no proven record of countries successfully using tax holidays to achieve financial upgrading, especially in an already low-tax economy such as Mauritius. As it stands, there are few investment banks and private banks present in Mauritius, local firms have limited capabilities to launch new investment banking and wealth management divisions, and there have been few companies interested in the tax exemptions available in these spheres. An immediate solution would be to open the economy further to foreign financial workers, as advocated by interviewees such as the former Finance Minister (interview with Rama Sithanen, Mauritius,

2014). Yet, there is no track record of Mauritius being able to entice such workers, and it is doubtful whether financial professionals in Dubai, Hong Kong, or Singapore would exit those markets for Mauritius, given the slew of challenges and inconveniences that await them there. According to one disillusioned foreign executive (Yann Duchesne, as quoted in Fortado, 2016), whose highly critical comments appeared in the *Financial Times*, residents of Mauritius are faced with "a lack of outbound and inbound flights, a dearth of suitable housing, a non-existent social life and daily traffic jams, as well as prohibitive government bureaucracy when trying to hire foreigners." A local executive (Richard Arlove, as quoted in Fortado, 2016) concedes: "Are we a global financial centre that encourages people to live here? We still have a way to go." In summary, few OFCs have moved beyond their specific offshore segments. It will take greater effort and more time for Mauritius to break from this mold.

The potential of new entry points into the Indian market

When the revised DTA with India was announced, the offshore industry in Mauritius vociferously expressed its displeasure. In our discussions with offshore practitioners, there were two messages: first, that Mauritius was targeted by Indian negotiators because the country holds less power than Singapore or the UAE, and second, that Mauritius failed to gain assurances from India that it would negotiate similar DTAs with other partners. The offshore sector's reasoning proved mistaken when India effectively negotiated the same tax deal with rival jurisdictions after Mauritius. These changes established a level playing field for jurisdictions mediating foreign investment into India. However, there was one exception. The deals signed by other jurisdictions mirrored the Mauritius DTA, except the Mauritian agreement included a lower withholding tax on debt transactions. In contrast with the expectations of Mauritian offshore actors, it was Singapore, Mauritius's principal competitor, that ended up with the slightly worse agreement.

Mauritius was left with one small advantage: the tax rate on debt interest income for a Mauritius-registered investment is lower than for similar investments made through other jurisdictions. Any debt transaction through a Singaporean company into India must pay a tax rate double that of a Mauritian company. India's demand for debt in corporate transactions is potentially sizable given that Indian debt markets are shallow compared to equity markets. Foreign expertise to supply debt services could be demanded. The more optimistic elements of the public and private sectors of Mauritius look excitedly at the resultant business prospects. Nevertheless, structuring a deal with debt is significantly different than structuring a deal with equity and Mauritian operators only have experience and networks in equity deal-making. As the head of an offshore financial services provider told us, despite his Master's degree in finance and years of offshore experience, he lacks any specialized training or familiarity with structuring debt deals generally, and specifically with regard to India's debt markets (interview with Roshan Boodhoo, Mauritius, 2016). He estimated that it would take years to develop this knowledge and to foster new business. It is therefore unrealistic to expect Mauritius to be able to seize this tax advantage to a great extent. The scale of this challenge is evident when one examines the assets held by Mauritius companies operating in the global economy, predominantly in India. Only 4% of these assets are held in debt securities (FSC, 2020a; 2020b). In the two years since the beneficial provisions of the DTA with India were removed, Mauritius has fallen behind Singapore in channeling capital into India. According to DPIIT (2021) data, in 2019, Singapore captured double the market share of India's inward investment (36% of total FDI) compared with Mauritius (18% of total FDI), and in 2020, it came close to doing so again (29% of total FDI compared with 16% of total FDI).

Mauritius's comparative advantages

Although the Mauritian OFC is diminished, it will not disappear. It still carries particular advantages in the regional and global political economies. First, Mauritius is better placed than its African financial competitors. One investor bemoaned the currency controls in place across Africa, noting by way of contrast how "I can do 20 African currencies in Mauritius" (anonymous interview with a foreign investor, Mauritius, 2014). It is significantly more difficult for large economies, such as those of Nigeria, Kenya, and South Africa, to remove exchange controls. In these contexts, where exchange controls are still widespread, small states in the global economy step in and service regional/global business demand by handling multiple currencies. Second, Mauritius has one of the most open travel systems in the region, with extensive visa exemptions, enabling African investors to enter Mauritius with ease. Third, Mauritius has a high per capita rate of trained offshore services professionals. It has over 3,300 registered professional accountants (Mauritius Institute of Professional Accountants [MIPA], 2021), with skills that are increasingly in demand in the global economy. The human resources of Mauritius related to global finance are also on the rise, with some of the most oversubscribed university programs being joint programs combining financial services with law and management run by the University of Mauritius and the University of Technology, Mauritius. Fourth, the costs for an offshore company to establish a minimally defensible presence in Mauritius are far lower than those in Dubai or Singapore. Fifth, Mauritius offsets the economic and political risk of doing business in Africa cheaper than most of its direct competitors. Some global investors are wary of domestic regimes. Fairly or not, a corporate lawyer who guides foreign capital into Africa explains that "no one wants to be a shareholder in a Ghanaian company" (anonymous interview, Hong Kong, 2015). Instead, foreign investors structure deals offshore through Mauritius. While the notion that African deal-making is risky is perhaps exaggerated, it is nonetheless a view that is still commonly held (see Table 6.1).

Table 6.1 Mauritius – Significant Presence (Top 5) by FDI Stock in African Countries* – 2015–2019 (Billions of USD)

		2015	2016	2017	2018	2019
		(#) $ bn (%)	*(#) $ bn (%)*	*(#) $ bn (%)*	*(#) $ bn (%)*	*(#) $ bn (%)*
Botswana	**Inward**	(4) 0.57 (17%)	(3) 0.58 (11%)	(3) 0.70 (14%)	(3) 0.60 (12%)	(3) 0.34 (6%)
	Outward	(1) 0.23 (37%)	(1) 0.28 (26%)	(1) 0.35 (26%)	(1) 0.32 (25%)	Ø
Côte d'Ivoire	**Inward**	N/A	(4) 0.29 (6%)	Ø	(4) 0.46 (5%)	Ø
	Outward	N/A	Ø	Ø	Ø	Ø
Morocco	**Inward**	Ø	Ø	Ø	Ø	Ø
	Outward	N/A	Ø	(4) 0.32 (7%)	(5) 0.24 (5%)	(5) 0.23 (4%)
Mozambique	**Inward**	(3) 3.86 (14%)	(2) 6.96 (20%)	(3) 5.86 (15%)	(3) 6.09 (15%)	(3) 6.41 (15%)
	Outward	Ø	N/A	N/A	N/A	N/A
Namibia	**Inward**	(3) 0.14 (3%)	Ø	Ø	Ø	(2) 0.45 (7%)
	Outward	N/A	N/A	N/A	N/A	N/A
Rwanda	**Inward**	(1) 0.38 (27%)	(1) 0.54 (32%)	(1) 0.63 (32%)	(1) 0.80 (35%)	(1) 0.92 (35%)
	Outward	N/A	N/A	N/A	N/A	N/A
Seychelles	**Inward**	(1) 0.36 (37%)	(1) 0.32 (37%)	(1) 0.33 (39%)	(1) 0.42 (44%)	(1) 0.34 (45%)
	Outward	N/A	N/A	N/A	N/A	N/A
South Africa	**Inward**	Ø	Ø	Ø	Ø	Ø
	Outward	(4) 9.97 (6%)	(3) 10.79 (6%)	(3)** 11.44 (4%)	(3) 20.61 (8%)	(4) 11.23 (5%)
Tanzania	**Inward**	(5) 0.54 (4%)	N/A	N/A	N/A	N/A
	Outward	N/A	N/A	N/A	N/A	N/A

(Continued)

Table 6.1 (Continued)

		2015			*2016*			*2017*			*2018*			*2019*		
		(#)	*$ bn*	*(%)*	*(#)*	*$ bn*	*(%)*	*(#)*	*$ bn*	*(%)*	*(#)*	*$ bn*	*(%)*	*(#)*	*$ bn*	*(%)*
Togo	**Inward**	(4)	0.09	(5%)	(5)	0.07	(3%)		Ø			Ø			N/A	
	Outward		Ø			Ø			Ø			Ø			N/A	
Uganda	**Inward**	(5)	0.52	(6%)	(5)	0.37	(4%)	(5)	0.52	(6%)	(5)	0.65	(7%)		N/A	
	Outward		N/A			N/A			N/A			N/A			N/A	
Zambia	**Inward**		Ø			Ø			Ø			Ø			Ø	
	Outward	(1)	0.30	(24%)	(2)	0.23	(13%)		Ø			Ø			Ø	

Note: **(#)** = Mauritius's position in the Top 5 for that country/year/direction; **$ bn** = The amount of Mauritius's FDI stock for that country/year/direction; **(%)** = Percentage of the total FDI stock for that country/year/direction; **Inward** = From Mauritius into the applicable African country; **Outward** = From the applicable African country into Mauritius; **Ø** = Mauritius is not in the Top 5 for that country/year/direction; **N/A** = Data not available.

* Aside from Mauritius, the IMF Coordinated Direct Investment Survey (CDIS) data set features the following 24 African countries: Algeria, Benin, Botswana, Burkina Faso, Cabo Verde, Côte d'Ivoire, Eswatini, Ghana, Guinea, Guinea-Bissau, Mali, Morocco, Mozambique, Namibia, Niger, Nigeria, Rwanda, Senegal, Seychelles, South Africa, Tanzania, Togo, Uganda, and Zambia.

** The IMF CDIS data set lists Mauritania here instead of Mauritius. However, given the clear trend exhibited by Mauritius in the previous as well as the following years, and the fact that Mauritania is a much smaller economy, is not an OFC, and does not appear in South Africa's Top 5 as either a source or a host in any other year on record, it is most likely a mistake, and has been treated here as such.

Source: (IMF, 2021).

Finally, Mauritius has so far faced relatively little OFC competition from other parts of Africa. Broadly speaking, scholars note that aside from Johannesburg, cities in sub-Saharan Africa are "largely disconnected" from the global economy (Geyer, 2019, p. 233). South Africa is the natural rival to Mauritius in providing financial services to African and foreign investors striking deals in the region. However, South Africa has not yet established itself as a financial center to global investors due to its economic fragility, domestic governance weaknesses, and dangers to the personal security of residents. In fact, as Oguttu (2017, p. 15) writes:

> South African companies also often route investments into other African countries via Mauritius because it has negotiated better benefits (such as lower withholding tax rates) in its tax treaties with some African countries than is the case with South Africa.

Officials in Mauritius report growing levels of interest among South African companies in establishing regional headquarters for non-South African operations in Mauritius, in addition to interest among HNWIs, funds, and family offices in exploring Mauritian offshore financial domiciles (anonymous interview with a FSPA official, Mauritius, 2016). We can add that during fieldwork we observed South Africans as highly visible business owners in the tourism and real estate sectors of Mauritius. Other African countries are implausible candidates to displace Mauritius. One Mauritian official correctly points out that "No one is worried about Morocco as financial centre competition" (anonymous interview, Mauritius, 2014). Some potential OFCs have shelved their plans (e.g., the Gambia and Ghana), and others (e.g., the Seychelles) have suffered scandals severely damaging their reputation (Robertson, 2020). Kenya bears watching, but its OFC initiative to date has amounted to little (Waris, 2014). The greatest threat to Mauritius actually lies outside of Africa, coming from consolidated survivor OFCs such as Dubai, and core OFCs such as the Netherlands (see Table 6.2).

Dubai has a wide tax treaty network through the UAE and better DTAs with African countries than both South Africa and Mauritius (multiple interviews). Importantly, the UAE's tax treaty with South Africa is slightly more favorable than the equivalent Mauritius–South Africa DTA. One interviewee, a UK transfer pricing expert, added that "people actually want to live there" (anonymous interview, Mauritius, 2019), and this is important for clients who have to demonstrate a degree of substance when setting up an offshore financial structure. Another trend to follow is core OFCs further afield that are looking to Africa as their normal client base declines. Mauritius has been a proverbial "big fish in a little pond," but that is about to change. Going forward, it is likely to face competitive challenges from core OFCs seeking to expand into the next big growth markets, especially European OFCs that are more hamstrung than before by EU regulations.

Is there still room in the global economy for offshore finance-led development strategies among small economies? The answer to this question is yes. Similarly, the answer to the question of whether Mauritius holds continuing advantages in

Table 6.2 Mauritius and Its OFC Competitors – Total FDI Stock of Their Significant Presence in African Countries[*] – 2015–2019 (Billions of USD)

		Significant Presence (Top 5) in African Countries by FDI Stock	*Total FDI Stock – 2015–2019*[**]	
			Inward	*Outward*
Mauritius	12	Botswana, Côte d'Ivoire, Morocco, Mozambique, Namibia, Rwanda, Seychelles, South Africa, Tanzania, Togo, Uganda, Zambia	41.11	66.54
UK	18	Algeria, Botswana, Burkina Faso, Cabo Verde, Côte d'Ivoire, Eswatini, Guinea, Mali, Morocco, Mozambique, Namibia, Nigeria, Senegal, Seychelles, South Africa, Tanzania, Uganda, Zambia	337.85	110.67
Netherlands	6	Morocco, Mozambique, Nigeria, Rwanda, South Africa, Uganda	254.33	111.41
UAE	5	Ghana, Guinea, Morocco, Mozambique, Zambia	91.02	0.46
Bermuda	2	Burkina Faso, Nigeria	73.35	3.75
Ireland	3	Cabo Verde, Ghana[***], Zambia	21.82[***]	0
BVI	6	Ghana, Mali, Namibia, Nigeria, Seychelles, Zambia	17.58	0
Switzerland	5	Algeria, Benin, Guinea, Morocco, Zambia	17.12	0.96
Cayman Islands	3	Côte d'Ivoire, Ghana, Nigeria	8.76	2.69
Barbados	2	Burkina Faso, Mali	3.27	0
Luxembourg	6	Botswana, Côte d'Ivoire, Guinea-Bissau, Morocco, South Africa, Zambia	1.08	21.66

Note: **Inward** = From Mauritius or its applicable OFC competitors into the applicable African countries; **Outward** = From the applicable African countries into Mauritius or its applicable OFC competitors.

[*] Aside from Mauritius, the IMF Coordinated Direct Investment Survey (CDIS) data set features the following 24 African countries: Algeria, Benin, Botswana, Burkina Faso, Cabo Verde, Côte d'Ivoire, Eswatini, Ghana, Guinea, Guinea-Bissau, Mali, Morocco, Mozambique, Namibia, Niger, Nigeria, Rwanda, Senegal, Seychelles, South Africa, Tanzania, Togo, Uganda, and Zambia.

[**] Subject to data availability, which can vary significantly across countries/years/directions in the IMF CDIS data set.

[***] For 2017 and 2018, the IMF CDIS data set attributes 5.72 billion and 6.68 billion in Ghana's inward FDI stock to the UK instead of Ireland. However, given the clear trend exhibited by Ireland in the previous years, the fact that the UK does not appear in Ghana's Top 5 as either a source or a host in any other year on record, and that the UK's Department for International Trade (DIT) has itself reported the UK's outward FDI stock in Ghana to only have been 0.32 billion in 2018 and 0.20 billion in 2019 (DIT, 2021), it is most likely a mistake, and has been treated here as such.

Source: (IMF, 2021).

the global offshore economy is also yes. Nevertheless, the central point remains that despite this room to maneuver, the Mauritius–India offshore relationship was a unique one that Mauritius will be unable to replicate with Africa.

Arrested development and OFCs

Waris and Seabrooke (2018) argue that OFCs in Africa represent a form of "arrested development." There are undoubtedly problems with such OFCs, and recent leaks about the nature of offshore financial behavior by individuals and companies have further reinforced this point. Just as global accounting firms surreptitiously serviced demand for offshore financial structures, as discussed in Chapters 2 and 3, most recently the Luanda Leaks revealed the number of corporate services providers (CSPs) in Mauritius that are willing to operate in the "grey zone" of the global offshore economy. In a real-life repeat of the well-known experiment of testing the due diligence practices of CSPs (Findley et al., 2014), a Portuguese lawyer contacted a small number of Mauritius CSPs on behalf of the dos Santos business empire and explained that the ultimate beneficial owner who was seeking to design Mauritian offshore structures was a PEP (Fitzgibbon, 2020a). Three CSPs quickly replied and offered their services to create and administer a Mauritian corporate structure. In another instance, a family friend of dos Santos, who had won a US$3 billion investment from Angola's sovereign wealth fund, approached Mauritian CSPs for company formation assistance, after being turned down by CSPs in Jersey and the Isle of Man (Khan, 2020). This individual (Jean-Claude Bastos do Morais) and his financial entity (Quantum Global Fund) found willing CSP partners in Mauritius.

While these practices are disappointing, they are also par for the course among OFCs. Nonetheless, ICIJ's Shiel and Fitzgibbon (2019) may have gone too far in asserting of Mauritius that "the island's economic success has been built on offering investors tax advantages." Mauritian elites continually reject the notion that the country is a tax haven, with one retort being that "Mauritius is not a tax haven and we have nothing to hide; the money is not kept here and it flows elsewhere" (interview with Nikhil Treebhoohun, Mauritius, 2016). This is really more of a technicality, because shell companies employed in treaty shopping tax structures are also a problematic feature of global finance, not just offshore bank accounts. Another common rejoinder from Mauritian elites is that the offshore sector is a small percentage of the national economy. This is a fairer reply. Mauritius boasts a more diversified economy than many small conduit economies. The offshore sector only contributed to 5.8% of Mauritius's GDP in 2019 (Bank of Mauritius, 2020); it was never the principal driver of Mauritius's economy as the ICIJ makes it out to be.

Moreover, this is a country lauded by political scientists (Sandbrook, 2005) and economists (Subramanian & Roy, 2021) alike for "successfully building a diverse economy, a democratic political system and a strong safety net" (Stiglitz, 2011). These achievements of the Mauritian economic policy are partly the result of high-salary employment and high profits generated by the offshore financial sector. Over a decade ago, Frankel (2010, p. 11) asked: "Is the move to banking a wishful-thinking pursuit of a mirage in the desert?" The answer was not reassuring for Mauritius: "Not quite. But neither can the island realistically see itself as the next Singapore . . . If the financial center is built on Indians using a bilateral investment treaty for round-tripping, it is unlikely to be durable" (Frankel, 2010, p. 11). Today, the evidence suggests that this prediction was mostly correct.

The capital gains exemption with India has been eliminated, and with all likelihood, this will cause a net loss to Mauritius, particularly because it is doubtful that Africa will produce a larger economic contribution to the Mauritian economy than India did over the previous decades, or that new financial industries, such as captive insurance and wealth management, will develop substantively in the jurisdiction. While the Mauritian case is not quite arrested development, it is nonetheless accurate to say that the influence of the financial sector has detracted from more strategic investment in other sectors. Had Mauritius chosen to strategically invest in the information technology sector, for example, that sector could have become more integral to the contemporary Mauritian economy. Now, Mauritius is confronting a middle-income trap with weak productivity growth, rising youth unemployment, and insufficient research and development investment (Tandrayen-Ragoobur & Kasseeah, 2018).

However, the end of the capital gains exemption with India is not the complete end of Mauritius as an OFC. Although Mauritius fails to live up to its depiction in commercials broadcast on CNN and on social media, it will continue to perform an intermediation role in the global economy. Just as in its earlier history with India, a Mauritian offshore vehicle nearly always offers lower capital gains taxes for foreign investors than would be paid if the enterprise invested directly in many of Africa's economies. Mauritius is a consolidated survivor OFC, which has pushed aside less viable OFCs. Despite this, neither the government nor the private sector in Mauritius appear to be well-positioned for a major advance into African markets. The few top Mauritian MCs are the exception. These are professionalized firms with extensive networks outside of Mauritius and they are finding new sources of profit in Africa. They are dynamic, profitable, and growing fast. The prospects of attracting new financial industries to locate themselves in Mauritius are similarly frustrated, in this instance by the exclusivity of offshore niches in the global economy. Finally, the execution of debt deals in India via Mauritian companies, while incentivized in the revised DTA, is hampered by the shortage of financial experience in debt structuring within Mauritius. Given the advantages that Mauritius holds and the likelihood that foreign capital and pan-African capital will seek out deals in African markets, Mauritius will continue to serve as a mid-tier OFC. However, the enormous amounts of capital that have flowed into India via Mauritius in the last two decades represent a unique moment in the history of the global offshore economy and an unrealizable future for the Mauritius–Africa relationship.

This chapter has detailed both optimistic and pessimistic trend lines concerning the integration of India, Africa, and Mauritius in the global economy. Optimistic trends are becoming more noticeable and there are grounds to think that these geographies will feature more just tax systems in the future than in the past, even though there are clear divisions in Africa, and Mauritius appears to be a status quo economy.

Note

1 Unlike in the past, the OECD nowadays generally does not use the term "tax haven."

7 Conclusion

Unknown to many experts outside India, the small island state of Mauritius has served as the offshore financial gateway to India for over two decades, turning Mauritius into a significant site within global capitalism. Since 1993, India and Mauritius have been closely linked through a capital-friendly treaty that enabled Mauritius to become the largest investor in India's economy, by a wide margin. Mauritius offered an economical option for investors to deploy capital in India, while also gaining tax benefits and a faster and more welcoming business and legal environment than in India. India's resolute action against offshore finance, including the long-standing Mauritius route, is an important case study to reflect upon, given the uncertainty over whether the global offshore financial system is unraveling. In the wake of India's decision to take a harder line against the Mauritian OFC, Mauritius has chosen to market itself as the financial gateway to Africa. Mauritius is, therefore, at the forefront of an active attempt by OFCs to capture a share of the market of investment flows that are rising in emerging markets. Africa represents a test for whether Mauritius can maintain a key place in the global economy as a jurisdiction servicing demand for offshore financial services. One of the central questions that this book has sought to answer is: does the Mauritius–Africa relationship exhibit continuity, suggesting that there is still space for offshore flows in global finance, or alternatively, does it exhibit similar fault lines to the Mauritius–India relationship?

Turning first to the contest over the bilateral tax deal between India and Mauritius, Indian tax authorities, social movements, CSOs, and journalists persistently applied pressure by questioning the Mauritian OFC, but the pressure generated was insufficient to induce the parties to amend the DTA. Elites in both India and Mauritius weathered these challenges and maintained the Mauritian offshore channel. Partly as a result of the seismic changes taking place at the global level, shifting views surfaced at the start of the Modi regime. As Indian officials surveyed the Indian economy and its global competitors, they concluded that India's market was sufficiently attractive that the special treatment of offshore-based foreign investors was no longer justifiable. For its part, Mauritius was forced to agree to renegotiate the DTA on the basis of new global policy pressures and the erroneous strategies of new Mauritian elites. The newly appointed Minister of Financial Services and Good Governance in Mauritius clung to the impractical notion that

DOI: 10.4324/9781003161011-7

Mauritius could rapidly upgrade its financial sector without relying on the Indian market. Structural change also shaped the decision-making of political elites. India had become a different economy by 2016, with a healthier capital position. At the same time, the international community united to a surprising degree to craft new guidelines on the taxation of global business and India committed to following and in some aspects even surpassing these guidelines, having served as a particularly active participant during the G20/OECD negotiations. In particular, India shaped the BEPS agenda in multilateral negotiations and then committed itself more fully to the BEPS deliverables than other emerging markets.

The question then becomes whether India's stricter line with Mauritius is indicative of a more tightly regulated global economy, in which offshore business will wane. More specifically, is the Mauritius–India case replicable in other parts of the developing world, all of which are engaged to some extent with offshore finance? Clearly, the 2016 Mauritius–India pact is one step forward in the global movement toward tax justice. Shell companies should not be treated as Mauritius-resident companies and India has the right to collect its own capital gains taxes. Nevertheless, settling these issues took over two decades, which suggests that despite India having made progress, caution should prevail before larger conclusions are drawn. The analysis in the preceding chapters demonstrates that India represents an exceptional case among emerging markets, and that its experiences are not fully applicable to other settings.

Although African countries are under pressure to conform to the new global standards and norms, significant leeway remains for these countries to continue business-friendly agreements with Mauritius in the pursuit of foreign investment inflows. OECD processes are fashioning norms but they are not yet transformative in practice. Large parts of the African economy remain integrated in the global offshore financial system. However, the scale of the region's involvement in offshore flows needs to be contextualized. Africa's market for inbound offshore-registered investment is much smaller than that of India and it is difficult to foresee Africa soon approaching the capital volumes that India has generated over the last two decades. Clearly, Africa is not a panacea for Mauritius's financial sector in the wake of India's tougher stance on offshore finance.

The broader significance of these developments is that the offshore financial network is no longer as unobstructed as in its earlier incarnation. Its demise, however, is surely exaggerated. The global politics of offshore financial reform are inextricably linked to decisions taken at a national level and how national decision-makers translate global norms into national reforms. BITs and DTAs are financial texts that enable substantially higher flows of finance within the global economy. The largely liberal and pro-investment rules enshrined in BITs and DTAs are being renegotiated, but the modification and implementation of these agreements in the Mauritius–Africa case do not prohibit the use of offshore financial services. In addition, the boldest proposals for global tax reform are constrained by the nationally rooted international system and the lack of binding global law. Consider proposals such as the global wealth tax advanced by Thomas Piketty or the global asset registry advanced by Gabriel Zucman.

Two keen observers argue that such far-reaching initiatives "require too much global cooperation among governments to be realistic" (Avi-Yonah & Xu, 2016, p. 15). And yet, as the CRS, the BEPS project, and perhaps most of all BEPS 2.0 have demonstrated, significant global cooperation among governments in the area of taxation is possible. Although Piketty's and Zucman's proposals may be too ambitious in the foreseeable future, it was only recently that the same was true of automatic exchange of tax information, beneficial ownership registers, country-by-country reporting, and worldwide unitary taxation with formulary apportionment. Today, the first three, while imperfect in their execution and unevenly applied, have essentially become global standards, and as for the fourth, even many skeptical observers concede that the prospects for at least some form of unitary taxation with formulary apportionment have risen considerably (Avi-Yonah & Kir, 2019). Still, as impressive as this pace of progress has been, the road ahead is long and filled with uncertainty.

Developments that would put into question the findings of the book

Should the analysis in this book be flawed, then other developments may materialize in the coming years. The global movement against offshore tax evasion and avoidance may gain political strength faster than anticipated here, and global change would crystallize in a near-universally held tougher approach, including in Africa. This scenario could be ignited by one factor in particular in the African region. As many foreign investments in Africa are relatively nascent, only a small number of African deals with an underlying Mauritian offshore structure have been sold. However, in the coming five to ten years, a substantial number of Mauritius-led African investments will be exited, many of which will be subject to low or zero rates of capital gains taxation and many of which may be highly profitable transactions in the natural resources and telecommunications sectors. Inevitably, this will spark a degree of tension domestically and regionally. Offshore tightening could be spurred by deepening opposition within African societies, fueled by discontent over profits being withdrawn from these countries with virtually no taxes paid. African societies are increasingly asking hard questions about the political economy of the mining industry and the paltry tax rates paid by the biggest mining companies (Moore et al., 2018). Recently, a Senegalese official told a journalist that one of the reasons that Senegal withdrew from its DTA with Mauritius was out of a concern for tax losses from its newly unearthed oil and gas fields (Fitzgibbon, 2020b).

There are high-profile precedents outside the African region. Three US private equity firms – the Carlyle Group, Newbridge Capital, and Lone Star Funds – probably thought they were playing a highly strategic hand by structuring their investments in Korea during the Asian financial crisis through lower-tax jurisdictions with DTAs with Korea. When these highly profitable investments were exited without any capital gains taxes paid in Korea, the subsequent public uproar led to multi-year investigations and legal challenges for these private equity funds.

Negative stories on African corporate transactions could be published by newly emerging investigative journalists and CSO leaders and widely shared, resulting in more extensive domestic criticism. This would also be a PR challenge for Mauritius. Senior Mauritian figures fear two outcomes most: for the country to be blacklisted and for DFIs to pull out of Mauritius. Hosting DFIs in Mauritius, and having them structure deals via Mauritius, provides credibility to the Mauritian OFC, which could be imperiled by such African developments.

In contrast to this possible scenario, other future factors may support accommodative forces over resistant forces. First, post-Brexit UK may undermine global standards by seeking to entice global capital with further corporate tax breaks and incentives, thereby providing a demonstration effect to other countries. Second, there is uncertainty about China's trajectory with regard to the global offshore economy going forward. Over the last two decades, China has served as "the rising engine of global offshore finance" (Haberly & Wójcik, 2015b, p. 271). Facing US pressure on its international economic relations, China may become even more permissive toward the offshore world to ensure inward and outward capital accessibility. Third, the entrance of SMEs into global markets with new technologies may create a new source of demand for OFCs. As Sheng (2015) notes: "Never have so many SMEs been able to access so much knowledge and markets with such speed and ease. The time of small companies in new markets is only just beginning." Fourth, structural conditions are worsening for African countries, which empowers those elites advocating for accommodation and the status quo. The widespread collapse of commodity prices, which began before the COVID-19 pandemic but worsened significantly as a result of it, increases the need to attract capital inflows to mend deteriorating public and private finances. This is doubly true at a time when African countries are likely to experience decreasing disbursements of foreign aid. In this context, the likelihood increases that African countries will sign and maintain tax agreements with Mauritius and other OFCs rather than step away from them.

Future research questions

The next step in expanding the analysis of the uneven offshore world is a better understanding of China's standing, not least because of China's African ambitions. Cotterill (2017) effectively captures the significance for Mauritius: "relations with New Delhi and Beijing appear to be pulling Mauritius in different directions. The island aims to maintain political and security links with India, and to have China play a very important part in plans to re-orient Mauritius's role as a financial centre towards Africa." Two research questions warrant close attention over the next five to ten years: first, will Chinese enterprises increase their use of offshore financial mechanisms, and second, will Chinese actors use Mauritius to carry out deal-making in Africa?

Whether Chinese actors will travel offshore more or less than in the past is an important question for understanding the overseas strategies of state-owned enterprises (SOEs) and the quasi-private sector, and for determining whether the recently tightened capital controls are functioning. As is typical for a country of China's size, it does not exhibit a single pattern but rather a number of co-existing patterns. Three such patterns are observable in a preliminary analysis.

First, Chinese enterprises have moved from ambivalence to a greater interest in the use of offshore financial vehicles. Bräutigam (2012) describes two models of the China–Africa relationship. There is the older Chinese model, defined by "risky joint investments with host governments in fragile states" (Bräutigam, 2012, p. 25). Much of the earlier growth of Chinese investment in the developing world took place through direct investments rather than being intermediated by offshore corporate structures. Often, these investments were marked by relationship-based business where the African side, keen to build relationships with Chinese actors for the long-term, acceded to most Chinese requests (Lee, 2014) and the Chinese side pursued less due diligence than is common among Western investors. Such deals have mostly been struck between Chinese enterprises and the central governments of African countries. In the other, newer model, which according to Bräutigam (2012, p. 25) is now more prevalent, "Chinese companies are looking more and more like 'normal' investors in Africa," with the growing trends including "mergers and acquisitions, as well as joint ventures with private Western firms and syndicated loans with big global banks." This list of business strategies can be supplemented with the use of offshore transactions. There is in principle no incompatibility between state-dominant capitalism and engagement with the offshore world. Cross-border deals have grown in recent decades and firms from emerging markets have, as smaller participants, been exposed to the practitioners and processes of global finance. The more they expand, the more they interact with global capital, and thus they face a choice of either embracing offshore financial channels or lobbying their governments to tackle tax avoidance by their competitors. The incentive to embrace offshore financial services has increased in light of the missteps, overpayments, and unprofitable deals struck in the first wave of Chinese overseas investment, especially by SOEs. As one indication of this, we attended the China Offshore Summit in Shanghai and Shenzhen and observed sold-out conferences with over 400 Chinese attendees seeking out offshore financial services providers.

Second, China's taxation approach has become geared toward supporting Chinese MNEs. Hearson and Prichard (2018) published an analysis contending that China grants no leeway to developing countries in tax negotiations. The picture they paint, especially when set against the context of the India case presented in this book, is that China is less interested than India in global tax leadership and instead is pursuing a narrow promotion of its own interests. These authors make several pointed claims. First, they write that China has pursued a "self-interested approach to bilateral tax treaties," and that "insiders claim that China has likewise abandoned support in recent years for proposals designed to strengthen the ability of developing countries to tax technical service fees and digital firms" (Hearson & Prichard 2018, pp. 1304–1305). In other words, China is not granting any development breaks to developing countries. They then argue that China's larger strategy lies in "trying to tax OECD MNCs, without risking the imposition of additional taxation on Chinese MNCs operating in developing countries" (Hearson & Prichard, 2018, p. 1305). Given China's policy of advancing the interests of Chinese enterprises in tax treaty negotiations and given that Chinese enterprises have suffered significant failures in their initial overseas investments, it would follow that these Chinese firms would more carefully consider the toolkits of global business, namely offshore financial vehicles. The combination of China's assertive tax diplomacy to promote the interests of its enterprises, its continuing tolerance of OFCs, its web of DTAs and BITs, and the rise of emerging market offshore investors brings into question the model of a new and more progressive Global South.

Third, and most important for future research, is that just as Chinese actors are starting to more seriously study the offshore system, the Chinese government has started cracking down on capital outflows by both individuals and companies (Robertson, 2021). Should inequality within China continue to rise at its current alarming pace and threaten domestic stability, the Chinese government may find it prudent to boost its legitimacy among the general population and intensify this crackdown on the offshore world in a similar fashion that India and many of the EU institutions and member states have been attempting over the last few decades. It is also possible that China's potential retreat from the offshore world could be prompted more by the actions of its geopolitical rivals than by its own choice. Given that the global offshore infrastructure is still almost completely controlled by the UK, the US, and a few continental European powers, should the hegemonic competition between the US and China escalate, China may find its access to the offshore world significantly curtailed. Fine-grained analysis will be needed on the business activities of SOEs and the quasi-private sector, as well as on governmental policies of several key actors in this complex national, regional, and global environment.

Are Chinese companies starting to use Mauritius more as part of their investment strategies in Africa? To date, the level of Chinese economic involvement in Mauritius has been relatively limited and several informants in Mauritian MCs have expressed surprise that Chinese clients are such a small proportion of their client base (multiple interviews, Mauritius, 2016). One of the challenges for Mauritius is that Chinese clients have been loyal users of BVI and Cayman Islands structures. As the former Mauritian Finance Minister remarked: "We go to China and they say 'We know BVI'" (interview with Rama Sithanen, Mauritius, 2016). However, Mauritius has been presented with a new opportunity to market itself to China, as the BVI's OFC has been damaged by leaks about offshore financial dealings, and along with the Cayman Islands and other Overseas Territories will be subject to more stringent regulations on transparency imposed by the UK government (Robertson, 2021).

A number of new developments suggest that Mauritius may be positioning itself to try and capitalize on this opportunity. One interesting development is the preparation of the Variable Capital Companies (VCCs) Bill, which would introduce a new type of investment vehicle to complement the current range of fund structures offered by Mauritius. This vehicle is very popular with Chinese clients, and is currently offered only by a very small number of OFCs, such as the Cayman Islands, Luxembourg, and more recently Singapore. Whether Mauritius will be able to compete in this niche area dominated by more established and experienced OFCs remains to be seen. Another interesting development is that the Bank of China has opened its first branch in Mauritius, about which informants told us two different stories. Most commonly, it was stated that the Bank of China is focused on SOEs and financing infrastructure deals in Africa. However, the picture that emerged from further inquiries is that China's quasi-private sector is the primary source of demand for the Mauritius branch (anonymous interview with a Bank of China official, Mauritius, 2016). This is due to China's SOEs requiring multiple levels of approval, and gaining this approval to structure an investment using a Mauritius vehicle can be painstakingly slow. Whereas SOEs are more open than before to considering offshore financial structures, their senior leaders adopt a highly cautious posture, partly due to their concerns about the reputational risks of OFCs. As much as Mauritius would like to guide Chinese capital flows into Africa, it is doubtful that China will fill the vacuum left in the wake of India's offshore shift.

As a final word, change is undeniably afoot in global tax reform. The global economy still carries strong neoliberal underpinnings even though it has become less globally footloose than before. A nuanced view that takes full account of the numerous historical and systemic determinants is necessary to understand how the changing global and regional contexts influence national action and vice versa, leading to different outcomes in differently positioned geographies: there has been less tightening in emerging markets than in developed markets, but larger emerging markets are more likely to have moved away from full accommodation with Mauritius than smaller emerging markets, while the developing world is once again largely left behind. As such, the global offshore economy is not on life support: it is a resilient system that is ongoing, albeit in an uneven fashion. The next decade will be telling, and students of IPE in general, and world-systems analysts in particular, should pay close attention as civil society actors and their allies develop new strategies to keep the spotlight on the offshore world and devote even more resources to holding offshore financial suppliers and their users to account.

References

ActionAid. (2012, April). *Calling time: Why SABMiller should stop dodging taxes in Africa*. www.attac-paderborn.de/wp-content/uploads/2014/12/Calling-Time.pdf

ActionAid. (2013a, May 23). *How tax havens plunder the poor*. https://actionaid.org/publications/2013/how-tax-havens-plunder-poor

ActionAid. (2013b, February 10). *Sweet nothings: The human cost of a British sugar giant avoiding taxes in southern Africa*. https://actionaid.org/publications/2013/sweet-nothings#downloads

ActionAid. (2014, September 18). *Double taxation treaties in Uganda: Impact and policy implications*. https://uganda.actionaid.org/publications/2014/double-taxation-treaties-uganda-impact-and-policy-implications#downloads

ActionAid. (2015, July 6). *Levelling up: Ensuring a fairer share of corporate tax for developing countries*. https://actionaid.org/publications/2015/levelling-ensuring-fairer-share-corporate-tax-developing-countries

ActionAid. (2016, February 23). *Mistreated: The tax treaties that are depriving the world's poorest countries of vital revenue*. https://actionaid.org/publications/2016/mistreated

Ahmed, A., & Kumar, M. (2021, August 7). India to scrap retrospective tax law in olive branch to global firms. *Reuters*. www.reuters.com/world/india/india-proposes-refunds-retrospective-tax-disputes-2021-08-05/

Alstadsæter, A., Johannesen, N., & Zucman, G. (2019). Tax evasion and inequality. *American Economic Review*, *109*(6), 2073–2103.

Altshuler, R., & Grubert, H. (2005). The three parties in the race to the bottom: Host governments, home governments and multinational companies. *Florida Tax Review*, *7*(3), 153–173.

Amin, S. (1976). *Unequal development: An essay on the social formations of peripheral capitalism*. Monthly Review Press.

Anyangwe, E. (2015, July 16). Glee, relief and regret: Addis Ababa outcome receives mixed reception. *The Guardian*. www.theguardian.com/global-development/2015/jul/16/outcome-document-addis-ababa-ffd3-financing-for-development

Armijo, L. E., & Echeverri-Gent, J. (2014). Brave new world? The politics of international finance in Brazil and India. In L. E. Armijo & S. N. Katada (Eds.), *The financial statecraft of emerging powers: Shield and sword in Asia and Latin America* (pp. 47–76). Palgrave Macmillan.

Arrighi, G. (2010). *The long twentieth century: Money, power, and the origins of our times*. Verso.

Aryan, A. (2020, September 27). Retrospective taxation: The Vodafone case, and the Hague court ruling. *The Indian Express*. https://indianexpress.com/article/explained/retrospective-taxation-the-vodafone-case-and-the-hague-court-ruling-6613799/

Asen, E. (2020, December 9). Corporate tax rates around the world, 2020. *Tax Foundation*. https://taxfoundation.org/publications/corporate-tax-rates-around-the-world/

Avi-Yonah, R. S. (2009). Double tax treaties: An introduction. In K. P. Sauvant & L. E. Sachs (Eds.), *The effect of treaties on foreign direct investment: Bilateral investment treaties, double taxation treaties, and investment flows* (pp. 99–106). Oxford University Press.

Avi-Yonah, R. S., & Kir, A. (2019). *A break in the dam? India's new profit attribution proposal and the arm's length standard* (Research Paper). University of Michigan, Law & Economics.

Avi-Yonah, R. S., & Xu, H. (2016). *Global taxation after the crisis: Why BEPS and MAATM are inadequate responses, and what can be done about it* (Research Paper No. 494). University of Michigan, Public Law & Legal Theory.

Axis & BLC Robert. (2020, June 9). *EU list of high-risk countries and its implications on Mauritius* [Video]. Axis Fiduciary Ltd and BLC Robert & Associates Ltd. www.youtube.com/watch?v=BlVYg4QGcmw

Bank of Mauritius. (2020). Financial stability report – December 2020. *Bank of Mauritius*. www.bom.mu/financial-stability/financial-stability/reports

Baruch, J., Ferrer, M., Vaudano, M., & Michel, A. (2021, February 8). OpenLux: The secrets of Luxembourg, a tax haven at the heart of Europe. *Le Monde*. www.lemonde.fr/les-decodeurs/article/2021/02/08/openlux-the-secrets-of-luxembourg-a-tax-haven-at-the-heart-of-europe_6069140_4355770.html

BBC. (2012, November 12). Starbucks, Google and Amazon grilled over tax avoidance. *BBC*. www.bbc.com/news/business-20288077

Beer, S., & Loeprick, J. (2018a, October 24). *The costs and benefits of tax treaties with investment hubs: Findings from sub-Saharan Africa* (Working Paper No. 18/227). International Monetary Fund. www.imf.org/en/Publications/WP/Issues/2018/10/24/The-Cost-and-Benefits-of-Tax-Treaties-with-Investment-Hubs-Findings-from-Sub-Saharan-Africa-46264

Beer, S., & Loeprick, J. (2018b, October 25). *The costs and benefits of tax treaties with investment hubs: Findings from sub-Saharan Africa* (Policy Research Working Paper No. 8623). World Bank. https://documents.worldbank.org/en/publication/documents-reports/documentdetail/325021540479671671/the-cost-and-benefits-of-tax-treaties-with-investment-hubs-findings-from-sub-saharan-africa

Bergin, T. (2012, October 15). Special report: How Starbucks avoids UK taxes. *Reuters*. www.reuters.com/article/us-britain-starbucks-tax-idUKBRE89E0EX20121015

Berglez, P., & Gearing, A. (2018). The Panama and Paradise Papers: The rise of a global fourth estate. *International Journal of Communication*, *12*, 4573–4592.

Bernstein, J. (2017). *Secrecy world: Inside the Panama Papers investigation of illicit money networks and the global elite*. Henry Holt and Company.

Blair, E. (2015, October 16). Mauritius eyes Africa as pressure mounts on offshore business. *Reuters*. www.reuters.com/article/us-mauritius-economy-insight/mauritius-eyes-africa-as-pressure-mounts-on-offshore-business-idUKKCN0SA1GJ20151016

Bloningen, B. A., & Piger, J. (2014). Determinants of foreign direct investment. *Canadian Journal of Economics*, *47*(3), 775–812.

Blustein, P. (2009). *Misadventures of the most favored nations: Clashing egos, inflated ambitions, and the great shambles of the world trade system*. PublicAffairs.

BMG. (2015, October 5). Overall evaluation of the G20/OECD Base Erosion and Profit Shifting (BEPS) project. *The BEPS Monitoring Group*. www.bepsmonitoringgroup.org/news/2018/5/10/overall-evaluation

Boffey, D. (2020, February 13). In wake of Brexit, EU to put Cayman Islands on tax haven blacklist. *The Guardian*. www.theguardian.com/us-news/2020/feb/13/eu-to-put-cayman-islands-on-tax-haven-blacklist

Bond, P. (2017). As the global commodity super-cycle ends, Africans continue uprising against 'Africa rising'. In N. Poku & J. Whitman (Eds.), *Africa under neoliberalism* (pp. 48–60). Routledge.

Bracking, S. (2012). Secrecy jurisdictions and economic development in Africa: The role of sovereign spaces of exception in producing private wealth and public poverty. *Economy and Society*, *41*(4), 615–637.

Bräutigam, D. (2012). Investors, not infesters. *China Economic Quarterly*, *16*(3), 22–27.

Bremner, B. (2017, November 15). The final days of a tax haven. *Bloomberg*. www.bloomberg.com/news/features/2017-11-15/the-final-days-of-a-tax-haven

Brunsden, J., Parker, G., & Houlder, V. (2016, April 7). David Cameron's EU intervention on trusts set up tax loophole. *Financial Times*. www.ft.com/content/0e7c0a20-fc17-11e5-b5f5-070dca6d0a0d

Bullough, O. (2018, July 12). Nevis: How the world's most secretive offshore tax haven refuses to clean up. *The Guardian*. www.theguardian.com/news/2018/jul/12/nevis-how-the-worlds-most-secretive-offshore-haven-refuses-to-clean-up

Bullough, O. (2019, November 14). The great American tax haven: Why the super-rich love South Dakota. *The Guardian*. www.theguardian.com/world/2019/nov/14/the-great-american-tax-haven-why-the-super-rich-love-south-dakota-trust-laws

Burgers, I. J. J., & Mosquera Valderrama, I. J. (2017). Corporate taxation and BEPS: A fair slice for developing countries? *Erasmus Law Review*, *10*(1), 29–47.

Cano, M. C. (2019, December 17). Global tax 50 2019: Gerard Ryle. *International Tax Review*. www.internationaltaxreview.com/article/b1jdvqyr84rn4s/global-tax-50-2019-gerard-ryle

Carlisle, R. (1980). The "American Century" implemented: Stettinius and the Liberian flag of convenience. *Business History Review*, *54*(2), 175–191.

Carter, P. (2017, October). Why do development finance institutions use offshore financial centres? *Overseas Development Institute*. https://odi.org/en/publications/why-do-development-finance-institutions-use-offshore-financial-centres/

Cavanagh, J. (2014, September 2). Africa: Who are you calling corrupt? Good governance begins at home. *allAfrica*. https://allafrica.com/stories/201409040563.html

Chancel, L. (2021). Ten facts about inequality in advanced economies. In O. Blanchard & D. Rodrik (Eds.), *Combating inequality: Rethinking government's role* (pp. 3–30). The MIT Press.

Chase-Dunn, C. (1998). *Global formation: Structures of the world-economy*. Rowman & Littlefield.

Chowdhary, A. M. (2018, August 29). Why is India the only country funding the United Nations Tax Committee? *The Wire*. https://thewire.in/economy/india-united-nations-tax-committee

Christensen, R. C., & Hearson, M. (2019a). The new politics of global tax governance: Taking stock a decade after the financial crisis. *Review of International Political Economy*, *26*(5), 1068–1088.

Christensen, R. C., & Hearson, M. (2019b, December 10). The future of global corporate taxation is more uncertain than ever. *Roosevelt Institute*. https://

rooseveltinstitute.org/2019/12/10/the-future-of-global-corporate-taxation-is-more-uncertain-than-ever/

Christians, A. (2009). *Global trends and constraints on tax policy in the least developed countries* (Research Paper No. 1086). University of Wisconsin, Legal Studies.

Cobham, A. (2017, May 5). Developing countries' access to CbCR: Guess who's (not) coming to OECD dinner. *Tax Justice Network*. www.taxjustice.net/2017/05/05/developing-countries-access-to-cbcr-guess-whos-not-coming-oecd-dinner/

Cobham, A., Faccio, T., & FitzGerald, V. (2019). *Global inequalities in taxing rights: An early evaluation of the OECD tax reform proposals*. https://osf.io/preprints/socarxiv/j3p48/

Cobham, A., Garcia-Bernardo, J., Palanský, M., & Mansour, M. B. (2020, November 20). The state of tax justice 2020: Tax justice in the time of COVID-19. *Tax Justice Network, the Global Alliance for Tax Justice, and Public Services International*. www.taxjustice.net/reports/the-state-of-tax-justice-2020/

Cobham, A., Janský, P., & Meinzer, M. (2019). A half-century of resistance to corporate disclosure. *Transnational Corporations*, *25*(3), 1–26.

Cooper, A. F., & Farooq, A. B. (2016). The role of China and India in the G20 and BRICS: Commonalities or competitive behavior? *Journal of Current Chinese Affairs*, *45*(3), 73–106.

Cotterill, J. (2017, October 5). Is Mauritius big enough for China and India? *Financial Times*. www.ft.com/content/bb658580-8434-11e7-94e2-c5b903247afd

Council of the EU. (2021a, June 1). *Public country-by-country reporting by big multinationals: EU co-legislators reach political agreement*. Council of the European Union. www.consilium.europa.eu/en/press/press-releases/2021/06/01/public-country-by-country-reporting-by-big-multinationals-eu-co-legislators-reach-political-agreement/

Council of the EU. (2021b). *Taxation: EU list of non-cooperative jurisdictions*. Council of the European Union. www.consilium.europa.eu/en/policies/eu-list-of-non-cooperative-jurisdictions/

Crawford, D. (2001). Globalisation and Guanxi: The ethos of Hong Kong finance. *New Political Economy*, *6*(1), 45–65.

Damgaard, J., Elkjaer, T., & Johannesen, N. (2019). The rise of phantom investments. *Finance & Development*, *56*(3), 11–13.

Daurer, V., & Krever, R. (2014). Choosing between the UN and OECD tax policy models: An African case study. *African Journal of International and Comparative Law*, *22*(1), 1–21.

Davies, W. (2014, March 7). Neoliberalism: A bibliographic review. *Theory, Culture & Society*. www.theoryculturesociety.org/william-davies-a-bibliographic-review-of-neoliberalism/

De Groen, W. P. (2017, April). Role of advisors and intermediaries in the schemes revealed in the Panama Papers. *European Parliament*. www.europarl.europa.eu/RegData/etudes/STUD/2017/602030/IPOL_STU(2017)602030_EN.pdf

Deloitte. (2013, June 11). *Investing in Africa through Mauritius*. www.aph.gov.au/DocumentStore.ashx?id=a12bb150-a320-4380-82cf-81627cf110fb&subId=303237

Desai, M. A., Fritz Foley, C., & Hines, J. R., Jr. (2006). *Taxation and multinational activity: New evidence, new interpretations* (Survey of Current Business Article No. 1402). University of Michigan.

Desai, N., & Sanghavi, D. (2008, December 1). The travails of the India Mauritius tax treaty & the road ahead. *Nishith Desai Associates*. www.nishithdesai.com/

fileadmin/user_upload/pdfs/The_Travails_of_the_India_Mauritius_Tax_Treaty_and_the_Road_Ahead.pdf

Devereux, M., & Vella, J. (2014). Are we heading towards a corporate tax system fit for the 21st century? *Fiscal Studies*, *34*(4), 449–475.

DIT. (2021, April 9). Trade & investment factsheets: Ghana. *Department for International Trade*. https://assets.publishing.service.gov.uk/government/uploads/system/uploads/attachment_data/file/976539/ghana-trade-and-investment-factsheet-2021–04–09.pdf

Dooley, M. P. (1986, March 11). Country-specific risk premiums, capital flight and net investment income payments in selected developing countries (Departmental Memorandum No. 86/17). *International Monetary Fund*. https://people.ucsc.edu/~mpd/risk-premia.pdf

Doward, J. (2013, November 3). Deloitte promotes Mauritius as tax haven to avoid big payouts to poor African nations. *The Observer*. www.theguardian.com/business/2013/nov/03/deloittes-tax-savings-investments-in-poor-countries

DPIIT. (2021). FDI Statistics Archives. *Department for Promotion of Industry and Internal Trade, Government of India*. https://dipp.gov.in/publications/fdi-statistics/archives

Drucker, J. (2010, October 21). Google 2.4% rate shows how $60 billion is lost to tax loopholes. *Bloomberg*. www.bloomberg.com/news/articles/2010-10-21/google-2-4-rate-shows-how-60-billion-u-s-revenue-lost-to-tax-loopholes

DTOS. (2020, June 10). *Mauritius on the EU blacklist: Consequences and the way forward* [Video]. DTOS Group. www.youtube.com/watch?v=QIR_aj7PTZ0

Duff, D. G. (2018). Tax treaty abuse and the principal purpose test – Part I. *Canadian Tax Journal*, *66*(3), 619–677.

Duhigg, C., & Kocieniewski, D. (2012, April 28). How Apple sidesteps billions in taxes. *The New York Times*. www.nytimes.com/2012/04/29/business/apples-tax-strategy-aims-at-low-tax-states-and-nations.html

Durst, M. C. (2019, February). Taxing multinational business in lower-income countries: Economics, politics and social responsibility. *Institute of Development Studies and the International Centre for Tax and Development*. www.ictd.ac/publication/taxing-multinational-business-lower-income-countries-economics-politics-social-responsibility/

Dyreng, S. D., Hoopes, J. L., & Wilde, J. H. (2016). Public pressure and corporate tax behavior. *Journal of Accounting Research*, *54*(1), 147–186.

EC. (2016). *Common Consolidated Corporate Tax Base (CCCTB)*. European Commission. https://ec.europa.eu/taxation_customs/business/company-tax/common-consolidated-corporate-tax-base-ccctb_en

EC. (2021). *Tax rulings*. European Commission. https://ec.europa.eu/competition-policy/state-aid/tax-rulings_en

Eden, L., & Kudrle, R. T. (2005). Tax havens: Renegade states in the international tax regime? *Law & Policy*, *27*(1), 100–127.

Emmenegger, P. (2017). Swiss banking secrecy and the problem of international cooperation in tax matters: A nut too hard to crack? *Regulation & Governance*, *11*(1), 24–40.

EP. (2019, March 8). *Report on financial crimes, tax evasion and tax avoidance* (Document No. A8-0170/2019). European Parliament. www.europarl.europa.eu/doceo/document/A-8-2019-0170_EN.pdf

Errico, L., & Musalem, A. (1999, January 1). Offshore banking: An analysis of micro- and macro-prudential issues (Working Paper No. 99/5). *International*

MonetaryFund. www.imf.org/en/Publications/WP/Issues/2016/12/30/Offshore-Banking-An-Analysis-of-Micro-and-Macro-Prudential-Issues-2867

Etter-Phoya, R., Lima, S. N., & Meinzer, M. (2019, August 28). Corporate income taxation in the digital age: Africa in the Corporate Tax Haven Index 2019. *Tax Justice Network*. www.taxjustice.net/wp-content/uploads/2019/08/CORPOR1.pdf

EY. (2015, October 14). *EY's attractiveness survey: India 2015 – Ready, set, grow*. https://pdfslide.net/documents/eys-2015-india-attractiveness-survey-ready-set-grow.html

EY. (2020, July 22). *Worldwide corporate tax guide*. www.ey.com/en_gl/tax-guides/worldwide-corporate-tax-guide-2020

FACTI Panel. (2021, February 24). *Financial integrity for sustainable development*. High Level Panel on International Financial Accountability, Transparency and Integrity for Achieving the 2030 Agenda. www.factipanel.org/reports

FATF. (2000, June 22). *Review to identify non-cooperative countries or territories: Increasing the worldwide effectiveness of anti-money laundering measures*. Financial Action Task Force. www.fatf-gafi.org/media/fatf/documents/reports/1999%20 2000%20NCCT%20ENG.pdf

Findley, M. G., Nielson, D. L., & Sharman, J. C. (2014). *Global shell games: Experiments in transnational relations, crime, and terrorism*. Cambridge University Press.

Finér, L., & Ylönen, M. (2017). Tax-driven wealth chains: A multiple case study of tax avoidance in the Finnish mining sector. *Critical Perspectives on Accounting*, *48*, 53–81.

Fitzgibbon, W. (2017, November 7). Tax haven Mauritius' rise comes at the rest of Africa's expense. *International Consortium of Investigative Journalists*. www.icij.org/investigations/paradise-papers/tax-haven-mauritius-africa/

Fitzgibbon, W. (2019, July 23). Treasure island: Leak reveals how Mauritius siphons tax from poor nations to benefit elites. *International Consortium of Investigative Journalists*. www.icij.org/investigations/mauritius-leaks/treasure-island-leak-reveals-how-mauritius-siphons-tax-from-poor-nations-to-benefit-elites/

Fitzgibbon, W. (2020a, February 25). How Isabel dos Santos went shopping in Mauritius for shell companies, secrecy and a tax dodge. *International Consortium of Investigative Journalists*. www.icij.org/investigations/luanda-leaks/how-isabel-dos-santos-went-shopping-in-mauritius-for-shell-companies-secrecy-and-a-tax-dodge/

Fitzgibbon, W. (2020b, May 26). Senegal nixes 'unbalanced' tax treaty with Mauritius. *International Consortium of Investigative Journalists*. www.icij.org/investigations/mauritius-leaks/senegal-nixes-unbalanced-tax-treaty-with-mauritius/

Forstater, M. (2018, February 8). Tax and development: New frontiers of research and action (Policy Paper 118). *Center for Global Development*. www.cgdev.org/publication/tax-and-development-new-frontiers-research-and-action

Fortado, L. (2016, September 29). Realities of being an expat in Mauritius. *Financial Times*. www.ft.com/content/9c332db0-75b3-11e6-bf48-b372cdb1043a

Fouche, G. (2017, May 11). Norway's $940 billion wealth fund eyes possible repatriation of tax haven subsidiaries. *Reuters*. www.reuters.com/article/us-norway-budget-swf-idUSKBN187268

Fouche, G. (2021, February 1). For first time, Norway's wealth fund ditches firms over tax transparency. *Reuters*. www.reuters.com/article/us-norway-swf-idUSKBN2A11TR

Frank, A. G. (1978). *Dependent accumulation and underdevelopment*. Macmillan Press.

Frankel, J. A. (2010, December). Mauritius: African success story (Working Paper 16569). *National Bureau of Economic Research*. www.nber.org/papers/w16569

Frick, S. A., Rodríguez-Pose, A., & Wong, M. D. (2019). Toward economically dynamic special economic zones in emerging countries. *Economic Geography*, *95*(1), 30–64.

FSC. (2020a). Annual statistical bulletin 2019. *Financial Services Commission of Mauritius*. www.fscmauritius.org/en/statistics/statistics/statistical-bulletins

FSC. (2020b). Value of investment (2012–2019). *Financial Services Commission of Mauritius*. www.fscmauritius.org/en/statistics/statistics/global-business

FSD Africa & EMPEA. (2015, October 1). Conduits of capital: Onshore financial centres and their relevance to African private equity. *Financial Sector Deepening Africa and the Emerging Markets Private Equity Association*. www.fsdafrica.org/wp-content/uploads/2019/08/15-10-21-FSDA_EMPEA_Conduits-of-Capital_web_version.pdf

FSF. (2000, May 26). *Financial Stability Forum releases grouping of offshore financial centres (OFCs) to assist in setting priorities for assessment*. Financial Stability Forum. www.fsb.org/2000/05/pr_000526/

FTC. (2017, April 28). Every government that's supported a UN tax body, in one table. *Financial Transparency Coalition*. https://financialtransparency.org/list-governments-supported-un-tax-body-one-table/

Fundira, T. (2015, April 26). The G-20 tax agenda and Africa's taxation needs. *South African Institute of International Affairs*. https://saiia.org.za/research/the-g-20-tax-agenda-and-africa-s-taxation-needs/

G20. (2009, April 2). *G20 Leaders' statement: Global plan for recovery and reform*. G20 Summit, London. www.g20.utoronto.ca/2009/2009communique0402.html

G20. (2015, November 16). *G20 Leaders' communiqué*. G20 Summit, Antalya. www.g20.utoronto.ca/2015/151116-communique.html

Garcia-Bernardo, J., Fichtner, J., Heemskerk, E., & Takes, F. (2017). Uncovering offshore financial centers: Conduits and sinks in the global corporate ownership network. *Scientific Reports*, *7*(6246).

Gardner, M., McIntyre, R. S., & Phillips, R. (2017, March 9). The 35 percent corporate tax myth: Corporate tax avoidance by Fortune 500 companies, 2008 to 2015. *Institute on Taxation and Economic Policy*. https://itep.org/the-35-percent-corporate-tax-myth/

Gardner, M., & Wamhoff, S. (2021, April 2). 55 corporations paid $0 in federal taxes on 2020 profits. *Institute on Taxation and Economic Policy*. https://itep.org/55-profitable-corporations-zero-corporate-tax/

Geyer, H. S. (2019). Gateway cities, under-connected cities and largely disconnected cities in global value chains in sub-Saharan Africa. In S. Scholvin, A. Black, J. R. Diez, & I. Turok (Eds.), *Value chains in sub-Saharan Africa: Challenges of integration into the global economy* (pp. 221–234). Springer.

Gilleard, M. (2011, May 23). Eight member states show CCCTB yellow card. *International Tax Review*. www.internationaltaxreview.com/article/b1fbs016lv43gx/eight-member-states-show-ccctb-yellow-card

Gowrea, G. (2009, May 31). Mauritius: Not a tax haven and white listed by OECD. *International Tax Review*. www.internationaltaxreview.com/article/b1f7b800yw8g8c/mauritius-not-a-tax-haven-and-white-listed-by-oecd

Grady, K. A. (1983). Income tax treaty shopping: An overview of prevention techniques. *Northwestern Journal of International Law & Business*, *5*(3), 626–657.

Grant, W., & Wilson, G. K. (Eds.). (2012). *The consequences of the global financial crisis: The rhetoric of reform and regulation.* Oxford University Press.

Griffiths, I. (2012, April 4). Amazon: £7bn sales, no UK corporation tax. *The Guardian.* www.theguardian.com/technology/2012/apr/04/amazon-british-operation-corporation-tax

Haberly, D., & Wójcik, D. (2015a). Tax havens and the production of offshore FDI: An empirical analysis. *Journal of Economic Geography, 15*(1), 75–101.

Haberly, D., & Wójcik, D. (2015b). Regional blocks and imperial legacies: Mapping the global offshore FDI network. *Economic Geography, 91*(3), 251–280.

Hakelberg, L. (2016). Coercion in international tax cooperation: Identifying the prerequisites for sanction threat by a great power. *Review of International Political Economy, 23*(3), 511–541.

Hakelberg, L. (2020). *The hypocritical hegemon: How the United States shapes global rules against tax evasion and avoidance.* Cornell University Press.

Hakelberg, L., & Schaub, M. (2018). The redistributive impact of hypocrisy in international taxation. *Regulation & Governance, 12*(3), 353–370.

Hall, B., Parker, G., & Houlder V. (2009, April 2). Stage set for tax havens battle. *Financial Times.* www.ft.com/content/8439875c-1f00-11de-a748-00144feabdc0

Hallman, B., Gurney, K., Alecci, S., & de Haldevang, M. (2020, January 19). Western advisers helped an autocrat's daughter amass and shield a Fortune. *International Consortium of Investigative Journalists.* www.icij.org/investigations/luanda-leaks/western-advisers-helped-an-autocrats-daughter-amass-and-shield-a-fortune/

Hampton, M. P. (1996). *The offshore interface: Tax havens in the global economy.* Macmillan Press.

Hampton, M. P., & Christensen, J. (2002). Offshore pariahs? Small island economies, tax havens, and the re-configuration of global finance. *World Development, 30*(9), 1657–1673.

Harrington, B. (2016). *Capital without borders: Wealth managers and the one percent.* Harvard University Press.

Harrington, B. (2017). Trusts and finacialization. *Socio-Economic Review, 15*(1), 31–63.

Harvey, D. (2005). *A brief history of neoliberalism.* Oxford University Press.

Hattingh, J. (2017). The legal and related challenges, and emerging solutions for implementation of the BEPS Multilateral Instrument. *Global Taxation*, 29–36.

Hearson, M. (2018a). Transnational expertise and the expansion of the international tax regime: Imposing 'acceptable' standards. *Review of International Political Economy, 25*(5), 647–671.

Hearson, M. (2018b). When do developing countries negotiate away their corporate tax base? *Journal of International Development, 30*(2), 233–255.

Hearson, M. (2020, January). Corporate tax negotiations at the OECD: What's at stake for developing countries in 2020? *International Centre for Tax and Development.* www.ictd.ac/publication/corporate-tax-negotiations-oecd-developing-countries/

Hearson, M., & Prichard, W. (2018). China's challenge to international tax rules and the implications for global economic governance. *International Affairs, 94*(6), 1287–1307.

Helleiner, E. (1994). *States and the reemergence of global finance: From Bretton Woods to the 1990s.* Cornell University Press.

Helleiner, E. (2014). *The status quo crisis: Global financial governance after the 2008 meltdown.* Oxford University Press.

Henry, J. S. (2012, July). The price of offshore revisited: New estimates for "missing" global private wealth, income, inequality, and lost taxes. *Tax Justice Network.* https://static1.squarespace.com/static/579e90ef46c3c4b32bf7ecc9/t/57b3889 7e6f2e189cfaa33e6/1523489835871/The+Price+of+Offshore+revisited.pdf

Henry, J. S. (2016, April 12). Taxing tax havens: How to respond to the Panama Papers. *Foreign Affairs.* www.foreignaffairs.com/articles/panama/2016-04-12/ taxing-tax-havens

Hers, J., Witteman, J., Rougoor, W., & van Buiren, K. (2018, May). The role of investment hubs in FDI, economic development and trade: Ireland, Luxembourg, Mauritius, the Netherlands, and Singapore. *SEO Amsterdam Economics.* https://25cjk227xfsu3mkyfg1m9xb7-wpengine.netdna-ssl.com/wp-content/ uploads/2020/04/2018-40_The_Role_of_Investment_Hubs_in_FDI__Economic_ Development_and_Trade.pdf

Hopewell, K. (2018). Recalcitrant spoiler? Contesting dominant accounts of India's role in global trade governance. *Third World Quarterly, 39*(3), 577–593.

Houlder, V. (2016, September 29). Mauritius rides wave of Asian investment in Africa. *Financial Times.* www.ft.com/content/929f41d0-75b3-11e6-bf48-b372cdb1043a

ICTD. (2021a). *The tax treaties explorer.* www.ictd.ac/dataset/tax-treaties-explorer/

ICTD. (2021b, January 15). *At the table, off the menu?* [Video]. www.youtube.com/ watch?v=LZFHMsazAbM

ICIJ. (2021a). *Investigations.* www.icij.org/investigations/

ICIJ. (2021b). *Offshore leaks database.* https://offshoreleaks.icij.org/

ILO. (2014, December 1). *Trade union manual on export processing zones.* www.ilo. org/actrav/info/pubs/WCMS_324632/lang--en/index.htm

IMF. (2000, June 23). *Offshore financial centers: IMF background paper.* www.imf. org/external/np/mae/oshore/2000/eng/back.htm

IMF. (2013, October). *Fiscal monitor: Taxing times.* www.imf.org/en/Publications/ FM/Issues/2016/12/31/TaxingTimes

IMF. (2021). *Annual data 2009–2019: Coordinated direct investment survey.* https://data.imf.org/?sk=40313609-F037-48C1-84B1-E1F1CE54D6D5& sId=1482186404325

ITF. (2021). *Flags of convenience.* www.itfglobal.org/en/sector/seafarers/flags-of- convenience

Jaiswal, S. (2017). Foreign direct investment in India and role of tax havens. *Centre for Budget and Governance Accountability.* www.cbgaindia.org/study-report/ foreign-direct-investment-india-role-tax-havens/

Jaiswal, S. (2018, April 20). Is Netherlands becoming the new 'Mauritius Route' for FDI flows into India? *The Wire.* https://thewire.in/macro/is-netherlands-becoming- the-new-mauritius-route-for-fdi-flows-into-india

Jenkins, R. (2003). International development institutions and national economic contexts: Neo-liberalism encounters India's indigenous political traditions. *Economy and Society, 32*(4), 584–610.

Jha, S. K. (2012). *Mauritius turns into a tax haven: A historical perspective.* www.shiva kantjha.org/openfile.php?filename=legal/mauritius_turns_into_tax_haven.htm

Johannesen, N., & Zucman, G. (2014). The end of bank secrecy? An evaluation of the G20 tax haven crackdown. *American Economic Journal: Economic Policy, 6*(1), 65–91.

Johnston, D. C. (2014, September 4). Corporate deadbeats: How companies get rich off of taxes. *Newsweek.* www.newsweek.com/2014/09/12/corporate-deadbeats- how-companies-get-rich-taxes-268303.html

Jones, C., Temouri, Y., & Cobham, A. (2018). Tax haven networks and the role of the Big 4 accountancy firms. *Journal of World Business*, *53*(2), 177–193.

Kar, D., & Spanjers, J. (2015, December 8). Illicit financial flows from developing countries: 2004–2013. *Global Financial Integrity*. https://gfintegrity.org/report/illicit-financial-flows-from-developing-countries-2004–2013/

Keaney, M. (2017). The aftermath of the financial crisis: Continuity and little change. *Political Studies Review*, *15*(1), 6–17.

Khan, I. A. (2020, February 7). Luanda leaks and beyond: Mauritius and the fall of the dos Santos empire. *L'express Maurice*. www.lexpress.mu/node/369730

Knobel, A. (2016, October 25). The OECD information exchange 'dating game'. *Tax Justice Network*. www.taxjustice.net/2016/10/25/oecd-information-exchange-dating-game/

Knobel, A., Meinzer, M., Harari, M., & Palanský, M. (2020, June 1). The state of play of beneficial ownership registration in 2020. *Tax Justice Network*. https://taxjustice.net/reports/the-state-of-play-of-beneficial-ownership-registration-in-2020/

Kohli, A. (2007). State, business, and economic growth in India. *Studies in Comparative International Development*, *42*, 87–114.

KPMG. (2015). *Status of Mauritius incorporation*. https://assets.documentcloud.org/documents/6206570/KPMG-Advice-Ubongo.pdf

Kvangraven, H. I., Koddenbrock, K., & Sylla, N. S. (2021). Financial subordination and uneven financialization in 21st century Africa. *Community Development Journal*, *56*(1), 119–140.

Lee, C. K. (2014). The spectre of global China. *New Left Review*, *89*, 29–65.

Lennard, M. (2008). The purpose and current status of the United Nations tax work. *Asia-Pacific Tax Bulletin*, *14*(1), 23–30.

Luce, E. (2009, April 3). Obama brokers pact on tax havens. *Financial Times*. www.ft.com/content/b75c6726-1fbe-11de-a1df-00144feabdc0

Mackintosh, S. P. M. (2014). Crises and paradigm shift. *The Political Quarterly*, *85*(4), 406–412.

Mascagni, G., Moore, M., & McCluskey, R. (2014, April 11). Tax revenue mobilisation in developing countries: Issues and challenges. *European Parliament*. www.europarl.europa.eu/RegData/etudes/etudes/join/2014/433849/EXPO-DEVE_ET(2014)433849_EN.pdf

Mehta, K. (2014, July). How developing countries can take control of their own tax destinies. *Tax Justice Network*. www.taxjustice.net/wp-content/uploads/2014/07/Krishen-How-Developing-Countries-can-take-Control-of-their-own-Tax-Destinies.pdf

Meisel, A., & Grossman, D. (2017, November 8). Paradise papers: Fishy smell about Namibian tax affairs. *BBC*. www.bbc.com/news/world-africa-41901872

Metaxas, B. N. (1981). Flags of convenience. *Marine Policy*, *5*(1), 52–66.

Michira, M. (2014, October 14). Lobby sues treasury CS over 'illegal' tax deal with Mauritius. *The Standard*. www.standardmedia.co.ke/business/article/2000137645

Ministry of Financial Services and Good Governance. (2020, May 9). Communiqué: European Commission list of high risk third countries. *Government of Mauritius*. https://financialservices.govmu.org/Communique/Press%20release%20-09.05.2020.pdf

MIPA. (2021). About MIPA. *Mauritius Institute of Professional Accountants*. www.mipa.mu/MIPA/About+MIPA

Mirowski, P., & Plehwe, D. (Eds.). (2009). *The road from Mont Pèlerin: The making of the neoliberal thought collective*. Harvard University Press.

Moore, M. (2013, February). The changing politics of tax policy reform in developing countries. *World Bank*. https://openknowledge.worldbank.org/handle/10986/29695

Moore, M. (2014a, January 1). Will changes to the international tax system benefit low-income countries? *Institute of Development Studies*. www.ids.ac.uk/publications/will-changes-to-the-international-tax-system-benefit-low-income-countries/

Moore, M. (2014b). Revenue reform and statebuilding in anglophone Africa. *World Development*, *60*, 99–112.

Moore, M., Fjeldstad, O. H., Isaksen, J., Lundstøl, O., McCluskey, R., & Prichard, W. (2015, July 5). Building tax capacity in developing countries. *Institute of Development Studies*. www.ids.ac.uk/publications/building-tax-capacity-in-developing-countries-2/

Moore, M., Prichard, W., & Fjeldstad, O. H. (2018). *Taxing Africa: Coercion, reform and development*. Zed Books.

Mosquera Valderrama, I. J. (2015). The OECD-BEPS measures to deal with aggressive tax planning in South America and Sub-Saharan Africa: The challenges ahead. *Intertax*, *43*(10), 615–627.

Mossack Fonseca. (2016, April 5). Statement regarding recent media coverage. *Mossack Fonseca*. www.independent.co.uk/news/world/americas/mossack-fonseca-statement-full-law-firm-responds-panama-papers-report-and-defends-its-high-standards-a6968961.html

MRA. (2020, September 29). Double taxation avoidance agreements. *Mauritius Revenue Authority*. www.mra.mu/index.php/taxes-duties/international-taxation/double-taxation-agreements

Mukherji, R. (2013). Ideas, interests, and the tipping point: Economic change in India. *Review of International Political Economy*, *20*(2), 363–389.

Murphy, R., & Stausholm, S. N. (2017, July 5). The big four: A study of opacity (GUE/NGL). *European Parliament*. https://guengl-panamapapers.eu/guengl-report-lays-bare-the-secretive-tax-evasion-practices-of-the-big-four/

Mutava, C. N. (2019, December). Review of tax treaty practices and policy framework in Africa. *International Centre for Tax and Development*. www.ictd.ac/publication/review-tax-treaties-policy-framework-africa/

Mutegi, M. (2014, June 15). Kenya now woos Mauritius companies with lower taxes. *Business Daily*. www.businessdailyafrica.com/bd/economy/-kenya-now-woos-mauritius-companies-with-lower-taxes-2060634

Ndikumana, L., & Boyce, J. K. (2003). Public debts and private assets: Explaining capital flight from sub-Saharan African countries. *World Development*, *31*(1), 107–130.

Ndikumana, L., & Boyce, J. K. (2011). *Africa's odious debts: How foreign loans and capital flight bled a continent*. Zed Books.

Ndikumana, L., & Boyce, J. K. (2018, June 1). Capital flight from Africa: Updated methodology and new estimates. *Political Economy Research Institute*. www.peri.umass.edu/publication/item/1083-capital-flight-from-africa-updated-methodology-and-new-estimates

Neighbour, J. (2002). Transfer pricing: Keeping it at arm's length. *OECD Observer*, *2002*(1), 29–30. www.oecd-ilibrary.org/economics/oecd-observer/volume-2002/issue 1_observer v2002-1-en

Nguegan, F. (2019, May 6). Kenya Mauritius double tax avoidance agreement. *Tax Justice Network Africa*. https://taxjusticeafrica.net/kenya-mauritius-double-tax-avoidance-agreement/

Norad. (2015, February). Evaluation of the Norwegian Investment Fund for Developing Countries (Norfund). *Norwegian Agency for Development Cooperation.* www.norad.no/en/toolspublications/publications/2015/evaluation-of-the-norwegian-investment-fund-for-developing-countries-norfund/

NOU. (2009, June 18). *Tax havens and development: Status, analyses and measures.* Official Norwegian Reports, Government Commission on Capital Flight from Poor Countries. www.regjeringen.no/en/dokumenter/nou-2009-19/id571718/

Observatoire des Multinationales. (2020, November 19). *CAC40: Le véritable bilan annuel – édition 2020.* https://multinationales.org/CAC40-le-veritable-bilan-annuel-l-edition-2020

OECD.Stat. (2021). *Revenue statistics.* Organization for Economic Cooperation and Development. https://stats.oecd.org/

Ogle, V. (2017). Archipelago capitalism: Tax havens, offshore money, and the state, 1950s–1970s. *The American Historical Review, 122*(5), 1431–1458.

Oguttu, A. W. (2016, June). Tax base erosion and profit shifting in Africa – Part 1: Africa's response to the OECD BEPS action plan. *International Centre for Tax and Development.* www.ictd.ac/publication/tax-base-erosion-and-profit-shifting-in-africa-part-1-africa-s-response-to-the-oecd-beps-action-plan/

Oguttu, A. W. (2017, February). Tax base erosion and profit shifting in Africa – Part 2: A critique of some priority OECD Actions from an African perspective. *International Centre for Tax and Development.* www.ictd.ac/publication/ictd-wp64/

Oguttu, A. W. (2018, November 13). Should developing countries sign the OECD Multilateral Instrument to address treaty-related base erosion and profit shifting measures? (Policy Paper 132). *Center for Global Development.* www.cgdev.org/publication/should-developing-countries-sign-oecd-multilateral-instrument-address-treaty-related

OECD. (1998a, February 24). *Tax sparing: A reconsideration.* www.oecd-ilibrary.org/taxation/tax-sparing_9789264162433-en

OECD. (1998b, May 19). *Harmful tax competition: An emerging global issue.* www.oecd-ilibrary.org/taxation/harmful-tax-competition_9789264162945-en

OECD. (2000, June 26). *Towards global tax co-operation: Progress in identifying and eliminating harmful tax practices.* www.oecd-ilibrary.org/taxation/towards-global-tax-co-operation_9789264184541-en

OECD. (2008, April 8). *Study into the role of tax intermediaries.* www.oecd.org/tax/administration/studyintotheroleoftaxintermediaries.htm

OECD. (2009, April 2). *A progress report on the jurisdictions surveyed by the OECD Global Forum in implementing the internationally agreed tax standard.* www.oecd.org/tax/exchange-of-tax-information/42497950.pdf

OECD. (2013, July 19). *Action plan on base erosion and profit shifting.* www.oecd.org/tax/action-plan-on-base-erosion-and-profit-shifting-9789264202719-en.htm

OECD. (2014, July 15). *Common Reporting Standard (CRS).* www.oecd.org/tax/automatic-exchange/common-reporting-standard/

OECD. (2015, October 5). *BEPS 2015 final reports.* www.oecd.org/ctp/beps-2015-final-reports.htm

OECD. (2017, December 18). *Model tax convention on income and on capital: Condensed version 2017.* www.oecd.org/tax/treaties/model-tax-convention-on-income-and-on-capital-condensed-version-20745419.htm

OECD. (2019, April 25). *Model Tax Convention on income and on capital 2017 (full version).* www.oecd.org/ctp/model-tax-convention-on-income-and-on-capital-full-version-9a5b369e-en.htm

OECD. (2020, December 9). *Peer review of the automatic exchange of financial account information 2020.* www.oecd-ilibrary.org/taxation/peer-review-of-the-automatic-exchange-of-financial-account-information-2020_175eeff4-en

OECD. (2021a, February). *OECD Secretary-General tax report to G20 Finance Ministers and Central Bank Governors.* www.oecd.org/tax/oecd-secretary-general-tax-report-g20-finance-ministers-february-2021.pdf

OECD. (2021b). *Action 1 tax challenges arising from digitalisation.* www.oecd.org/tax/beps/beps-actions/action1/

OECD. (2021c). *International framework for the CRS.* www.oecd.org/tax/automatic-exchange/international-framework-for-the-crs/

OECD. (2021d). *Multilateral convention to implement tax treaty related measures to prevent BEPS.* www.oecd.org/tax/treaties/multilateral-convention-to-implement-tax-treaty-related-measures-to-prevent-beps.htm

OECD. (2021e, July 1). *Statement on a two-pillar solution to address the tax challenges arising from the digitalisation of the economy.* www.oecd.org/tax/beps/statement-on-a-two-pillar-solution-to-address-the-tax-challenges-arising-from-the-digitalisation-of-the-economy-july-2021.htm

Osborne, H. (2016, February 29). Tax paid by FTSE 100 firms 'falls by nearly a quarter since 2010'. *The Guardian.* www.theguardian.com/politics/2016/feb/29/tax-paid-by-ftse-100-firms-falls-by-nearly-a-quarter-since-2010

Oxfam Intermón. (2020, November). *La hora del compromise: Las empresas del Ibex 35 ante el reto de la pandemia.* www.oxfamintermon.org/es/como-distribuyen-valor-empresas-ibex-35

Padilla, A., Biyani, N., Jaiswal, S., Buenaventura, M., Maranga, J., & Quantrill, T. (2020, January 15). Use and abuse of tax breaks: How tax incentives become harmful. *Financial Transparency Coalition.* https://financialtransparency.org/reports/31710/

Palan, R. (2003). *The offshore world: Sovereign markets, virtual places, and nomad millionaires.* Cornell University Press.

Palan, R. (2015). The second British Empire and the re-emergence of global finance. In S. Halperin & R. Palan (Eds.), *Legacies of empire: Imperial roots of the contemporary global order* (pp. 46–68). Cambridge University Press.

Palan, R., Murphy, R., & Chavagneux, C. (2010). *Tax havens: How globalization really works.* Cornell University Press.

Palan, R., & Wigan, D. (2014). Herding cats and taming tax havens: The US strategy of 'not in my backyard'. *Global Policy, 5*(3), 334–343.

Pew Research Center. (2014, September 16). *Faith and skepticism about trade, foreign investment.* www.pewresearch.org/global/2014/09/16/faith-and-skepticism-about-trade-foreign-investment/

Philip Morris Asia Limited v. Commonwealth of Australia. (2015, December 17). Permanent Court of Arbitration, Case No. 2012–12.

Phillips, R., Gardner, M., Robins, A., & Surka, M. (2017, October 17). Offshore shell games 2017: The use of offshore tax havens by Fortune 500 companies. *U.S. Public Interest Research Group Education Fund and the Institute on Taxation and Economic Policy.* https://uspirgedfund.org/reports/usp/offshore-shell-games-2017

Picciotto, S. (1992). *International business taxation: A study in the internationalization of business regulation.* Cambridge University Press.

Picciotto, S. (2013, September). Is the international tax system fit for purpose, especially for developing countries? *International Centre for Tax and Development.*

www.ictd.ac/publication/is-the-international-tax-system-fit-for-purpose-especially-for-developing-countries/

Picciotto, S. (2019). The interactions of national and international tax law and the Kenya – Mauritius tax treaty. *Journal on Financing for Development*, *1*(1), 1–32.

Pigeaud, F., & Sylla, N. S. (2021). *Africa's last colonial currency: The CFA franc story*. Pluto Press.

PMG. (2017, May 23). Rates and Monetary Amounts Bill & sugary beverages tax; BEPS Multilateral Instrument: briefing. *Parliamentary Monitoring Group*. https://pmg.org.za/committee-meeting/24430/

Prashad, V. (2012). *The poorer nations: A possible history of the Global South*. Verso.

Prichard, W., & Moore, M. (2018, June). Tax reform for low-income countries: Five ideas for simplifying tax systems to fit local realities. *International Centre for Tax and Development*. www.ictd.ac/publication/tax-reform-for-low-income-countries-five-ideas-for-simplifying-tax-systems-to-fit-local-realities/

Prime Minister's Office. (2020, June 2). Communiqué: Mauritius on the new EU List. *Government of Mauritius*. https://pmo.govmu.org/Communique/Communique%20English.pdf

PwC. (2021, February 25). *Worldwide tax summaries online*. https://taxsummaries.pwc.com/

Ranald, P. (2019, March 27). When even winning is losing. The surprising cost of defeating Philip Morris over plain packaging. *The Conversation*. https://theconversation.com/when-even-winning-is-losing-the-surprising-cost-of-defeating-philip-morris-over-plain-packaging-114279

Rawlings, G. (2005). Mobile people, mobile capital and tax neutrality: Sustaining a market for offshore finance centres. *Accounting Forum*, *29*(3), 289–310.

RBI. (2021). *Annual Reports of the RBI*. https://m.rbi.org.in/Scripts/AnnualReportPublications.aspx?year=2021

Rixen, T. (2008). *The political economy of international tax governance*. Palgrave Macmillan.

Rixen, T. (2013). Why reregulation after the crisis is feeble: Shadow banking, offshore financial centers, and jurisdictional competition. *Regulation & Governance*, *7*(4), 435–459.

Rixen, T., & Schwarz, P. (2012). How effective is the European Union's savings tax directive? Evidence from four EU member states. *Journal of Common Market Studies*, *50*(1), 151–168.

Roberts, S. (1994). Fictitious capital, fictitious spaces: The geography of offshore financial flows. In S. Corbridge, R. Martin, & N. Thrift (Eds.), *Money, power and space* (pp. 91–115). Blackwell.

Robertson, J. (2020). Global networks on the way up and the way down: Lessons from the rise and fall of the Seychelles as an offshore financial centre. *Global Networks*. Advance online publication. https://doi.org/10.1111/glob.12283

Robertson, J. (2021). Global financial networks confront headwinds: China's shifting offshore relationship with the British Virgin Islands. *The Pacific Review*, *34*(2), 177–205.

Rodney, W. (2018). *How Europe underdeveloped Africa*. Verso.

Rodrigue, J.-P. (2020). *The geography of transport systems*. Routledge.

Sandbrook, R. (2005). Origins of the democratic developmental state: Interrogating Mauritius. *Canadian Journal of African Studies*, *39*(3), 549–581.

Sauvant, K. P., & Sachs, L. E. (Eds.). (2009). *The effect of treaties on foreign direct investment: Bilateral investment treaties, double taxation treaties, and investment flows*. Oxford University Press.
Scholvin, S., Breul, M., & Diez, J. R. (2019). Revisting gateway cities: Connecting hubs in global networks to their hinterlands. *Urban Geography*, *40*(9), 1291–1309.
Schumann, B. (2017, January 23). Usual suspects? Co-conspirators in the business of tax dodging (The Greens/EFA). *European Parliament*. www.greens-efa.eu/files/doc/docs/d6bd745c6d08df3856eb6d49ebd9fe58.pdf
Seabrooke, L., & Wigan, D. (2016, April 6). The question behind the Panama leak: Why aren't international rules stopping offshore tax evasion? *The Washington Post*. www.washingtonpost.com/news/monkey-cage/wp/2016/04/05/heres-the-question-behind-the-panama-leak-why-international-rules-arent-stopping-offshore-tax-evasion/
Seabrooke, L., & Wigan, D. (2017). The governance of global wealth chains. *Review of International Political Economy*, *24*(1), 1–29.
SEATINI & ActionAid. (2014, September 18). Double taxation treaties in Uganda: Impact and policy implications. *Southern and Eastern Africa Trade Information and Negotiations Institute & ActionAid*. https://uganda.actionaid.org/publications/2014/double-taxation-treaties-uganda-impact-and-policy-implications#downloads
SEBI. (2021). *Foreign portfolio investors investments*. www.sebi.gov.in/statistics/fpi-investment.html
Shane, S. (2016, May 29). Panama Papers may inspire more big leaks, if not reform. *The New York Times*. www.nytimes.com/2016/05/30/us/politics/panama-papers-may-inspire-more-big-leaks-if-not-reform.html
Sharman, J. C. (2006). *Havens in a storm: The struggle for global tax regulation*. Cornell University Press.
Sharman, J. C. (2008). Regional deals and the global imperative: The external dimension of the European Union Savings Tax Directive. *Journal of Common Market Studies*, *46*(5), 1049–1069.
Sharman, J. C. (2009). The bark is the bite: International organizations and blacklisting. *Review of International Political Economy*, *16*(4), 573–596.
Sharman, J. C. (2012). Chinese capital flows and offshore financial centers. *The Pacific Review*, *25*(3), 317–337.
Sharman, J. C. (2017). Illicit global wealth chains after the financial crisis: Micro-states and an unusual suspect. *Review of International Political Economy*, *24*(1), 30–55.
Shaxson, N. (2011). *Treasure islands: Uncovering the damage of offshore banking and tax havens*. Palgrave Macmillan.
Shaxson, N. (2013, November 6). New index reveals UK runs biggest part of global secrecy network. *Tax Justice Network*. https://taxjustice.blogspot.com/2013/11/2013-financial-secrecy-index-press_6.html
Shaxson, N. (2015, June 19). Follow the money: Inside the world's tax havens. *The Guardian*. www.theguardian.com/business/2015/jun/19/tax-havens-money-cayman-islands-jersey-offshore-accounts
Shaxson, N. (2018). *Finance curse: How global finance is making us all poorer*. The Bodley Head.
Shaxson, N. (2019, May 16). No, corporate tax avoidance is not legal. *Financial Times*. www.ft.com/content/67cabeef-23a2-3601-a18d-5604880b109d

Shaxson, N., & O'Hagan, E. M. (2013, April). Mythbusters from nef and the Tax Justice Network: "A competitive tax system is a better tax system". *New Economics Foundation and the Tax Justice Network.* www.taxjustice.net/wp-content/uploads/2014/04/Mythbusters-2013-competitive-tax-system-is-bad-tax-system-.pdf

Sheng, A. (2015, November 2013). Foster ecosystem for innovation. *The Statesman.* www.thestatesman.com/opinion/foster-ecosystem-for-innovation-103712.html

Sheppard, L. (2009, March 24). Don't ask, don't tell, part 4: Ineffectual information sharing. *Tax Notes.* www.taxnotes.com/tax-notes-today-federal/tax-havens/news-analysis-dont-ask-dont-tell-part-4-ineffectual-information-sharing/2009/03/24/4824936

Shiel, F., & Fitzgibbon, W. (2019, July 23). About the Mauritius Leaks investigation. *International Consortium of Investigative Journalists.* www.icij.org/investigations/mauritius-leaks/about-the-mauritius-leaks-investigation/

Shrivastava, B., & Beniwal, V. (2016, May 11). Mauritius is now a tax paradise lost for investors in India: Q&A. *Bloomberg.* www.bloomberg.com/news/articles/2016-05-11/mauritius-is-now-a-tax-paradise-lost-for-investors-in-india-q-a

Sikka, P., & Willmott, H. (2013). The tax avoidance industry: Accountancy firms on the make. *Critical Perspectives on International Business*, *9*(4), 415–443.

Sithanen, R. (2019, August 1). Mauritius: Not a tax haven but a competitive and attractive cross-border investment platform. *L'express Maurice.* www.lexpress.mu/node/358225

Srinivasan, K. (2005). Capital flight recycling in India. *Tax Justice Network.* http://kannansrinivasan.org/wp-content/uploads/2013/04/Tax_Justice_Focus__vol_1_no_4___Q4__2005.pdf

Starrs, S. (2013). American economic power hasn't declined – It globalized! Summoning the data and taking globalization seriously. *International Studies Quarterly*, *57*(4), 817–830.

Stiglitz, J. E. (2011, March 7). The Mauritius miracle. *Project Syndicate.* www.project-syndicate.org/commentary/the-mauritius-miracle

Streeck, W., & Thelen K. (2005). Introduction: Institutional change in advanced political economies. In W. Streeck & K. Thelen (Eds.), *Beyond continuity: Institutional change in advanced political economies* (pp. 1–39). Oxford University Press.

Subramanian, A., & Roy, D. (2001, August 1). Who can explain the Mauritian miracle: Meade, Romer, Sachs or Rodrik? (Working Paper No. 01/116). *International Monetary Fund.* www.imf.org/en/Publications/WP/Issues/2016/12/30/Who-Can-Explain-The-Mauritian-Miracle-Meade-Romer-Sachs-or-Rodrik-15215

Tandrayen-Ragoobur, V., & Kasseeah, H. (2018). Mauritius' economic success uncovered. In R. Ramtohul & T. H. Eriksen (Eds.), *The Mauritian paradox: Fifty years of development, diversity and democracy* (pp. 85–106). University of Mauritius Press.

Taylor, P. J., & Derudder, B. (2016). *World city network: A global urban analysis.* Routledge.

The Economic Times. (2011, November 4). G20 summit 2011: India wants G-20 nations to share past banking and tax information. *The Economic Times.* https://economictimes.indiatimes.com/news/economy/foreign-trade/g20-summit-2011-india-wants-g-20-nations-to-share-past-banking-and-tax-information/articleshow/10605291.cms

The Economist. (2018, November 24). Treaty-shopping is about to get more expensive. *The Economist*. www.economist.com/finance-and-economics/2018/11/24/treaty-shopping-is-about-to-get-more-expensive

Thurbon, E., & Weiss, L. (2016). The developmental state in the late twentieth century. In E. S. Reinert, J. Ghosh, & R. Kattel (Eds.), *Handbook of alternative theories of economic development* (pp. 637–650). Edward Elgar.

TJN. (2015). *The greatest invention: Tax and the campaign for a just society*. Commonwealth.

TJN. (2020a). *Financial secrecy index*. https://fsi.taxjustice.net/en/

TJN. (2020b). *Taking back control of our tax systems: A visual report by the Tax Justice Network*. www.taxjustice.net/take-back-control/

TJN. (2021). *Corporate tax haven index*. www.corporatetaxhavenindex.org/en/

TJN Africa. (2019, May 29). UAE and Mauritius are the most corrosive corporate tax havens against African countries. *TJN Africa*. https://taxjusticeafrica.net/wp-content/uploads/2019/05/TJNA-Press-release_UAE-and-Mauritius_Tax-Haven-Index.pdf

TJN Australia & United Voice. (2014, October). Who pays for our common wealth? Tax practices of the ASX 200. *TJN Australia & United Voice*. https://cictar.org/who-pays-for-our-common-wealth-tax-practices-of-the-asx-200/

Tørsløv, T., Wier, L., & Zucman, G. (2020). *The missing profits of nations database*. https://missingprofits.world/

TUAC. (2016a, June 30). *The G20/OECD Base Erosion and Profit Shifting package – Assessment by the TUAC Secretariat*. Trade Union Advisory Committee to the Organization for Economic Cooperation and Development. https://tuac.org/wp-content/uploads/2017/12/1606t-beps_assess-1.pdf

TUAC. (2016b, June 27). *The case for making country-by-country reporting public*. Trade Union Advisory Committee to the Organization for Economic Cooperation and Development. https://tuac.org/wp-content/uploads/2017/12/1606t_beps_cbc-rev-1.pdf

Turner, G. (2015, October 9). Finance Uncovered investigation: MTN's Mauritian billions. *Finance Uncovered*. www.financeuncovered.org/investigations/finance-uncovered-investigation-mtns-mauritian-billions/

UK Foreign and Commonwealth Office. (2012, June 28). The overseas territories: Security, success and sustainability. *Government of the United Kingdom*. www.gov.uk/government/publications/the-overseas-territories-security-success-and-sustainability

UK Ministry of Justice. (2013, April 12). Fact sheet on the UK's relationship with the Crown Dependencies. *Government of the United Kingdom*. www.gov.uk/government/publications/crown-dependencies-jersey-guernsey-and-the-isle-of-man

UN. (1974a, May 1). *Declaration on the establishment of a new international economic order*. United Nations, Resolution 3201 (S-VI). www.un-documents.net/s6r3201.htm

UN. (1974b, May 1). *Programme of action on the establishment of a new international economic order*. United Nations, Resolution 3202 (S-VI). www.un-documents.net/s6r3202.htm

UN. (2017). *United Nations model double taxation convention between developed and developing countries 2017 update*. United Nations, Department of Economic & Social Affairs. www.un.org/esa/ffd/wp-content/uploads/2018/05/MDT_2017.pdf

UNCTAD. (2015, June 25). *World investment report 2015: Reforming international investment governance.* https://unctad.org/webflyer/world-investment-report-2015

UNCTAD. (2019, June 12). *World investment report 2019: Special economic zones.* https://unctad.org/webflyer/world-investment-report-2019

UNECA. (2015). *Illicit financial flows: Report of the High Level Panel on illicit financial flows from Africa.* https://repository.uneca.org/handle/10855/22695

Union of India v. Azadi Bachao Andolan. (2003, October 7). Supreme Court of India, Case No. 8161–8162 & 8163–8164.

US Department of the Treasury. (2016, February 11). Letter from the US Secretary of the Treasury to the President of the European Commission. *US Department of the Treasury.* www.treasury.gov/resource-center/tax-policy/treaties/Documents/Letter-State-Aid-Investigations.pdf

Vervynckt, M. (2014, November 1). Going offshore: How development finance institutions support companies using the world's most secretive financial centres. *European Network on Debt and Development.* www.eurodad.org/going_offshore

Vieira, M. A., & Alden, C. (2011). India, Brazil, and South Africa (IBSA): South-South cooperation and the paradox of regional leadership. *Global Governance, 17*(4), 507–528.

Vlcek, W. (2011). Offshore finance in Ghana: Why not? *Review of African Political Economy, 38*(127), 143–149.

Vlcek, W. (2014). From road town to Shanghai: Situating the Caribbean in global capital flows to China. *The British Journal of Politics and International Relations, 16*(3), 534–553.

Vlcek, W. (2017). *Offshore finance and global governance: Disciplining the tax nomad.* Palgrave Macmillan.

Vlcek, W. (2019). Tax avoidance. In T. M. Shaw, L. C. Mahrenbach, R. Modi, & X. Yi-chong (Eds.), *The Palgrave handbook of contemporary international political economy* (pp. 345–357). Palgrave Macmillan.

Wallerstein, I. M. (1974a). *The modern world-system: Capitalist agriculture and the origins of the European world-economy in the sixteenth century.* Academic Press.

Wallerstein, I. M. (1974b). The rise and future demise of the world capitalist system: Concepts for comparative analysis. *Comparative Studies in Society and History, 16*(4), 387–415.

Wallerstein, I. M. (1979). *The capitalist world-economy.* Cambridge University Press.

Wallerstein, I. M. (1984). *The politics of the world-economy: The states, the movements and the civilizations.* Cambridge University Press.

Wallerstein, I. M. (2004). *World-systems analysis: An introduction.* Duke University Press.

Walter, A. (1998). Do they really rule the world? *New Political Economy, 3*(2), 288–292.

Walter, A. (2008). *Governing finance: East Asia's adoption of international standards.* Cornell University Press.

Waris, A. (2014, September). *Tax haven or international financial centre? The case of Kenya.* U4 Anti-Corruption Resource Centre. www.u4.no/publications/tax-haven-or-international-financial-centre-the-case-of-kenya

Waris, A., & Seabrooke, L. (2018). Arrested development in Africa's global wealth chains: Accountability and hierarchy among 'tax havens'. In N. Hashimzade & Y.

Epifantseva (Eds.), *The Routledge companion to tax avoidance research* (pp. 267–286). Routledge.

White, J. (2021, February 2). European Commission accuses EU court of 'errors' in Apple case. *International Tax Review*. www.internationaltaxreview.com/article/b1qd6b9qjyp73x/european-commission-accuses-eu-court-of-errors-in-apple-case

Williamson, J. (2004, January 13). The Washington Consensus as policy prescription for development. *Peterson Institute for International Economics*. www.piie.com/commentary/speeches-papers/washington-consensus-policy-prescription-development

Woodward, R. (2016). A strange revolution: Mock compliance and the failure of the OECD's international tax transparency regime. In P. Dietsch & T. Rixen (Eds.), *Global tax governance: What is wrong with it and how to fix it* (pp. 103–122). ECPR Press.

Wright, T., & Hope, B. (2018). *Billion dollar whale: The man who fooled Wall Street, Hollywood, and the world*. Hachette Books.

Zirnsak, M. (2013, May). Secrecy jurisdictions, the ASX100 and public transparency. *Uniting Church in Australia*. https://silo.tips/download/secrecy-jurisdictions-the-asx100-and-public-transparency

Zucman, G. (2015). *The hidden wealth of nations: The scourge of tax havens*. The University of Chicago Press.

Zucman, G. (2017, November 8). The desperate inequality behind global tax dodging. *The Guardian*. www.theguardian.com/commentisfree/2017/nov/08/tax-havens-dodging-theft-multinationals-avoiding-tax

Index

Note: Page numbers in bold indicate a table on the corresponding page. Page numbers in italics indicate a figure on the corresponding page. Page numbers followed by "n" indicate a note.